Oct?

BAGELS, BARRY BONDS,
AND ROTTEN POLITICIANS

to Jim
You are
"the Gold-Standard"
of pals.

Burt Blum

BAGELS, BARRY BONDS, AND ROTTEN POLITICIANS

BURTON S. BLUMERT

EDITED WITH AN INTRODUCTION BY
DAVID GORDON

Ludwig
von Mises
Institute

AUBURN, ALABAMA

ISBN: 978-1-933550-30-5

TABLE OF CONTENTS

THE WAR BETWEEN THE SEXES AND EMULATING "MR. FIRST NIGHTER"

REMINISCENCES OF MURRAY ROTHBARD AND OTHER GREAT MEN

FOREWORD

Since the hyper-statist Progressive Era especially, American intellectuals have tended to disrespect and even hate business people. Instead of troubling themselves to learn about the real world of commerce, and the entrepreneurs who are responsible for the material well-being of the world, intellectuals have tended to promote everything evil, from Communism to perpetual neocon wars. Business people in turn have rightly suspected that anything smacking of scholarship might pose a mortal threat. But this split is not inevitable. As Murray N. Rothbard noted, it was Ludwig von Mises who saw that the free society had no future without an alliance between capitalist intellectuals and the far-seeing business leaders who could make their work possible.

Burton S. Blumert is an example of what Mises and Rothbard hoped for, an entrepreneur dedicated to the intellectual cause of freedom and free enterprise. That cause started to become clear for Burt when he enlisted in the Air Force to avoid being drafted into Truman's slave army during his war on North Korea. As a member of a socialist organization, Burt saw that a society organized in that fashion would be catastrophic for humanity.

After the war and NYU, Burt began his private-sector experience, and learned that this sector is the one and only key to social progress. It was also in this period that Burt was exposed to the writings of Ayn Rand, Mises, and Rothbard. In fact, he knew Mises, and was later Murray's closest friend.

After managing a chain of millinery shops in the South—he has loved the region ever since for its manners and traditions—

Burt was transferred to California, and then entered the coin and precious metals business, eventually establishing the Camino Coin Company and running it for almost fifty years. Burt always felt blessed to be dealing in collector coins, a hobby he had enjoyed his whole life. Camino, while always important, was central to monetary affairs in the 1960s and 1970s, decades of dramatic changes in the precious metals market.

The US had abandoned the domestic gold standard and then the coinage of silver. Ever since FDR, it had been illegal for Americans to own gold. That finally changed, and people needed a reliable business to make that ownership real. Camino became the most respected name in the industry. Burt's buy-sell spreads consistently beat the competition, his attention to the consumer was famous—his long-term customers became his friends—and he fought against unethical practices, as recognized by various industry groups. Burt was also a Silicon Valley pioneer: in 1970, he founded the first computerized price and news network that knit together dealers all over country, and made the coin market more efficient. Xerox recognized Burt's entrepreneurial achievement when it bought the network.

As a collector, Burt would use real examples of hard money and depreciated paper money for the most engaging lessons in monetary history and theory I've ever heard. He especially enjoyed teaching young people about inflation, and the direct connection between monetary deprecation and tyranny. Among his tools were zero-filled Yugoslavian notes, and paper currency printed and used in Nazi concentration camps.

Burt helped Murray Rothbard found the Center for Libertarian Studies in 1976, later becoming its president. In this role, he was publisher of the *Journal of Libertarian Studies* and the *Austrian Economics Newsletter*, and the benefactor—materially and in friendship—to many libertarian intellectuals. His offices were a kind of home base for thinkers in the movement. He also became the chairman of the Mises Institute, succeeding Margit von Mises, and then the publisher of the *Rothbard-Rockwell*

Report and its successor, LewRockwell.com, where these funny and profound essays first appeared.

Burt Blumert has been charitable, far-seeing, and steadfast in his role as Misesian-Rothbardian entrepreneur. As a man, he is funny, charming, decent, and generous. As a writer, as you will see from this book, he is a talented satirist who can teach the truths of liberty and life while making you laugh out loud. Most of all, he has shown how the Mises-Rothbard dream of drawing together commerce and ideas can be achieved.

LLEWELLYN H. ROCKWELL, JR.
AUGUST 18, 2008

PREFACE

Anna Marie Robertson, "Grandma" Moses, lived 101 years and was recognized as one of America's great Folk artists in the twentieth century. Her work continues to be exhibited in fine galleries throughout Europe and the US.

Amazingly, she had never painted a stroke until her early 70s!

Well, move over Grandma. Here comes Blumert.

In my first seventy years I had written letters, a handful of articles for trade publications, and my share of angry missives to the Editorial Page. I had composed subscription pleas for the old *Rothbard-Rockwell Report* (*RRR*) newsletter and proudly produced fund raisers for lewrockwell.com (LRC).

All good stuff, I must admit, but not exactly creative writing.

And then a fateful day. I was complaining bitterly to Lew Rockwell how shabbily the media was dealing with Pat Buchanan.

"They're playing the ant-Semitism card against poor Pat and it makes me mad AS hell."

Lew's response was typically terse.

"Write it up," he grumbled.

On November 1st, 1999, my first article appeared on LRC, followed by more than a hundred others, many included in these pages. I'll not earn any literary awards, blue ribbons, or Pulitzer prizes, but that doesn't mean a twit. It's the rush you experience when editor Rockwell advises that your submission meets his demanding standards, and that you've made the LRC page.

Look, we all know that Lew Rockwell stands alone as a libertarian thinker and writer. His prose is crisp, clear, and he never wavers on principle. A wag once wryly observed that Murray N. Rothbard would never win a Noble Prize in economics because he wrote too clearly. Lew shares that precision with Murray, his great mentor.

But, I have news for you; writing is just another skill for Lew. He is the most exacting and creative editor on the Internet and is proficient in every phase of that craft. I've watched him cast his editing magic since 1990 at the old *RRR* and now at LRC, but what amazes most is Lew's impact on his writers.

Keep in mind that most LRC authors are amateurs who earn their livelihood in other venues. (I should add that Lew pays his writers nothing, zero, bupkis.) Sure, they glow when receiving friendly e-mails from appreciative readers, but winning approval from editor Rockwell is their true reward.

"Gee, Blumert," a pal observed, " you see things through a warped lens."

"Listen, Buster," I replied. "The only thing funny about you was when you came home from school to find that your parents had changed the lock on the front door."

What is humor? Why do we laugh? Steve Allen, the late, great humorist answers the question as follows; "Humor is the social lubricant that helps us get over the bad spots."

Steve's right. In most jokes the victim has been betrayed, robbed, maimed, or even killed. He is often stupid and always ridiculous.

Just like the fellow who arrives home early one day to find his wife in bed with his best friend. Our fool runs to another room, returns with a gun and proceeds to point the pistol to his own head. Waves of laughter come from the bed.

"What are you laughing about?," he shouts. "You're next!"

Political humor takes a different twist. The satirist studies these 'oft-dangerous politicians/bureaucrats, extends their cruel and calloused behavior to the absurd, and we laugh. If the satirist is too good at what he does, he may wind up with his head in a noose.

The "loveable" Transportation Security Administration (TSA) provides us with overwhelming evidence of such behavior every day at every airport, and we laugh through our tears.

Here is a snippet of pure satire from the essay "Revisiting The Friendly Skies" (p. 20). Blumert is at the Security Check Point and the young TSA agent is about to use the electronic wand on him.

" I hope you're in good health," she said. "Earlier today I short circuited an old dude's pacemaker."

"Good Lord," I stammered. "What happened to him?"

"Well, after a few scary moments we finally revived him. It was nice that they gave him a free upgrade to first class."

If you're going to write political satire, you had better be funny. Not necessarily, "falling off your chair, gasping for air, funny," but the bulk of your readers better, at minimum, be breaking a smile or two.

"Blumert, your last article was not funny. In fact, it was over the line and tasteless," wrote the e-mailer. His outrage was directed at my article, "Blumert Almost Qualifies As A Suicide Bomber" (p. 46).

I knew I was treading on hazardous ice with this piece. After all, nothing is conceptually more horrible than the image of innocent people being blown to bits.

I wrestled with the dilemma of submitting, or not and decided, Yes, that there was no better way to express my abhorrence of this dastardly act.

Dear reader, if you are troubled by anything in this volume, that's okay. I can handle it. But, if you don't laugh out loud at least ten times, I will be devastated. You wouldn't disappoint me, would you?

My deep appreciation goes to Dr. David Gordon for lending his brilliant editorial skills to these pages. Also, thank you, Lew Rockwell for your constant support and friendship through the years. Without your counsel and encouragement, this volume would not exist.

If there are any errors of commission, omission, or anything really stupid in the pages ahead, I would love to place the blame elsewhere, but I alone bear the responsibility.

BURTON S. BLUMERT
AUGUST 15, 2008

LET THEM EAT BAGELS

BLUMERT IS SO COOL
HE GETS TATTOOED

I t all began with a chance meeting at the local Social Security office. Although I'm no fanatic on the matter, I scrupulously avoid such places. Not because they are the very embodiment of the welfare state, but because they smell awful. It must be the combination of aging people sitting in decaying surroundings.

I had failed to fill out some Medicare form, and my private insurer stopped paying dental bills. The only way out of the morass was to go to the Social Security office and sign the paper. That should read, go to, get in line for several hours, and only then, sign the paper.

I first noticed the gent sitting 40 degrees to my left because he appeared to be smiling at me. There was something familiar about him, but the smile I remembered contained more teeth.

"Say don't you remember?
They called me Al.
It was Al all the time.
Why don't you remember?
I'm your pal,
Say, buddy can you spare a dime?"

He didn't sing that refrain from the great Gorney and Harburg, 1932, depression song, "Brother, Can You Spare a Dime?"

recorded by Bing Crosby. But, Al did remind me that we had downed a few Coor's 50 years earlier at an Air Force base in Colorado.

He insisted we share the afternoon and suggested the following choices:

- We can sit and watch the stock prices at Merrill Lynch and the coffee is free.
- There's a softball game in the park and sometimes the winning team buys hot dogs for everybody.
- At 2 o'clock there's a juicy custody case at the courthouse in Redwood City.
- We could go to the movies. *Seabiscuit* is playing and the afternoon rate for seniors is $4.

I signed Medicare Form 6829, and fled the scene, advising Al that I had already seen the movie and, anyway, I was late for my break-dancing lesson.

Meeting Al confirmed why any and all "Reunions" should be avoided like the plague.

I have no desire to see Greta, she of the flaming red-hair, and the first to break my heart, looking, not like her mother, but like her grandmother.

Maybe I should be at peace, mooching free coffee with my fellow codgers, or playing Bocce Ball at the Commons, but such is not my fate.

I blame Rockwell. Between LRC and the Mises Institute, I seem to be bumping into young people much of the time.

I'm not complaining, mind you. The kids that show up at Auburn for Mises University each summer are dazzlers and I don't have to tell readers at LRC about the quality of some of our columnists who are barely pubescent.

There is no doubt our culture is obsessed with "Youth." Women endlessly seek the elixir that will undo the years, and eventually, many succumb to the surgeon's blade.

Now the shameless hucksters have turned upon the male. "Whiten your teeth, seed your scalp, and take this pill to restore your manhood." Repeated often enough, messages that were once offensive become amusing and, finally, just another consumer option.

But I was caught up on the wave of youth much earlier. Brooks Brothers was of another time. I now find my clothes in the Portly department at Banana Republic. And although the hair stylists at Supercuts used to draw straws when I entered the door (the loser got me), they now enthusiastically cut my hair, all the while regarding me as an oddity.

But all this was nibbling at the edges. If I truly wanted to make the supreme sacrifice to youthful fashion, it was time to be decisive. It was time to get tattooed.

We are surrounded by tattoos. Almost every young woman I see has colorful birds, flowers, or insects permanently stenciled on every available inch of skin (not that I'm looking, mind you). Some athletes have even taken to selling their exposed skin areas to advertisers.

Surely, I could find some up-to-date, yet tasteful defacing that will mark me as "cool." Something my wife could tolerate, but at the same time, would win approval from the crowd at Starbucks.

Finding a reputable Tattooer was next and the Yellow Pages seemed the appropriate starting point. I was attracted by the candor of one company. They called themselves "The House of Pain," but I decided upon "The Indelible Tattoo" with their clever motto, "Our Tattoo is forever. At least through your first marriage."

It was clear "Charles the Artist" was the owner as he carried a needle like device that was constantly buzzing even while he ate his lunch. The blood stains covering his white tee shirt were merely evidence of his commitment to his craft.

The following dialogue ensued:

Charles the Artist: "Old man, if you are looking for a restroom, or change for a parking meter, you're in the wrong place."

Blumert: "I'm no tire-kicker, Buster. I'm in the market for a tattoo, and it might be more than one if the deal is right." (Calling him Buster lets him know that I'm tough as well as cool.)

C the A: "If you must know, I figured you for a cop from Weights and Measures checking on the purity of our vegetable dyes, but you sound OK, old man. I promise not to use the blunt needle."

Blumert: "I'm feeling more confident by the moment. What do you recommend? What's cool?"

C the A: "You want something smart, but not pretentious. Colorful, but not loud. A tattoo you'll be comfortable with during the day, or for evenings."

Blumert: Well, maybe something a bit more masculine. I don't want anyone to think I'm gay, you know a ho—, uh, one of those—"

C the A: "Say it, old man, you mean faggot."

Blumert: "I didn't say that, you did. Why, some of my best—"

C the A: "Forget it, nobody could ever mistake you for one of —them."

"Let me tell you about our Special for September. It's a barbed-wire arm bracelet in light purple and you get your ears pierced free. The bracelet is our best seller. It's from the Alan Iverson Collection."

Blumert: "Maybe something less contemporary. Something classical."

C the A: "Well, let's look at my 'golden oldies' file. Let's see: WWII, Korean War, Vietnam, the 60's. Anything strike you yet?"

Blumert: I was in the Air Force during the Korean thing, but I try to forget all of that."

C the A: "Tell you what, I have something perfect for you. As you walked through the door, YOUR tattoo flashed in my mind. Let the artist prevail. Let me pick your tattoo. You'll not be sorry."

Blumert: "I respect the artist in you and you can go ahead, as long as I get my senior discount."

C the A: "Please remove your shirt, old man."

Epilogue: Blumert is having his tattoo surgically removed next Thursday. He has been silent about the design, but, knowing Blumert, he will be blabbing about it as soon as he heals.

September 1, 2003

BLUMERT SURVIVES
SHOPPING AT THE MALL

Maybe it's because they were brought up as slaves to changing fashions. Whatever the reason, women don't have the proper respect for tradition and the institutions which render service to those traditions. Take my wife, for example,

"Look, Blumert, Thom McAn Shoe stores don't exist anymore. They're history. The one that was on Market Street in San Francisco probably closed during the Johnson administration."

I was going to make some crack about President Andrew Johnson being impeached in 1868, but, she wouldn't have laughed.

Instead, I pointed out that, "If the US Government had shown some spunk there'd still be an American shoe industry and a Thom McAn's store. All the jobs went to Tibet, I think. Pat Buchanan wrote all about it."

"I know you were fond of those $13 loafers Thom McAn sold, but let's go to the Mall and we'll find you something just as nice."

Going to the Mall is her solution to every problem.

It had been a while since I'd been to the Mall and I'm sure you'll be thrilled to death with my observations.

It took only moments to realize that there were more cars parked than there were people shopping. This suggests that many of the vehicles were abandoned.

I scratched a note on my shirt cuff to do an LRC article on the mystery of abandoned cars at the shopping Mall.

Well, there was one vehicle that wasn't abandoned; while snooping about, I inadvertently peered into a 1963 Chevy Station Wagon and startled a family of 6 having their dinner.

The back seat, which served as a bed for the children, had been converted to a dining table. (Their main course was Beef Wellington with wild rice and mushrooms) I was invited to join them, and later, while munching a zero carb sandwich at Subway, I regretted having declined.

You won't be surprised to learn that the "Handicapped" have more of the choice parking slots than ever before. I have

NEVER, EVER seen a single car parked in one of those Handicapped slots. That record remains intact.

It's time for some class action litigation. Look, my handicaps are just as important as anybody else's. What arrogant legislator or jurist gave them the cushy parking slots?

I look forward to giving testimony at the trial,

"Your honor, overeating is MY handicap. Every time I pass a "Handicap" parking slot I am forbidden to use, I get frustrated, and hungry, which leads to more overeating. Save me from that vicious circle and grant me a Handicap Parking Permit."

Whatever YOUR handicap, join me in this class action. (Sorry, a golf handicap is not applicable.)

The most significant change I observed at the Mall was that the folks manning the aisles and the computers were no longer "sales people." Salesmanship is dead. For purposes of this report they shall be known as "clerks".

Let's quickly dispense with the statistics:

- 37 percent of the clerks do not speak English.
- 29 percent of the clerks have English as their second language.
- 100 percent of the remaining 34 percent speak English, but hate the customers.

(margin of error for this poll, 3–4 percent).

In such an environment, it's no surprise that I didn't find anything like those old Thom McAn loafers. (Tomorrow, I'll look for them on eBay.)

I must admit that I was drawn to an astonishing Nike shoe that had lights and could be inflated by pressing a button.

The young clerk with the shaved head said they were a bargain at $285. He was unimpressed when I told him I paid less for my first family car (a 1957 Ford).

Now that my loafers were forgotten, I became a barely tolerated presence. Tolerated only if I stayed out of the way and spoke only when spoken to.

It was as though I had a Visitor's Day Pass in an enclave meant for Females Only.

Teenage girls were the dominant population. They giggled and raced from one store to the next, understanding every protocol. After all, they were in training, in transit to the lofty status of "Superior Shopper" that every woman achieves.

I was lost in such thoughts when my wife rattled me out of my torpor with a deadly question,

"Which dress (substitute, shoes, purse,) looks better on me, the red or the blue?"

There are a series of dreaded questions every man learns to fear:

"Do you think I'm looking fat? ("Truth MUST be avoided when dealing with this question.")

"Do you like this hair style? (If she's crying hysterically, the answer is, "No!")

"Does she look younger and prettier than I do? (The more beautiful the woman in question, the more vehement your, "No!")

Finally, back home to the safety of my Lazy Boy Recliner, I realized what a close call I had survived at The Mall.

I won't be going back there again soon.

July 2, 2004

WELCOME TO THE WRETCHED SKIES

The passengers carried the captain and crew on their shoulders cheering and popping bottles of cheap champagne as they disembarked the plane. They were followed by grim-faced stretcher-bearers rushing away the wounded.

The clean-up crew, wearing gas masks, prepared to board the aircraft and clear the debris. When they were done, our exhausted group of passengers for Flight 666 was finally ready to board.

This flight did not look promising.

Bad things had begun earlier in the terminal when I was "randomly selected" for special security clearance.

Blumert: "Why do you guys always pick on me? You see that I'm too old for this terrorism business. My bomb-throwing days are well behind me."

(The mere mention of the word "bomb" triggered sirens and the release of snarling German shepherds. They would have surely eaten me, but someone decided I was more valuable alive.)

Turban Wearing Agent (TWA): "To paraphrase George W., either you're with us, or you're with them. Which is it?"

Blumert: "Can I have my shoes, please? My feet are getting cold and the last time I caught Athlete's Foot from your filthy floors. Are you finally done with me?"

TWA: "Yes, but you will be on probation for the next sixty days.

You will report to the FreeRepublic website every fortnight and I advise that you give up eating halvah. It may be delicious, but it's un-American.

Finally, it would be wise if you forgot about wearing that ridiculous Lawrence of Arabia costume you exhibit every Halloween.

Find an American costume in which to do your 'trick or treating'."

Blumert: "All right already. This year I'll go as George Patton."

Back at Gate 12, we passengers of Flight 666 fought our way onto the plane. I thought my luck had changed as I plopped into an unoccupied window seat.

How could I know that I was soon to be in charge of the Emergency Exit?

The Captain, swore me in using a King James version of the Bible, gave me a forty-eight-page pamphlet outlining my duties, and then strapped a slightly used WWII parachute onto my back.

"You're in charge of that Emergency Exit Door, Blumert," said the Captain. "You've never once shown up for Jury Duty when called. Well, here's another opportunity for you to serve."

I could feel the glaring eyes of my fellow passengers. I was determined to win their respect.

Things brightened when the Flight Attendants started to serve lunch. This time, I would beat the system. "Order a kosher lunch," the travel experts recommended. "You won't get the same tired fare," they said.

Well, I got the same tired ham and cheese sandwich as everybody else, only mine was in a wrapper with Golda Meir's picture on it.

The fellow next to me had ordered vegetarian. His ham and cheese sandwich wrapper had a picture of a cauliflower.

We all munched in silence.

The reality of air travel these days is hardly less absurd than the above.

Southwest and America West may be the only money-making airlines in the nation. In fact, they may soon be the ONLY airlines in the nation.

Just as Kaiser Permanente became the model for today's HMOs in providing minimal levels of medical care, so Southwest and Jet Blue have established standards (or should I say substandards) to the misery of the air travel consumer.

Southwest ticket holders are given Boarding Passes, but no assigned seats. This is part of the "success" of Southwest. Get those seats filled. No frills, no comfort.

There are three categories of Boarding Passes, A, B, and C. Which you get depends on how early you arrived at the ticket counter. A's board first and so on.

Getting on board early means a place for your bag in the compartment above your seat. Getting on board early means avoiding the middle seat between two three-hundred-pound garlic eaters.

The flight would only last an hour and twenty minutes, but I waited almost that long to protect my "turf" in line B.

There is a democratic aspect to current and future air travel. Everybody is in steerage.

The fear that kept people from flying after 9/11 appears to have vanished. The terminals are jammed with travelers. They seem numb, surly if approached, but they're not afraid. At the airport, even fear has been stamped out.

Going through Security used to engender outrage and archives filled with horror stories. A genre of gallows humor developed and we laughed while we shared our humiliations at the hands of the security buffoons.

"I can top that," said the office comedian. "I had to explain why I wasn't wearing underwear and the security clerk hardly spoke English," he recounted, to roars of laughter.

Maybe it's since the feds took over the job, but there's an attitude at Security which says, "there is nothing humorous going on here."

Say the magic "woid" and you'll wind up in jail. Try, "box cutter," or "9/11," or, "I remember a time when you just walked to the gate and boarded the plane, without being set upon by bozos."

There's no illusion that anybody is safer for "their efforts." The purpose is to compress the passenger into a silent, obedient and docile lump.

"Since our flight is two hours from now, let's have some lunch," my wife suggested, recognizing my blackening mood. "Look," she said, " All the fast food restaurants are here now."

She was right. They were all there: Pizza Hut, Kentucky Fried, even Nathan's Hot dogs from New York. I don't remember airports having all the national fast food chains on site.

I'm not a big fan of these great American dining institutions, but, they are predictable in what they deliver.

Not at the airport! Their prices were higher than in the outside world and the food was markedly inferior.

"Blumert, you're on the brink of some conspiracy theory," she said, pretending that her slice of pizza was edible.

I made it sound as if I had some facts when I told her, "Look, almost all fast food places are operated by franchisers, small business men who try their best to provide a decent product. Who knows who is running these dumps at the airport?"

Maybe I guessed right.

I wanted to tell you about what happened at the Car Rental place in Phoenix, but the Judge said we can't discuss the case until after the trial.

I can tell you that I had ordered a luxury car and they delivered the winning vehicle from a Demolition Derby.

They're not getting away with it.

October 28, 2004

COFFEE, TEA, OR ME IN YOUR AGONY?

A friend, beer in hand, complained. "For the past twenty years you've predicted the collapse of real estate values, the stock markets, and the entire political apparatus. I'm fed up with your gloom-and-doom view of the world."

"True," I responded meekly, "but you must admit it's all twenty years closer now than when I first started to tell you."

My critical friend misses the point. We are swept along by a whirlwind of technology that brings change by the minute. It is a revolution brought to us by young innovators in the great American tradition. Simultaneously, we endure a loss of quality in the everyday aspects of life. In spite of assurances from government officials and social engineers, things are not always better than they used to be.

The last time I took an international flight was six or seven years ago, and when I recently booked an overseas trip it was with some trepidation. Does the consumer get more for his airfare dollars today than he did in, say, 1965? No, and the evidence is overwhelming.

Like every passenger destined for steerage, there is the knowledge that conditions are better on the other side of the curtain. I did not have bonus miles nor time and energy to search out a "deal." If I wanted a better seat I'd have to buy it. The price of a roundtrip San Francisco-London business class ticket was $3,500. I decided to suffer in economy, and suffer I did.

Thirty-five years ago a nonstop flight from San Francisco to London took approximately eleven hours. Today it remains eleven hours, but everything else is worse.

Today's "airbus" is austere, devoid of anything soft or comfortable. In fact, the interior seems designed to be cleaned between flights with a high-powered water hose.

Back in '65 an economy airline seat was fashioned for the average American male provided he was 4'11" and weighed less than 120 pounds. Seat #32F on my recent Swissair flight to London was configured for the backside of a marathon runner or a Tour de France cyclist.

As passenger space shrinks, one becomes territorial. My left arm-rest was shared with a gentleman from Cambodia, and for much of the flight we maneuvered for possession. At one point violence appeared likely, but western guile proved superior to Eastern mysticism and I prevailed for more than 50 percent of the time.

On the face of it, prices compared with years ago may appear at bargain levels, but many of today's passengers are "on the house." They are recipients of mileage plus coupons.

Upgrades, airline employees, their friends and family fill the bulk of the seats, often the choice ones up front. Someone has to pay the bills, and it's the poor bloke who doesn't have coupons or sufficient advance time who is the victim and pays through the nose.

An airport has been defined as a construction site where they land planes. That's always been true, but it's worse than ever today. Many overseas travelers will relate that their worst frustration involves getting in and around the airports. Delays plague almost every commercial carrier. Add to that the cumbersome and often unnecessary security measures bugging the traveler, which add hours to a scheduled flight.

In the old days they were called stewardesses, all single, husband-hunting attractive young women clearly on site to please the predominantly male clientele. Aka flight attendants, today they are more like matrons in a women's prison whose sole purpose is to herd the sheeple into compliance.

No, I have not forgotten airline food. Not only was what they served inedible, it was unidentifiable. My Swissair flight was under the auspices of Delta Airlines. The net result was that the Swiss have adopted Delta's menu and efficiency while Delta now exhibits Swiss charm and graciousness.

By hour six I was so degraded that a bag of peanuts seemed essential to my survival. Spirits rose as one of the prison guards appeared with a heavy cart filled with bags of peanuts lurching down the narrow aisle. An eighty-year-old woman headed for the lav had to dive to avoid being crushed by the deadly object. The rest of us were relieved. Had she been squashed, we might have been peanutless.

Needless to say, the passenger's mood darkens with each passing hour. I was unable to shake the notion that the air I was breathing had been filtered for everything but seven deadly viruses, and that we were on the radar screen of the missile-launching ships attached to the Seventh Fleet on maneuvers below.

The final hour of the ordeal becomes almost manageable. Survival seems assured and freedom imminent. For me, it meant I was an hour away from a steaming cup of strong English coffee, a package of Frothman's Biscuits, and the morning *Telegraph*.

The landing was bumpy, and on shaky legs we quickly cleared customs. In celebration, I rushed to get my coffee, biscuits, and *Telegraph*, quickly found a space at a long common table, and life seemed worth living again. I removed the wrappings from the Frothman's package, selected one, and was not disappointed. They were as delicious as I remembered.

Then my eye was distracted by the strangest occurrence. Seated across from me was a middle-aged gent wearing a bowler hat and certainly a denizen of Lombard Street in the old City.

He was taking one of my biscuits. He did it brazenly and deftly. I tried to dismiss what I had seen.

While consuming my second biscuit, I must admit, my focus was no longer drawn to the *Telegraph* but on my bowlered neighbor.

He seemed absorbed in his newspaper (the *Guardian*), and managed to extract the fourth biscuit in the package, his second. In New York or San Francisco, I might have fled the scene or summoned the police. But this was London.

We proceeded to complete the package of six biscuits, each in turn, without ever making eye contact. In a flash, he was gone, and I was left to consider the experience. I shrugged and concluded that even lunatics can wear bowler hats.

I crushed my empty coffee container and folded my newspaper in preparation to take leave. Covered by a section of the newspaper but now exposed was my unopened package of Frothman's biscuits.

Who knows? If the bowlered bloke has an Internet pal equivalent to LewRockwell.com, he may be relating his incredible encounter with a crazed American.

My short tour of London, Berlin, and Rome resulted in the same culture shock as always. A driver in Rome summed up a view that we encountered throughout our brief visit.

"You Americans are okay, but you don't have any culture."

He was wrong. His real complaint was that by comparison America has no history. We do have a culture, but it has fallen precipitously.

Now let me tell you about my return flight home . . .

July 28, 2000

REVISITING THE FRIENDLY SKIES

I t was like a WWII newsreel: the endless line of defeated people pushing their baggage, inching toward the inevitable checkpoint.

"Achtung! Achtung!" blared the sound system at peak volume. "Do not leave your baggage unattended. It will be confiscated and destroyed."

The smell of fear was pervasive.

"How long have you been in line?" I asked the weary gent who looked as though he might have slept in his clothes.

"I started my trip two days ago at the Bakersfield airport and last night I slept in my clothes," he said.

Our attention was suddenly drawn to a ruckus at the front of the line. Two uniformed men were struggling to remove a flowered hat from a little old lady's head.

"They are looking for her hat pin," someone whispered. "A hat pin can be a lethal weapon."

"Remember, hat pins don't kill. People kill," I smugly countered.

That remark obviously earned respect as everyone in the line stayed clear of me from that point on.

Finally, two hours and ten minutes later it was my turn at the security checkpoint.

"You're tickling me," I giggled as the electronic wand probed from one sensitive area to another.

The young security agent seemed like an animal trainer putting her charges through their paces.

"I hope you're in good health," she said. "Earlier today I short circuited an old dude's pacemaker."

"Good Lord!" I stammered. "What happened to him?"

"Well, after a few scary moments we finally revived him. It was nice that they gave him a free upgrade to first class."

Exhausted, those passengers who survive the security checkpoint enter the peaceful, serene world of the corridors leading to the gates.

It was a San Francisco International Airport never seen before. The few passengers seemed dazed and just going through the motions.

The one dramatic change was the attitude of all airport personnel: from the restroom porter to the counter ticket agents to the food servers to the flight crew. All were beaming, polite and conversational. It's as if they were atoning for years of cruelty and indifference toward the passenger.

The change is so dramatic that the passenger is bewildered. He is actually being treated like—what's the word?—like a customer.

The passengers on my Delta Airlines Flight 217 were collecting up near the gate. Now that racial profiling is allowable once again—and all government preferential programs have been set aside for the duration of the war—I can comfortably analyze, without fear, the racial, religious, national origin, age, and political persuasion of each traveler.

Here are some partial results of my survey of the 65 passengers: 37 were white, Christian males (easily identified by the vacant look in their eyes). Thirty-two of this group were married (the vacant look had become resignation).

There was one copper-colored woman who upon eye contact said to me: "I am not a Moslem, I'm a Hindu, and although I'm not a political person, I never was too crazy about Moslems. I happily join you, my Christian cousins, in smashing these unworthy Islamic savages." She ended by humming several bars of "America the Beautiful" and proceeded on to her next eye contact.

The only other non-whites were two young black men magnificently attired in business suits. The other passengers were puzzled why they dribbled basketballs wherever they went, even to the lavs.

One dribbled so poorly I challenged him "one-on one" and easily stole the ball.

"I hate this game," he admitted. "I just want everyone to know I'm an American Black and that I'm cool."

Leroy was as nice a lad as you can find.

"In the late 1980s I changed my name to Mustafa Mohammed, but I recently changed it back to Leroy Johnson. Please don't let on that you beat me 'one-on-one'."

Leroy's secret was safe with me.

According to any statistical survey, there should have been 2.7 Jews on board the flight. There weren't even any folks that were borderline, and it finally occurred to me, this was Yom Kippur. A serious day. The highest of holy days for the Jews. They don't play basketball, and they certainly don't travel.

Even famous baseball player Sandy Koufax needed rabbinical dispensation to pitch in the World Series against the Yankees on Yom Kippur.

I must admit I began to experience personal guilt at traveling on the Jewish holy day, but it was Lew Rockwell who requested that I come to Auburn, and that comes close to rabbinical dispensation. Well, doesn't it?

An hour or so into the flight food odors wafted from the rear of the Boeing 767 through the front cabins.

Was it possible that this new accommodating attitude toward the passenger would mean a superb dining experience at 35,000 feet?

In recent years, airline food disintegrated from being inedible to being unidentifiable. As the passengers started up their meal there was some rumbling.

"My spoon won't penetrate the jello," complained one woman.

"My knife just snapped in two when I tried to cut the butter," added another.

We all knew the truth: the plastic utensils were fashioned so thin and lightweight that they never could be used as weapons.

I respectfully suggest to future travelers that they add to their travel kits a pair of wooden chopsticks, but be certain they have dull ends.

I write this piece from a windowless room in the bowels beneath the Atlanta airport. They have taken my papers—and I am scheduled to be interrogated by the assistant airport commandant.

The humiliation doesn't matter as long as I know my flight home will be safe.

October 4, 2001

LAUGHING ALL THE WAY
TO THE GALLOWS
AND THE POORHOUSE

EXCHANGE OF EMAILS

From: Rockwell, Editor, LRC
To: Blumert, Former LRC satirist

Where is the funny article you promised about all the bursting bubbles in San Francisco?

From: Blumert
To: Rockwell

Well, I've accumulated a few one-liners like: Did you hear about the former dotcom billionaire who begs in downtown Mountain View with a sign that reads, "I Work For Gigabytes"?

Or, when I called the movie theatre to find out when the feature started, the voice asked, "What time would you like to get here, sir?"

Or, things are so bad in California that my bank returned a check stamped "Insufficient Funds. Us not you."

I realize this is some of my funniest material ever, Lew, but don't you think it's tasteless (this, even more than usual) to jest about people's suffering, particularly with a bloody war on prime time TV as a backdrop?

From: Rockwell
To: Blumert

If we are supposed to laugh all the way to the gallows, we can certainly laugh all the way to the poorhouse.

In deference to my editor, note the title of this piece.

All we needed in San Francisco is a war. As if the economy wasn't disastrous enough. Tourism, the number one industry, is a vague memory to most. Cab drivers and hotel doormen are plundering one another just to stay in practice.

Things are so bad for the fast-food restaurants that they even rolled out the red carpet for the antiwar demonstrators and the National Guardsmen who came to town last week.

The antiwar event was hardly mentioned in the media, but police admitted that the crowd was the largest in San Francisco in thirty years. The anti-war kids looked pretty much like their Vietnam War ancestors, and like those ancestors are totally sound on war, but illiterate when it comes to economics.

As for the Guardsmen, I had the impression they were in town to earn their Crowd-Suppression Merit Badges.

To McDonald's and other one star restaurants, these visitors were as hungry as regular tourists, although not quite as fashionable.

McDonald's was quick to put several new specials on the griddle:

"The Dissent Burger"—Half-price in case you're arrested in the middle of eating it.

"The Iraq Burger"—The usual pickle, onion, and special dressing on a poppy seed bun, all covered with a layer of sand.

Just as San Francisco prospered more than other American cities during the "Nostalgic 90s," it now sinks into an even more profound despair. If there's "a broken-heart for every light on Broadway," there has to be a "shattered mother-board for every cybernik in Silicon Valley." (I haven't the foggiest idea of the meaning of what I just said.)

I must admit the pervasive gloom hanging over Northern California is almost too much, even for a hardened gold dealer. Our own Jeff Tucker helped me through it all: His guidance in reminding that the collapse of "bubbles" built on excess, corruption and loss of values should be celebrated.

Here follows some of my notes while searching out those bursting bubbles requested by my editor.

As a suburbanite I don't get to San Francisco often, but last month I made the trip and decided to dine at my favorite restaurant, Stars. In the old days, you had to reserve months in advance, but with things so quiet in the City now, surely I might be able to squeeze in at the counter.

I drove up to the valet, advising the young attendant that we had no reservation and that he could have the car if he thought we would be served.

Puzzled, he turned to his associate: (The following is a translation from the Spanish):

First attendant: Can you believe this gringo asking for a reservation? He must be from another planet. Should I tell him that you haven't needed a reservation in any restaurant in town for over three years?

Second attendant: What do you expect from someone driving a Saturn?

After exacting a pledge that he would not scratch our 4-wheeled beauty, my wife and I entered the restaurant and there was not one other customer. Not one!

The food was OK, but it was like the final meal before an execution. At one point, I slurped my soup and the sound bounced from wall to wall, resonating for a full 30 seconds.

Stars closed for good last month. We may have been one of the last to pay final respects.

The landlord at my office building is a gentle fellow from Taiwan, and I was surprised to receive a luncheon invitation from him. It was clear he had important matters on his mind.

We dined at his favorite restaurant, the Tokyo House. (Dennis is proud to demonstrate that he has overcome the prejudices of his ancestors.) After we finished the last of the sliced, dead, cold fish, he announced the purpose of our meeting.

Landlord: Mr. B, he calls me. (He can't say Blumert; it comes out "Bwumert".) Your lease is up for renewal in a few months and I have a pleasant surprise. I'm building you a sauna and a wet bar. Also, my wife will be bringing tea everyday at 3 o'clock and one of the building's elevators will be for your use only.

Blumert: Dennis, that's all very nice, but you don't have to do all that.

I'm not about to move. And I'm happy to renew.

When I signed the new lease, Dennis hosted a party that lasted 4 days and the ambassador from Taiwan presented me with honorary citizenship to that energetic little country.

(Dennis owns several office buildings and they are 70 percent vacant.)

When I got home that night I remembered having saved a transcript from my last lease negotiations with him. Things were very different in those days.

Dotcommers were renting every available foot of office space in return for stock in their companies. Everybody was getting richer by the minute. Old-fashioned businesses, like mine, were not the most desirable tenants.

TRANSCRIPT OF LEASE NEGOTIATIONS 1999

(He had me wait for 2 hours in a room with no windows.)

Landlord: Bwumert, you have ten minutes to convince me to renew your lease with only a 50-percent increase in rent.

Blumert: Dennis, I've been a loyal tenant for 15 years. Frankly, I don't even understand this new lease. For example, why are clauses 7-11 in Chinese?

And you can't be serious in Par. 1: "All building tenants must attend daily Tai Chi exercises at 7 a.m. in the building parking lot"?

Well, I guess I can live with everything, Dennis, but I draw the line at changing our name from Camino Coin to Chiang Kai-shek Coin Company.

If there's a plus to San Francisco's economic woes, it's that all those traffic jams are a memory. You can now drive from San Francisco to San Jose without even slowing down. Unfortunately, the price of a gallon of gas in the Bay Area is $2.60. I find myself looking at the fuel indicator as I drive along.

Which reminds me of my very first date: It was the Junior Prom and I picked her up in a taxi. (Limos were reserved for funerals in those days.) As we were driving along, the pretty young thing asked me what the time was. Clearly distracted, with eyes glued to the taxi-meter, I responded, "It's $1.25."

March 29, 2003

LET THEM EAT BAGELS

Congratulations to Nancy Keates and the Wall Street Journal for "Mail-Order Bagels Gain Popularity With New York On Minds of Many." Ms. Keates provides the valuable results of a "taste-test" among New York City's five leading bagel producers. But, more important, this is an exposé confirming the nationwide epidemic of phony bagels.

In a way, the loss of quality of the bagel is a metaphor for our national loss of value and purpose.

We have sunk so low that there are some Americans who actually prefer something as profane as a raisin bagel. (I will not even mention our esteemed editor's name, and besides, that was in his pre-anti-carbohydrate days.)

As usual, however, the *Wall Street Journal* conceals the real issue. By concentrating on the perversion of mass-produced, frozen bagels, the warmongering daily diverts attention from a cabal that has existed for almost 100 years.

Focus the debate on the bagel. Does today's bagel measure up to the standards of the last century? Is it possible to export the art of bagel baking beyond the confines of NYC? Finally—

setting aside the raisin bagel—should those who promote such bastardizations as "blueberry," "hot-pepper," and "sun-dried tomato" bagels be shot?

Folks, let me reveal the truth: it's a scam. Keep the goyim busy with the bagel debate. Let them conduct contests and have the winning formula taken over by Sara Lee. Keep them distracted to make sure they never discover the real "manna from above," the *Bialy*.

I can say with certainty that no genuine bialy has ever been baked outside the Boroughs. Even Jews outside NYC know nothing of the bialy.

Mysteriously, there is something in the bialy that causes its total erasure from the memory banks if you allow 18 months to pass without eating one. This explains why even ex-New York Jews look blank when the bialy is mentioned.

By secret agreement, Jewish comedians pledge never to joke about the bialy. Waiters are quick to discourage any out-of-towner in NYC who might inadvertently select a bialy. "Eat the bagel—it's better."

In NYC, a small group of gentiles knows the truth. It is rumored that they have undergone some mysterious conversion—more rigorous than ultra-orthodox-that allows them access to the bialy.

Note: If you call one of the five NYC leading bagel vendors listed in the *WSJ* article, and make an effort to order bialys, your chances are "iffy." I am convinced there is a secret password, but I am no help. I've been away too long.

November 19, 2001

BAGELS AND GAS MASKS

B eing an ex-New Yorker is worse than being an ex-Marine. You're branded for life. Diction lessons, joining the Southern League, and marrying a girl from Idaho can camouflage the beast and it may lay dormant in the chest cavity for decades like the "Alien" in that scary movie.

But, it's only a matter of time, when, due to stress or elevated blood-alcohol levels, the brash, "know it all" Nooo Yawker worms its way out for all to see. It's not a pretty sight, but those who witness the event are invariably discreet (they are never New Yorkers), and the incident passes without mention.

However successful the ex-New Yorker might be in burying those roots, there remains a compelling need to stay connected with the "Rancid Apple." It's a form of masochism, I suppose, and remains unexplainable.

For many years the weekly *Village Voice* magnificently covered New York City's internal struggles and more than satisfied my need for linkage. Although, I despised every position the rag represented, I couldn't wait for the next edition. People like Alexander Cockburn, James Ridgeway, and Joe Conason often drove me crazy, but they were outstanding writers often critical of US foreign policy.

Unfortunately, "The Voice" became consumed with the plight of the under-classes. The paper was mired in a style more suited to the 1960s and what once passed for irreverence became tiresome. When some of their best writers moved on, "The Voice" lost its cutting edge and it was time for me to find a better link.

New York magazine panders to the prosperous and sophisticated Gothamite. Rather than bleating about police brutality in Brooklyn like "The Voice," *New York* readers are more interested in locating the best bagel in town, or learning which Park Avenue surgeon performs the ultimate in face-lifts.

New York kept me plugged in to "hot" restaurants I would never visit and supreme live theatre a non- or ex-New Yorker can only see taped on the "Bravo" channel.

It's not that I'm embarrassed about subscribing to *New York* magazine, but having it mailed in an unmarked brown envelope is simply exercising prudence. My postman once questioned my sexuality when I received a sample copy of *Architectural Digest*. (I'll save for another time the neighborhood's reaction to my "Buchanan For President" lawn sign.)

Ok, you've got the message and can see why there's not much to say about *New York* magazine. It's slick, the writing is first-rate, and it's a good place to visit if you want to know the prevailing neocon views. But things have changed at the magazine.

Last year's horrible events have smothered the confident swagger at *New York* magazine, but, I was not prepared for the August 12th edition. The front cover is usually reserved for photos of the beautiful people playing in The Hamptons, or celebrating the opening of a new bistro in the SoHo. Not this time.

The large box in the center of the front cover announces the lead story: "THE SURVIVALIST'S GUIDE TO LIVING WITH TERRORISM."

The box is surrounded with photographs of a gas mask, a solar-powered/wind-up radio, a radiation meter, and other essentials like "Radiation Blocking Tablets."

It was like reading an upscale version of *Soldier of Fortune* magazine.

The reader is asked, "Should you plan for the unthinkable?" It continues, "Some call it paranoia. Others call it preparedness."

Although the article seriously deals with some subjects like the vulnerability of the water supply and what to do if exposed to a "dirty-bomb," the overall tone seems like cocktail party chatter.

Finally, the article details their recommended "72-Hour Survival Kit." It contains, the gas mask ($170—children's mask $200), the radio ($95), Katayn water filters ($200 ea.), and dozens of other items totaling about $5,500.

It wouldn't be a *New York* magazine article if they did not ask, "Want to rough it in style?" Among the items in their Deluxe Survival Kit are; a HOPE (High office parachute escape—$899), and a Sea Eagle 14SR sport boat—for evacuation by the Hudson or East River—($3,200).

As an expert on the subject of Survival Kits (see Blumert's credentials below), I suggest that the following items be added to the *New York* list.

1. A white flag to surrender;

2. An English/Arabic dictionary;

3. An English/Hebrew dictionary;

4. A letter from a Rabbi complimenting the bearer for his good works;

5. A letter from a Mullah complimenting the bearer for his good works;

6. A poison pill should the quality of life in Manhattan plummet and become unbearable (e.g., the good restaurants are all over-booked).

MAY 28, 2002

WORLD WAR II AND OTHER
GLORIOUS EVENTS

You Can Even Sell a Soviet Missile at the Right Price

"Pssssst: I've got a terrific deal for you on a six-year-old Indian elephant. It's a steal at $1,000."

"You can't be serious. What would a city dweller possibly do with an elephant?"

"Tell you what. I'll lower the price to $800 and include one year's supply of hay."

"This is ridiculous. I live in a three-room apartment in Berkeley and they don't even allow a parakeet."

"My final offer: $500 and I'll throw in a second elephant."

"Two elephants for $500? . . . It's a deal but they both better be healthy and housebroken."

News Item: American businessman Dennis Tito paid a $20 million fee to blast-off on a space shot aboard a Russian rocket. Tito's fare amounted to more than a sixth of the Russian space program's annual budget.

The media have made a big deal out of Tito's expensive excursion. But it is well-known that with the right connections in the Brighton Beach section of Brooklyn you can purchase an entire Russian infantry division or arrange to have former Soviet MIG fighter pilots as waiters for your next party. (Whatever deal you make, you'll probably get cheated, or worse.)

There is something deliciously perverse in seeing a major world government selling or renting their military paraphernalia to any and all customers. Some folks express panic at the mere thought of Russian weapons in the hands of "unaccountables." Seems to me, that the risks are no greater than when the weapons are in the hands of government murderers with "legal sanction" (ask Chechnya).

Given the inevitable bloating and corruption of all government enterprises, and the negative view Americans have of their intrusive, imperial government, it's only a matter of time when the "For Sale" signs are rolled out on all US agencies, military and otherwise.

Here is a peek at a future GSA brochure advertising US Government products and services at bargain prices:

CHRISTMAS GIFTS
FOR THE MAN WHO HAS EVERYTHING

- The man in your life will be delighted to receive three live Minuteman missiles ready to launch. (He needn't worry about any "collateral damage" as he will be protected by the same exemption of responsibility enjoyed by the US Military.) Price: $5 million (some history of family violence is useful.)

- He will be excited to command the 82nd Airborne in any military exercise of his choice. To be used outside the US only. Price: $5 million. (This is the favorite gift for those with strong, negative feelings toward some country somewhere.)

- How surprised he will be when he learns the aircraft carrier USS *Yorktown* is available for any purpose he desires: a wedding, confirmation, or bar mitzvah. Price: $1 million (no

Clinton-like parties allowed as we are still cleaning up the mess from the last one.)

- And to satisfy the darker side of your man's personality, we will arrange for the IRS to "work over his enemies" (includes audits, threatening letters, and asset confiscation). Price: $1 million or simply provide the names of ten people you know who are not paying their fair share of taxes.

- And if the man in your life has had a rough time of it lately, what better way to relieve tensions than to have him select a Supreme Court Justice to torture over a weekend. Price: $1 million.

The GSA bargain offerings are not only for the rich. There are many fascinating gifts for the average American with a limited budget.

- Wouldn't he enjoy a week of Marine Corps basic training at Paris Island? Price: $1,000 (he might as well learn his killing skills from the best).

- For the pet lover, what could be more loving and useful than an aging, retired drug-sniffing dog from US customs? Price: $100. (Customs is not responsible if the dog you receive is an addict.)

- If it's travel he likes, you can get him a trip to a disaster area of choice, courtesy of FEMA. Price: $1,000. (Since Washington, DC is a constant disaster area, it is not eligible here.)

- For those who seek adventure, you can be a FBI infiltrator. Choose from any organization: Act Up, Jewish Defense League, KKK, Southern Poverty League et al. Price: $1,000. (The infiltrator will feel right at home, as most of the organization members encountered are also FBI infiltrators.)

- As a lifetime gift, you can have your loved one placed in the Witness Protection Program, and they will never be heard from again. Price: $5,000. (Those already in the Witness Protection Program are not eligible.)

- For those who are homebound, we have a full array of video tapes featuring US military atrocities on four different continents. You will know the tapes are authentic, as the narrators are all recipients of Medals of Honor and Bronze Stars. Price: $50 (tapes are not to be used for political purposes.)

- For those who appreciate humor, you can read the hilarious accounts of US citizens unwittingly exposed to experimental drugs administered by various US government agencies. Price: $50. (These are destined to be collector items.)

Watch for our next exciting GSA Auction Catalog. Here's your chance to buy government-owned land and national parks including Yosemite. If you are one of the successful bidders for Alcatraz, "you'll really own a piece of the rock."

April 30, 2001

BLUMERT IS SHEIK FOR A WEEK

Following the tragic events of September 11, the media rushed to report widespread instances of violence against Arab-Americans. As the days passed these reports abated, replaced by articles about the contributions and patriotism of Arab-Americans and Muslims.

But how reliable is the media in reporting such data, and do they reflect American attitudes?

If the media's performance is as poor in this quarter as in almost every other area, we must look elsewhere. How do we find truth? Stay tuned.

In the 1947 Academy Award Winning film, *Gentleman's Agreement*, screenwriter Moss Hart and director Elia Kazan rocked the country with the movie's study of anti-Semitism in New York's corporate offices and in ritzy Darien, Connecticut.

Gregory Peck portrays the waspy Skylar Green, a writer assigned by *Smiths Weekly* to do a series on anti-Semitism. Green adopts the strategy of pretending he is Jewish writer, Phil Green, and rubs shoulders with the elite, seeking to determine the extent and depth of their anti-Semitism.

I recently rented and revisited *Gentleman's Agreement*, concluding that the reason the film's characters despised Phil Green was not because he was Jewish but because he was totally humorless, inarticulate, and unbelievably boring.

In a similar vein—thirteen years after *Gentleman's Agreement*—brilliant white author John Howard Griffin uncovered racism in his book, *Black Like Me*. Darkening his skin, Griffin disguised himself as a black man and toured the Deep South.

Black Like Me was published to wide acclaim in 1961, but some critics held that the book revealed more about the author than race relations in the old South.

On October 18 I received the following email directive from headquarters, LewRockwell.com:

Attn: Blumert

Problem: We are not getting sufficient information on public attitudes toward Arab-Americans.

Although the value of *Gentleman's Agreement* and *Black Like Me* was questionable, we can learn from their failure.

Your mission: You will enter your community posing as Sheik Whoizze. Mix with the people.

Seek the truth.

Warning: If captured we will not pay any ransom for your return. In fact, LRC will deny any affiliation with you.

It had been years since my last assignment in the field. In 1998 I was the nude streaker at The Academy Award Ceremony. This experience made me the logical choice as Sheik For A Week.

My report follows: Sheik For a Week

DAY ONE:

Burt's wife: "Who are these women and what are they doing here?"

Burt: "I'm going to play my role all the way. These young women are going to be my other wives for 'Sheik Week'."

Burt's wife (aghast): "Good Heavens! Where did you find them?"

Burt: "From the Afghan War Relief Agency, of course. They're really nice, aren't they?"

Burt's wife: "Gregory Peck didn't bring any women home in the movie. Anyway, we don't have any room for them, and they don't even speak English. Aren't you carrying this too far?"

Burt: "It's clear you have been influenced by Israeli propaganda. I'm reminded of an Arab proverb: 'May the feathers of one million partridges rest beneath your head, and give you dreams that lead to the tolerance and bliss found only in a peaceful oasis'."

Burt's wife: "Lovely, but what has that got to do with anything?"

DAY TWO:

(Finding a Sheik Costume)

Unfortunately, it was near Halloween and costumes were almost impossible to locate. Only through a stroke of luck was I able to find the San Francisco equivalent of Omar the tentmaker. He assured me he would save the day.

Omar: "I'm going to save the day. You will need at least seven yards of billowing fabric."

Sheik Whoizze: "I want what Peter O'Toole wore in *Lawrence of Arabia*. It was a spotlessly white Arab/Harith robe that made him appear larger than life."

Omar: "Well, we can come close, but the only bolt of cloth I have is blushing pink."

Sheik Whoizze: "Blushing pink?"

Omar (with a wave of dismissal): "This is San Francisco. It'll work, it'll work."

DAY THREE

I was ready for my first encounter with the people of San Francisco.

Now, fully costumed as the Sheik, I began my research in the Marina District, an upscale neighborhood within sight of the Golden Gate Bridge. While walking along Chestnut Street I disregarded the rude, hard stares and those suspiciously sexist overtures.

Finally, a pleasant-looking middle-aged man tapped my shoulder.

Pleasant looking man: "Sheik, I represent a small group of Christian and Jewish men who want fairness and equity for Arabs and Muslims. We are embarrassed by the hostility shown to your people, and wish to protect you from angry bigotry. We insist on accompanying you on your way to the mosque."

Sheik Whoizze (using best imitation of Omar Sharif): "That's very nice of you and your group, but I'm not going to the mosque. I'm on my way to Safeway to pick up a live lamb."

Pleasant looking man: "You need not hide your devotion to your faith, Mullah. You can walk with pride to the mosque for the sundown services. We are happy to escort you."

Sheik Whoizze: "I really have to get to Safeway before someone else gets my live lamb."

Pleasant looking man (seizing the hem of Sheik Whoizze's pink robe):

"You're going to the mosque, and we're going to see that you get there safely."

After a bit of pushing and shoving, bruised, with my garment torn, I escaped this loving group of citizens and managed to get to Safeway.

DAY FOUR

Bart (Bay Area Rapid Transit) proved to be an excellent testing ground for learning about America's reaction to Arabs. All went smoothly until one lady, obviously distraught at having received her monthly oil bill that morning, tugged at my fake beard and pulled it off.

Angry lady (snarling): "How come they tell me on TV that the government will help us yet my fuel bill keeps going up? What do you have to say about that, Mr. Sheik?"

Sheik Whoizze: "Madam, my family has nothing to do with oil. We are in the camel-breeding business."

She was so angry it wasn't easy getting my beard back, but I'm convinced our exchange will lead her to a better understanding of Arabs.

FINAL DAY

I'm back home. Tired, robes torn, and famished, I was really looking forward to a magnificent meal blending Afghan and American cuisine.

Sheik Whoizze (hopefully): "Where's my dinner, dears?"

There were my four wives playing Mahjong. They had consumed my case of Chateau Lafite Rothschild and smoked my box of Cuban Monte Cristo cigars.

Sheik Whoizze (still hopeful): "What are we having for dinner?"

Afghan wife #3: "We made a reservation for Chinese."

Sheik Whoizze (disappointed and surprised): "How come you're speaking English?"

Afghan wife #2: "We spent the day at Neiman Marcus and Bloomingdale's. Those sales ladies were so nice giving us lovely American clothes because of that plastic card of yours. Learning English that way is easy."

Stunned, ex-Sheik Whoizze staggers to the bathroom where he finds sixteen pairs of just washed Donna Karan pantyhose drying on the towel racks.

OCTOBER 23, 2001

MEMO FROM ROCKWELL: "BLUMERT, JOIN THE SARS EPIDEMIC"

From: Lew Rockwell, Editor
To: Burt Blumert

It's no accident, Blumert, that you haven't received an LRC story assignment since you made such a fool of yourself on the last one.

You were supposed to be researching American attitudes toward Arabs, but impersonating a Sheik in San Francisco, wearing Arabian garb that was blushing pink instead of traditional, Lawrence of Arabia white, showed the poorest judgment.

And what possessed you to request four temporary marriage licenses at City Hall, explaining that the extra wives lent authenticity to your being "Sheik For a Week"?

The worst part was negotiating with the Jewish Defense League for your freedom. You are fortunate they accepted in trade an autographed photo of William Kristol. (I'm still worried about blowback in case they thought they were getting Billy Crystal.)

Finally, I would appreciate if you stopped closing your emails with, "May the fleas of 1,000 camels infest the beard of your enemy."

Let's get to your new assignment.

It's clear the government-sponsored media are blocking any real data on the "SARS epidemic." We need you to uncover the truth. This is an important story, Blumert and here is your chance to make amends for the sheik debacle in San Francisco.

Travel Arrangements

On Thursday night, May 29, at the Oakland Airport, Cathay Pacific counter, you will be approached by a representative of Stolen-Tickets.com. He will hand you a packet with tickets and boarding passes, San Fran to Taipei to Hong Kong to Toronto to San Fran.

As you might surmise, these are the cheapest tickets available anywhere. Yours were issued in the name of Sister Mary Margaret of the Ursuline Order. Let's do better with the costume and impersonation this time. Okay?

Hotels

"The Final Destination Travel Agency" booked your hotel rooms as part of a terrific, cheap package deal. Your rooms will be on a floor with folks who have a slight cough, but no fever.

Meals

Business is so bad in the "SARS" cities that you should be able to get your meals at super low prices. May I suggest that, in Chinese restaurants, you negotiate the price of each item on the menu.

If the Egg Roll is priced at US$3.95, offer them $3.25. Initially, they might get upset, but persist. Morale is so low, you will wear them down and the bargains will flow.

In Toronto, when presented with the restaurant bill, have a coughing spasm. They will be so relieved to see you exit, it won't matter that the bill goes unpaid.

Interviews

We have obtained for you a highly prized, World Health Organization Green Badge. This allows the bearer full access to all Quarantined SARS Areas.

Imagine: you will be able to talk to SARS victims in each city, at every stage of the disease. This could mean a Pulitzer Prize.

MASK

Incidentally, you will be receiving via UPS (COD, of course) an historic surgical mask from the Spanish Influenza Epidemic of 1918.

This treasure is part of the LRC collection, so use it carefully, and please have it dry-cleaned before you return it (or leave instructions to have it returned).

May 28, 2003

BLUMERT ALMOST QUALIFIES AS A SUICIDE BOMBER

From: Editor Lew Rockwell
To: Burt Blumert
Subject: Your next assignment

I regret to advise you, Blumert, that your article on Katrina and the tragic flooding in New Orleans is unsuitable for LRC.

Interviewing the waiters at the Mardi Gras Bar and Grille in San Francisco hardly qualifies as adequate research.

Your revisionist theory that a clique of renegade CIA agents created Katrina so that damning JFK assassination evidence would be destroyed by the rampaging floodwaters is fascinating. But naming Waldo, the bartender at the Mardi Gras as your primary source for the story also falls short as proper investigative reporting.

Incidentally, the $125 charge on your expense account for "2 rounds of drinks for Katrina's victims at the Mardi Gras Bar" is also rejected.

This next assignment gives you a chance to regain your status as LRC's #7 investigative reporter.

It's predictable that people will react violently to foreign invaders on their soil, but to see them blowing themselves up as "suicide bombers" is beyond the ability of most Americans to fathom.

Who are these people that blow themselves up?

How are they chosen?

We need answers, Blumert.

Infiltrate their organizations,

sign on if you must;

do whatever it takes to get us the facts.

Following is a transcription of Blumert's interview at the Your Last Job Agency, located in the hills of Marin County.

Simon Rasputin is the Agency interviewer; Simon earned international notoriety as the Kool-Aid dispenser at the People's Temple in Guyana.

Rasputin: Hello, Blumert. And thanks for using Your Last Job Agency. We are an equal opportunity, nonsectarian agency seeking qualified suicide bombers (SBs) from all walks of life, regardless of their political or religious biases.

I don't wish to sound like an ageist but aren't you a little old to be applying for this kind of work?

Blumert: Well, being old may be part of it. The current costs of dying have skyrocketed and a suicide bombing might save my estate thousands of dollars. In fact, don't some SBs earn up to $25,000 for their family survivors?

Rasputin: Yes, that's true, less, of course, our 18 percent agency fee.

At the risk of being rude, Blumert, may I ask why are you wearing that ridiculous, pink Lawrence of Arabia costume? Are you making some political statement, or is it left over from Halloween? (See "Sheik for a Week.")

Blumert: No political statement intended, but there are so few occasions when I can wear it and my wife says that the flowing lines are flattering and make me look thinner.

As to the color, don't jump to any conclusions, Buster. The tailor ran out of white and all he had left was pink. Do you have trouble with that?

Rasputin: Well, Excuuuuuse me! Let's move on.

Your application is impressive, Blumert. It's hard to imagine anyone so consistently identified with losing causes. This is a very positive indicator for us. You just may be one of those "naturals" we encounter every now and then.

Are you ready to start talking about an assignment?

Blumert: Not so fast. There are several things that trouble me. First, I read that the strap-on bombs are getting bigger and more powerful. Please, make a note that my bomb can't be too heavy as I have a chronic bad back.

Can you imagine if my back went out just when I was pushing the button, or pulling the ripcord, or whatever it takes to set the thing off?

Rasputin: OK, OK. So noted. Now, are you ready to talk assignment?

Blumert: Well, let's see. I have a dental appointment on Tuesday and on Thursday I'm scheduled for a Karate lesson. How about after Christmas?

Rasputin: Some of the clients we represent might be hiring extra people for the Christmas season, but I'm confident we could place you after the holidays.

Blumert: Now, the first reports I heard on the hotel suicide bombings in Jordan indicated that a husband and wife team were involved. I know that some employers don't approve of hiring married couples, but it seems like a romantic idea to me.

Rasputin: I suppose it would be all right if we teamed the two of you up, but your wife will have to go through the same training course and don't try to get another $25,000 out of us. It's $25,000 per family.

Blumert: You just made that up. We should get at least $35,000 for the two of us,

Rasputin: All right, already. $35,000 it is. Call your wife and have her come down to sign up.

Blumert: Well, it's not quite that simple. She hasn't the foggiest notion I'm here or what we're discussing. She might very well be against this whole thing. You know how difficult women can be sometimes.

Rasputin: This interview is not going well. Tell me, Blumert, what other problems might you have as a suicide bomber?

Blumert: For one thing, I'm crazy about animals. I'd need total assurance that not a hair on any kitty or doggy would be singed.

Rasputin: I'm certain that somewhere, someone would be happy to see you become a suicide bomber, Blumert, especially if you are the only casualty. I'll give some thought to locating such a client. In the meanwhile, as they say, "Don't call us. We'll call you."

November 15, 2005

WORLD WAR II AND
OTHER GLORIOUS EVENTS

*The following was an enclosure with last month's credit card
bill with a solicitation for the WWII Monument in Washington, DC, and a promotional piece for the movie, Pearl Harbor.*

Are you bored with those phony, contrived TV survival
shows? Had enough watching photogenic showbiz
wannabes eating slugs and stabbing every back in sight?

Greats Wars and Other Glorious Events is proud to
announce the opening of our super theme park: World War II:
The Last Great War.

The park offers entertainment for the entire family, so pull
the plug on your TV, join us at our fabulous Theme Park, and
actually live World War II.

If you were not fortunate enough to have been part of the
"Greatest Generation," here is your opportunity to experience
the exhilaration of that wondrous time.

All the famous bloody battles will be recreated: from the
deserts of North Africa, to the invasion of Sicily, from Anzio to
the Battle of the Bulge. (Sorry, at this writing our permit to
explode atomic bombs has not been approved. Only films and
tapes of that epic event will be shown.)

And you can be part of it.

For those bravehearts who want to actually share the experience of the Great Generation, and defeat Shicklgruber and Tojo,
you will be fully equipped with 1940s weapons and gear, and
undergo a brief training period that will include hand-to-hand combat. From that point it is up to you to "Be All That You Can Be."

You will be under the constant eye of Theme Park employees who will direct the combat from our air-conditioned offices in Boca Raton.

Of course, family members are not required to participate directly and can watch the grand spectacle from reinforced bunkers and closed-circuit television near the front lines. (In war, even in recreated battles, there are casualties, and our heartfelt regrets go in advance to those innocents who will be victims.)

- Bloody battles are meticulously recreated. (On the Guadalcanal set, for example, the mosquitoes carry malaria.)

- The field medics have been trained and supervised by the producers of MASH.

- The Germans and Japanese, who portray enemy troops, have been recruited from maximum-security prisons in those countries. To ensure that they are appropriately surly, they have been barred from visiting Disneyland, and have eaten all their meals at fast-food restaurants.

- Acts of heroism will be properly recognized, but those committing atrocities can earn no award higher than the Bronze Star.

- The World War II Theme Park has been highly recommended by the following great Americans:

    Janet Reno says she has not been so moved since that exciting day in Waco, when the outgunned BATF and FBI agents courageously overcame the Branch Davidian cultists.

    General Westmoreland says after his visit, "It was nice to see us win some battles for a change."

    William Kristol enjoyed his visit to the World War II Theme Park, but grumbled that since we were doing it all over again, this time we should occupy Teheran, London, Moscow, and Peking.

As a Grand Opening special, we will conduct an Anne Frank lookalike contest. The winner gets to spend the month of August in an attic in Amsterdam.

(In fine print) Disclaimers and Warnings upon your visit to the World War II Theme Park.

- If you are wounded or get a combat-related disease, you will automatically be dispatched to a Walter Reed Hospital.

- If you are captured by the enemy, we will negotiate for your release, and even resort to a prisoner exchange (for example, you for Arnold Schwarzenegger).

- Under no circumstances will there be any refunds nor do guests at the World War II Theme Park qualify for the GI Bill of Rights.

May 30, 2001

BLUMERT PRODUCES HIS MILITARY RECORDS

From: Editor Rockwell
To: Blumert

"These are dangerous times. Since it's an election year, everybody's military record is being examined with a fine-tooth comb.

"There are questions about your commitment to liberty, Blumert.

"It's time to come clean. And don't tell me again that your records were lost in the San Francisco earthquake.

"You've given us different versions about your military career.

"Once, you dazzled a group of young libertarian women with an absurd tale about being America's ace fighter pilot during the Korean War.

"That you'd shot down 15 MIGs and reached the rank of Major General upon retiring. (For your information, the women weren't dazzled. They were nauseated.)

"I also recall, during a discussion about John McCain, you had to outdo his epic tale by recounting your experience in Korea. You told the group you were a POW for NINE years, finally released in a trade for a Russian ballerina who had defected to the West. (It was later learned she was a female impersonator.)

"I want the truth, Blumert. I expect an immediate response."

From: Blumert
To: Editor Rockwell

"All right, I admit it. Some of those reports of my being an Air Force ace, shooting down 15 Russian MIGS are greatly exaggerated.

"Actually, the closest I ever came to combat during the Korean War was getting airsick in an Air Force Transport and barfing all over the pilot's dress uniform carefully folded on the seat next to me.

"It required all my negotiating skills to survive that close call.

"Before finally winding up in Air Force blue, like all other thinking cowards, including Dick Cheney, I did everything to avoid the draft.

"Dick Cheney's five deferments are chicken feed. I had at least eight. The first seven were related to student deferments.

"Then, disaster. The rules changed. The only deferments left were for war related research, like PhDs working on Hydrogen Bombs.

"I had run out of options. It was like waiting for the executioner to beckon. Korea, here I come.

"Then, a glimmer of hope.

"Get a job in a factory doing war-related things," some unremembered faceless fellow said. "This can get you out of the draft and it won't cost you much."

"Details are blurry and I don't recall the price, but I have a faded recollection of depositing money in somebody's Swiss Bank account. My next image is of sitting in a windowless interview room in a Long Island City factory.

"I later learned that they produced pretty little precision objects that made bombs more deadly.

"Management consisted of seven ex-Nazi tool and die makers. After five minutes with me it was clear that I had to be kept away from any task that required dexterity, or tool and die making skills.

"There's only one job here for you, Blumert," SS Officer Schmidt said, "Cutting the aluminum bricks, that's your job. An average person can cut six bricks in a day. You might do four."

"It took three days, six band saws and a gallon of cooling fluid to produce my first (and last) cut brick. All of a sudden, combat in Korea seemed less horrible than another day at the band saw.

"There must be some way other than the band saw to avoid the draft?

"Yes, flunk the pre-induction medical and get the magical '4-F' status.

"The setting for this medieval ritual was a cavernous stone building on Whitehall Street on Lower Manhattan, clearly built for earlier wars. Hundreds of thousands of shivering American kids in their skivvies were herded through the drafty old facility during WWII—and those with a sense of irony were later able to make the experience part of a comedy routine.

Nobody was spared the indignities.

"Bend over," the rear-end doctor ordered.

"Do you like girls?" the psychiatrist inquired.

"Can you see the eye chart on the wall?" If you located the wall, this doc was satisfied.

The doc in search of hernias said, "Cough, but not on me."

"I didn't get the cherished '4-F'" rating, but had they awarded a 3-E status, I might have come close. But, you know the old bromide—'close' only counts in horseshoes.

"I was resigned to my fate: Korea here I come. Only divine intervention could save me now.

"I don't know if the US Air Force qualifies as an agent for divine intervention, but they came to the rescue.

"During the Korean War, the Air Force was having a tough time acquiring and keeping pilots. No surprise. Some functionary at 'military intelligence' decided that if the enlistment period were cut from four to two years they would net more volunteers.

"Well, they netted one more, me, Blumert.

"The prospect of serving in the Air Force for two years instead of being killed or maimed on a desolate Korean mountainside was irresistible.

"The draft board was indifferent. Air Force/Army, it was all the same to them. 'Go to the Air Force, my son, with our blessings.' Maybe those weren't the exact words, but I was off to Basic Training and Aviation Cadet school.

"This is the end of Part I."

Part II will reveal Blumert as a glamorous Aviation Cadet.

You will learn that he was the only Cadet in his class who didn't know how to drive a car. (The other Cadets could disassemble and assemble a motorcycle in two hours.)

You will get the details when, Blumert, wearing Air Force Blue, almost won $16,000 on a popular TV Quiz Show.

You will be fascinated (yawn) learning of other notable incidents in Blumert's Air Force career.

"Finally, Editor Rockwell, I trust that making this information public will put those ugly rumors to bed, once and for all.

("I'm having some difficulty locating the negatives of those horrid photographs that keep popping up on the Internet. I assure you, they have all been digitally altered.")

May 3, 2004

THE NEXT GENERATION REMOTE CONTROL— ZAPPING PEOPLE

If you hang by the neck long enough, you get used to it.

Adjusting is part of the human condition. If there is a germ of truth in the "hanging by the neck" maxim, imagine how quickly we adopt new devices and innovations when they bring improvement to the human condition.

There are those walking among us who actually celebrated the arrival of indoor plumbing, and how soon we have forgotten those funny little houses on street corners where people made telephone calls.

But technology's greatest triumph goes hardly noticed. We can only shudder thinking about the uncivilized, sub-human practice of manually changing TV channels. A process so gross it has been erased from the collective memory.

There are countless instances of the frustrated viewer, unable to lift himself out of the stuffed armchair quickly enough, throwing a shoe at the screen and even some recorded cases of desperate "TV rage" resulting in a gun being fired at the magic box.

In my judgment there is no more essential symbol of human progress than the wondrous "remote control" device that automatically changes TV channels. We affectionately dub it as the "zapper."

What follows is my TV log for the past week demonstrating how the "zapper" protected my soul and sanity.

BLUMERT'S TV LOG

"We're lucky this morning at Channel 4 to have Father O'Connor, Rabbi Levy, and Reverend Miller with us discussing the need for additional homeless shelters in the downtown area . . ."

Zap.

"Tom, it's a thrill to work with you this afternoon at ESPN. Lacrosse has been played far longer than baseball and is truly an American sport. Unfortunately, it has only gained real popularity with an elite group of Northeast colleges. Our game today is between two old rivals . . ."

Zap.

"Zambi's remarkable mastery of the zither has thrilled music lovers the world over. His CDs and tapes are not available in local stores. If you order now you will not only receive Zambi's interpretation of the complete works of Beethoven but as a bonus we will include his collection of Indian rhythms from the Brazilian rain forest. Call 800 . . ."

Zap.

"Dr. Teitlebaum has counseled Hollywood stars on their weight problems for decades. His 'Miracle Diet' is now available to you. We guarantee you will need an entire new wardrobe in two weeks. (Dr. Teitlebaum denies charges by the FDA that his formula employs the use of tapeworms.)"

Zap.

"At 3 p.m. on C-SPAN 2, we will air the Prohibition Party convention. The session lasts fifty-four minutes and ends with a drunken brawl . . ." (I made that up.)

Zap.

"Today on Meet the Press we have Senator John McCain. He will discuss his heroic effort to institute campaign finance reform. David Broder, Clarence Page, and William Safire make up our distinguished panel . . ."

Zap.

A brilliant high-tech pal has programmed my remote so that it automatically "zaps" the instant the name, image, or voice of any of the following is detected on my TV: Bill O'Reilly, Christiane Amanpour, Wolf Blitzer, Bill Maher, et al.*

I anxiously await the next generation of remote control devices. You point it at any offensive person or group whether on the street, in an office, or anywhere, you click, and they disappear.

A friend suggests that we already have such devices and they are called guns. He misses the point completely. I don't wish to hurt or maim. I just want the object to disappear from my life.

Others are free to keep my zapped victims or not. Let them do their own zapping.

April 3, 2001

---

*Send $1.99 and I will send you Blumert's V-Chip which blocks out and thus protects your family from these undesirables.

WHY IS THERE A CIRCUS TENT ON MY HOUSE?

W hen our front door disintegrated upon a neighbor's slight knock, it was evident we had a termite problem.

"California termites are bad," a friend reported. (This fellow provides impeccably accurate data as long as you never check him out.) "Some of those critters have mutated and are consuming metal," he added. (You needn't check that one out, but things were bad enough.)

Critics indict those on "the Right" as being mean-spirited and unfeeling. Single-handedly, I shatter that myth by maintaining a positive, almost childlike view of the world, which, often, approaches innocence.

For example, when I would see a house completely covered by a tent, I assumed that there was a happy American family putting on their own circus. Now I know better.

The Yellow Pages turned up dozens of pest control firms, but, none with as catchy a name as "Yougottem-Wekillem."

Their senior technician arrived in minutes and emerged from our basement, his wooden clipboard half consumed, proclaiming, "Dude, you have one terrific case of termites."

I might have been more confident in him had he not been wearing his flash-lit coal-miner's hat backward.

Next stop was the Internet. Surely, it would provide truth and guidance. I employed every search engine for "termites" and they all dead-ended with "fumigation." I didn't learn much, but my file of recipes now includes four gourmet-quality lethal gases.

For termites, Vicane (sulfuryl fluroide) manufactured by Dow Elanco is the poison gas of choice.

Dow's warnings on Vicane are scarey. "Exposure to high concentration causes excessive fluid in the lungs, pneumonia, and convulsions." The EPA adds additional danger signals when reentering after the fumigation. "Reduced awareness, slowed movement, garbled speech, or difficulty in breathing." (These warnings are very similar to those on the label of my antihistamine.)

A final caution: if you are rendered unconscious, wear a nametag so they'll know who you were. (I made this one up.)

It was time for action as the eating machine army of bugs had already sent advance scouting parties to taste my antique Brunswick billiard table. An emergency appointment at Yougottem-Wekillem's pest control center was scheduled and we should have been suspicious when we were advised to wear old clothes.

As we arrived, the police Swat Team prevented the pickets surrounding the facility from harassing us, but the crude picket signs were ugly and conveyed their message: "Extermination equals murder." "Today termites, tomorrow??"

Still shaken by the protestors from PETI (People for the Ethical Treatment of Insects), I said to the director, "I've read all the literature. Let's go ahead with my tent and the fumigation."

"Not so fast," he cautioned, "Before we can 'tent' you, there is a five-day waiting period and you have to face the state-mandated panel waiting in the next room. All of the arguments pro and con the extermination of termites will be presented and only then can you make the decision to forge ahead or not. You can be represented by counsel if you wish."

"This is ridiculous," I sputtered. "Let's move this along. They're eating my pool table!"

As we entered the windowless hearing room, the director donned a powdered wig, and actress Susan Sarandon rose to present the case for the termites.

"What is she doing here?" I stammered in disbelief.

"You're lucky. Last week they sent Barbra Streisand."

Sarandon made the same tired argument about all species having equal claim to the planet, but I stopped her in her tracks when I said, "What about the fact that your shoes are made of leather?"

Everybody's eyes focused on her feet. How could I have known that her feet were bare?

The fellow from the "Altered Genes Will Save The Planet Committee" was next, and his presentation was science at its best. Some were troubled by the notion of sterilizing one termite at a time, but he did get a standing ovation.

Last was a representative from Dow who was a bit difficult to understand because of his gas mask. His message was clear.

"If we follow the advice of those two crazies, what would Dow do with all this poison gas we have inventoried?"

A silent shudder passed through the room.

My concerns were more immediate than his and I quickly voted thumbs up.

Next week the circus tent will cover my house, and the fumigation will proceed.

By the way, can anybody out there take care of my two cats?

February 27, 2001

I HATE BED & BREAKFASTS

In the last episode, our termite-infested house was covered with a giant circus-like yellow tent, and the fumigators were prepared to pump in vicane, a deadly poison gas.

"A real man doesn't leave his home; a captain never abandons his ship; a shepherd doesn't desert his flock; a king always . . ."

"Enough, enough already," my wife sputtered. "The poison gas kills every form of life in seconds. Not even a termite could survive." (How quickly she forgot the purpose of the fumigation.)

"What about those gas masks I've ordered from the Whole Earth Catalog?" I asked smugly.

"That has to be the most ridiculous thing you've ever done, particularly the special order gas masks for the cats. Anyway, I made reservations at the bed and breakfast for four days."

"Bed and breakfast? I'll need more than a gas mask to survive that. Cancel the B&B, and book Motel Six."

"None of the hotels takes pets, you know that."

"Well, send the cats to the B&B," I said sarcastically.

A friend, widely known for his prudence in not spending money, presents a strong case for the bed and breakfast concept.

"In most instances," he says, "the B&B is cheaper than a hotel. Also, you're not just a customer passing through. At the B&B you are a guest, and after you've been there awhile, you're part of the family."

"Part of the family? I've got enough trouble with my own family, particularly some marginal folks on my wife's side. The one thing I don't need is a new family. As far as being somebody's houseguest, I prefer being a customer. At the Ritz Carlton, it's always clean and nobody gives a damn who I am."

I had never set foot in a B&B, so it was with trepidation that we entered "Mi Casa Es Su Casa," one of the better known B&Bs in our area. I couldn't stop thinking how much the man behind the desk looked like Norman Bates, particularly since he was wearing a dress that was clearly his mother's.

"Welcome," he said, embracing me. "Remember, you're part of our family. There's no smoking, no roller skating, no surfing, no phone calls, no faxes, no computers, and no paleo-libertarians."

How could he possibly have known that I was an inveterate roller skater?

"This key is for the front door," he continued, "this one is for the side door, this one for the basement, and this whistle, only heard by dogs, will alert Killer, the German Shepherd, that you are family and not to be attacked.

"Breakfast is served between 7 a.m. and 7:15, and if you miss it, you lose points."

"Points?"

"Yes, points. And we will have to check out your blood alcohol levels. By the way, if you are caught with a bottle of booze, you face the death penalty."

"Death penalty? Why not just take away points?"

"There's no point in that." (Collapsing in mirth at his joke.)

"You're assigned to room 3, the one with the orange door. We call it 'old Yosemite'." The air conditioner and the heater are on all the time. We just let them fight it out."

(He didn't really say that, I made it up.)

As we entered room 3, it was clear they had made an error as an elderly couple was in the bed.

"Welcome," the old codger said. "I am Elijah and this is Sarah, and we're your family. We're warming up the bed for you, and I can tell you that we like you already. Right, Sarah?"

Sarah burped.

"This is absurd. You folks are going to have to leave and get your own room."

"We already have a room. We're in 2. The one with the blue door they call, 'Donner's Pass'."

"Well, what are you doing here?"

Elijah smiled and said, "I told you, we're family, and we're earning points."

Our cats, being much more family-oriented, took to Elijah and Sarah and joined them in the bed.

I don't know how much I slept that first night, but my new family was remarkably energetic given that their average age was 75. I once thought I heard roller-skating up and down the corridor outside my door and I was tempted to join them, but then I remembered Rule 9.

At 6 a.m. I decided that Starbucks was the most important place in the world. Ladened with a caddy brimming with steaming coffee and bear claws, I attempted to enter my family home, unnoticed, through the side door, but was caught and surrounded by hostile people. My family had turned surly.

"No food from the outside, Rule 8. You lose three points and the food," said cousin Julius.

At 4 a.m. the following morning we were packing and planning our escape.

"But we can't go back into the house yet. The poison gas needs another day to dissipate," said my wife.

"Well," I said, "what are the chances we'll survive there?"

"Probably, fifty-fifty."

"Sounds like pretty good odds to me."

March 10, 2001

BEWARE THE PHONE CALL
FROM THE SHERIFF

My secretary trilled, "Sgt. Preston from the Sheriff's Department on line 4 for Blumert." I'd never heard her page me with such joy.

What could they possibly want?

It's folklore that your entire life flashes before you when faced with imminent death. Getting a call from the sheriff's department isn't quite that serious, but my brain conjured up every horrible reason why they wanted me:

Could it be that parking ticket I got in Las Vegas in 1991 that was "lost" and never paid?

No, there is a statute of limitations on old parking tickets and they must have known that I lost $800 on that trip. Anyway, Las Vegas would never use the sheriff's department to collect a debt.

Oh Lord, now I know, it was the Gore Vidal speech I attended in San Francisco last year. The creep next to me was surely CIA and, like a dummy, I spent the entire evening establishing my anti-war credentials.

He still would never have remembered me, but "old swifty" Blumert made sure to give him a business card.

No, this is still America. They don't drag you away because you listened to a speech and tried to sell a gold coin to a CIA agent. Not yet.

"Face it, Blumert," I said to myself. "You know damn well why they want you. It's because of LRC and those ridiculous articles you write attacking doctors, Rudy, and almost every sacred aspect of contemporary American culture. Well, you've finally gone too far and now they're coming to get you."

That's ridiculous. Why would they want me? I'm too much trouble. I need a nap every afternoon, and at 3:00 p.m. there's a chat group on line that expects to hear from the "Freedom Stud." They could never take me away from all that.

This was false bravado. I was panicked. My fingers quivered as I grasped the phone.

Blumert: "Sgt. Preston, I would like to serve my time in the federal prison near Palm Springs. Do you know if an inmate can have a low-carb menu? And like Martha Stewart, I'd like to start this Monday and get it over with."

Sgt. Preston: "Gee, Mr. Blumert, as far as I know the food is better in San Quentin, but the reason I'm calling is to see if we can count on you for 4 tickets for the Sheriff's Department Annual Square Dance. Can I stop by and pick up a $100 check right now?"

Blumert: "Who is this? Sgt, Preston? You sound like a child. In fact, you sound like my paper boy, Billy Preston."

Sgt. Preston: "It's me, Billy. I started on the phones as a lowly Officer on Thursday and I got my Sgt's stripes yesterday when I sold 400 tickets to the Sheriff's Square Dance.

"It's amazing how frightened people are when I call and how easy it is to sell them tickets. A few more sales and I'll be up for Lieutenant.

"When can I come by to pick up a check?"

Blumert: "Billy, I'll take 8 tickets if you promise not to mention any of this to my wife when you deliver the paper tomorrow morning."

I grind my teeth when I take a call from a tele-marketing "slickster." I suppose they have a place in this world and I oppose any government restrictions on their activities (unless they're outright crooks). But they sure get under my skin.

On most occasions I won't take their calls. But sometimes I get trapped and I'll decide to challenge them—you never win. (See Billy Preston above.) After all, they have a wealth of experience in overcoming the lame protests from their phone victims. The longer the conversation, the weaker my resolve, so I've devised an exit strategy.

It goes something like this: "My wife won't let me talk to you anymore."

It almost always works. Either they have a wife like that themselves, or they feel so much sympathy that they click off, leaving me to my miseries.

In the old days setting up a "boiler room" to sell securities, collectibles, swamp land, or "worthy causes" was expensive and time consuming.

Obtaining "hard-lined" phone equipment and getting on line was a major project. The phone companies, anxious for new business, generally managed to push the order along, while remaining oblivious to the true activities of the "new customer."

Next, the "boiler-room" needed people to man the phones. Rounding up an experienced team of "tele-marketers" wasn't easy. It often meant scouring cheap hotels and other haunts of the "specialty salesman."

They had to get the word out that "here was a new pitch to separate folks from their money." The salesmen came from all points, answering the siren's call.

Things are different now.

Technology has altered the world of the tele-marketing scam. No "boiler room" needed, no phone banks necessary. The tele-marketing enterprise can be reduced to a series of $49 cell phones, located anywhere and changed as frequently as underwear.

The cell phone is the magic key into the land of limitless victims.

The tele-marketing salesman can be operating from Calcutta, or even from prison.

There may be legitimate tele-marketing operations, but how does the consumer know the difference? I'd like to believe that the "market" will weed out the bad apples.

Meanwhile, it's prudent to avoid ALL tele-marketers, but if one of these phone slicksters gets you, don't feel too stupid. It happens to the best of us.

By the way, can I interest you in some tickets to the Sheriff's Square Dance?

October 11, 2004

HOORAY, ITS LEAP YEAR AND WE HAVE AN EXTRA DAY

It seemed like just another Sunday.

237 TV channels competed for my attention. The Food Channel promised a "life/death" cook-off between the Japanese Master and an American Interloper. Squid was featured in every course. A very tempting show.

For an instant, I almost settled in at the "E" (Entertainment) channel where they were readying for the Academy

Awards. (This year I actually saw one of the nominated movies and had heard of two others).

I should have been using the time researching the Infomercial on the Exo-Cize Machine for Seniors. (I'm close to making a decision on one of those babies.)

But viewing habits are hard to break. There I was, glued to the same old channels catching middle-aged men in bald-faced lies (politicians), and watching death and destruction in Haiti, the US foreign policy disaster of the week. (It's Haiti AGAIN, fellas.)

"Something isn't right," I muttered. "It must be my new high blood pressure pill."

"Look, Blumert, it's February 29th, Leap Year Day, that disorients you. Every four years we go through the same thing," advised my encyclopedic wife. "For some reason, you lose it on 'Leap Year Day'."

"In 1996 you sued the bank for an extra day's interest. And I don't even want to think about 1992, when you told the police that they could not legally issue parking violations on Leap Year Day."

As usual, her recollections are infallible when it comes to criticizing me, and she's right about February 29th.

There are certain events that people can handle only once in four years.

The Olympics; two solid weeks of observing drug-driven athletes, "up close and personal" and then having to endlessly endure the strains of that inferior music known as National Anthems.

The World Soccer Cup: praise the Lord, Americans have not yet fully succumbed to that disease. But, have no fear. It won't be long before the USA, USA (delivered with gusto) will be exporting our drunken rowdies to "exciting" soccer matches the world over. (Exciting? Watching a zero-zero soccer match is like watching Pakistan vs. Australia in Cricket.)

American Presidential Elections; It takes four years for the foul air to become breathable again.

Leap Year Day doesn't even measure up to such events. Because it is so unimportant, it surprises us every time.

Someone tell me, please, why Leap Year Day comes in February? You can always trust politicians to give you snow in the winter. Why not an extra day in May? Or, how about a different month for Leap Year Day each time?

And don't tell me that February gets it because it's a short month. Considering it's horrid weather, February deserves to be a short month.

We're a democracy aren't we? Let's put it to a vote.

Personally, I'm against government being involved at all in determining when we celebrate Leap Year Day.

Let people decide themselves when they want that extra day. Can you imagine the commerce that choice would engender?

You could gift "The Day" to a loved one. If you're broke, you could sell your extra day on eBay. The potential is endless.

I have some other thoughts on the subject, but I'll wait until February 29th, 2008, to fill you in.

March 1, 2004

THANKS A LOT RON PAUL—
MY HOUSE IS NOW A CAMPAIGN
HEADQUARTERS

THANKS A LOT, RON PAUL–
YOU'VE MADE MY HOME A
POLITICAL CAMPAIGN
HEADQUARTERS

My wife said, "Look, Blumert, you'll have to whip up your own dinner tonight. Ron Paul is on CNN with Larry King and later, PBS is showing their terrific, 'Now' documentary featuring Ron for almost the full hour. I can't miss that, and then, according to LRC's 'Breaking News' blog, O'Bnoxious O'Riley has a segment discussing Ron's foreign policy. So you're on your own this evening, and it wouldn't kill you to miss a meal once in awhile anyway."

There are times when negotiating with my beautiful wife is pointless. This was one of those times, and I was ready to nuke the popcorn.

Ron Paul's amazing political odyssey has turned the lives of many people topsy-turvy. It could not be more so than in my own home. My life companion had never been that interested in the political process and she certainly wasn't much of a television fan. Her interest in TV diminished as the size of the sets increased.

After "Best Buy" covered our living room wall with a 73" HDTV, her viewing was rare. The only time the giant box won her attention was when she was dusting the furniture, and that only occurred during the summer solstice. (This revelation will insure many popcorn dinners in my future.)

But, that was then.

Now, since Ron Paul's heroic mission, my dear wife is never more than six feet from the giant Hitachi. Her daily schedule breaks down as follows; fourteen hours for essentials like sleep, meals, shopping, and ministering to me, three hours at her blog, three hours of intense internet search on anything Ron Paul (I must say that lewrockwell.com has made that aspect of her life easier).

The excitement begins when the TV political shows take over the tube. That's where she spends the remaining four hours of her day. She switches from CNN to MSNBC to CNBC, to FOX to PBS with an occasional visit to NBC, CBS, and ABC, the old-fashioned channels.

There are days when the phones ring off the hook as she compares notes with other Paulian junkies. Supporters of Ron from the neighborhood are invited to join in the viewing, and the 73" screen is very attractive on debate nights. Last night, we had a full house for the New Hampshire debate. One fellow actually arrived clutching a Ron Paul for President sign.

My wife is a gentle person, but nowadays, I'll often hear her snarling at a talking head and on one occasion she came close to hurling a shoe at the screen. That was before we bought the new 73-incher. She's now required to wear soft slippers during TV time.

The entire rotten establishment is terrorized by Ron's campaign, and they have employed every strategy to derail him. Initially, they pretended that he wasn't there. If he isn't there, they reasoned, maybe he'll go away. Next, they decided to marginalize Ron. During the earlier debates, while Ron was making a point, the cameras would scan the faces of the sorry crop of contenders as they smirked, rolled their eyes, and did everything but stick out their tongues to show disdain.

Then they initiated frontal attacks to pound Ron down. Rudy did it in South Carolina and Huckaboob tried it during a later debate. Not only did every one of these strategies fail, the Paul campaign seemed to feed on and grow with each failure.

A TV reporter pal in San Francisco analyzed it as follows:

"In the war against Ron, the establishment has the five following areas in which to attack him:

1. THE DEBATES. Attacking him here hasn't worked out too well and is fraught with risk. When someone hits Ron, the moderators are compelled to allow him to respond. This is where Dr. Paul shines. (As I point out above.)

2. THE PRINT MEDIA. Ron is well-received by local newspapers when he hits town and since nobody pays attention to the national opinion mags these days, any hit pieces from them are futile.

3. THE INTERNET. Ron wins every skirmish on the net. (His dazzling array of supporters make sure of that.)

4. TV. As with the hometown newspapers, Ron does very well with local TV coverage. It is only through the national networks and cable that Ron's enemies can effectively try to destroy his remarkable run.

5. THE REPUBLICAN APPARATUS. In most instances, a single word from an upper-level Party functionary can stop a candidate in his tracks. Ron Paul has never been part of their "club," and thus is immune to their dictates.

My TV reporter pal's logic is irrefutable. National TV is the only effective weapon they can use against Ron. The "talking heads" continue to ridicule and marginalize him, and it will get worse. Future elections may be decided otherwise, but this presidential election will, unfortunately, be affected by the images transmitted by the networks and cable.

"TV is where the people live," my wife says. "I don't know how we can neutralize their venom, but we have to watch them every minute and expose every evil thing they do."

She has been meticulous in monitoring the "heads" and I couldn't help peeking at her scribbled notes from last week. Included below are some cogent observations about the media "stars."

George Stephanopoulos—He will one day choke on his own words—definitely a drone without an original thought. He is not as dangerous as some of the others.

Tim Russert—A slick performer, but not slick enough to conceal the strings that control him. He should be considered deadly dangerous.

Chris Matthews—Constantly playing the "choir boy" while seeking "truth and justice." He has been assigned to promote Obama and will most likely be his Press Secretary. Matthews is an embarrassment to his profession.

The Fox Boys—Combined brainpower would barely light a bulb. They are bullies, have no sense of morality and are simply "hit-men."

Frank Luntz—Probably once had a brain, but he sold it along with his soul. It's a wonder he can sleep at night.

Wolf "the Blitzer"—Although fully bought and paid for, on rare occasion he displays some reportorial integrity.

Pat Buchanan—Of course, he should endorse Ron, but he does have to make a living hanging around the NBC studios.

This is no excuse, but it's difficult not to like Pat and wife Shelly, so Pat gets a partial pass.

Tucker Carlson—Tucker is top of the short list for Ron's running mate. He's smart, young, and would lend balance to the ticket.

Frankly, it's not easy to watch inferior people degrading Ron Paul from one TV channel to the next. Except for that one time when she almost hurled her shoe at the screen, my beautiful wife has remained stoic under the avalanche of innuendo and lies.

That was until yesterday. I don't know whether it was Russert's mean-spirited interview on *Meet the Press*, or David Shuster's smug effort to assassinate Ron on MSNBC, but she finally lost it. "How dare these pygmies malign a man like Ron Paul," she said with disgust.

"Look," I tried to explain, "as Ron brings the message of freedom from one state to the next, the attacks will intensify. They will call him a racist, a Nazi, a neo-Confederate, and Lord knows what else. I'm not talking about crazed fringe websites. It will be the MSM leading the charge."

These evildoers have at least one serious problem. The guy they are trying to destroy is a giant. Bigotry is not in Ron's makeup, and those who make such charges know it. The hundreds of thousands (soon to be millions?) of young people who listen to Ron's words know the real thing when they encounter it.

Here's a vignette I've recounted before; Please don't hold me to precise dates, but I think it was the summer of 1988, at the California LP Convention, and Ron announced his decision to run for President as the Libertarian Party candidate. Those of us close to Ron celebrated. We saw it as an incredible opportunity to spread the message of freedom.

Former Congressman Paul "Pete" McCloskey, a maverick Republican and Korean War hero, came to the hotel to congratulate Ron and wish him well. McCloskey was no libertarian, but he was a true patriot and told me that Ron Paul was the most principled man he had served with in the US Congress.

I later learned that McCloskey carried some advice for Ron and his campaign. He knew that Ron's noninterventionist foreign policy views precluded US foreign aid for ANY country. Lew warned Ron that this would ire the Israeli lobby in the US, and he suggested that Ron have some Jews represented in his campaign to demonstrate that he was not anti-Semitic.

Ron mentioned McCloskey's warning to Lew Rockwell. He laughed and told Ron, "Well you have nothing to worry about. Blumert *is* your campaign chairman and Murray Rothbard *is* your economic advisor." "Oh, OK," said Ron.

Yes, this was twenty years ago and we were all a bit more innocent, but it does say something about Ron and the way his mind works.

Well, here it is Sunday after the New Hampshire debates. McCain is on *Meet The Press* and Romney will be on with Stephanopoulos. I don't know how my dear wife will be able to stomach all of it, but she will persevere.

One day they will tell the truth about Ron Paul. The United States will be a better place when that happens.

January 7, 2008

I HATE RUDY GIULIANI— YOU SHOULD TOO

I've always hated Rudy Giuliani—but never more than now.

His face fills the screen on every TV channel. Even watching the World Series on the tube provides no sanctuary. Between every inning, there he was, grinning, wearing his silly Yankee baseball cap, seated next to one of my other favorites, warmonger Senator John McCain.

The soon-to-be ex-mayor raises the temperature and gets a standing ovation every time he enters a room. Cameras pass over presidents and governors to focus on Rudy when he comes on stage. He seems ready for sainthood. It's enough to make you sick.

How did all this happen?

On that horrid day in September, Giuliani was trapped in a corridor in one of the World Trade Center buildings and was almost a casualty. This close brush with death energized him, propelling him tirelessly from every newly discovered horror to the next. Rudy was everywhere. The media, impressed, anointed him the icon of the disaster: the brash, *bona fide* New Yorker with his *bona fide* New York accent became a stand-in symbol for the city's courage and resolution.

The shell-shocked Gothamites were easy to persuade. Here was an untested, verbally bumbling president in the White House and a fast-talking New Yorker, both doing terrific jobs, weren't they? With each passing day, the mythology fed upon itself, and King Rudy reigned supreme.

Actually, Rudy Giuliani doesn't represent the spirit of New York City. Sanctified by the media, the only thing Giuliani represents is the government itself. To listen to the media, one would think that the only casualty of September 11 was the government. Giuliani filled the role of a functionary who roamed from one funeral to the next, a sort of toastmaster general helping bury New York's uniformed dignitaries.

It was a top-down event. The mayor represented the upper echelons of the city's apparatus, with an occasional moment of grieving for the hardworking, tragic victims from the real world of commerce.

Politically, Giuliani is like the horror film monster who refuses to stay dead. His prostate surgery forced him to drop out of the much anticipated senate race against Hillary. Pundits have little doubt, however, that Rudy would have fared no better against La Clinton than poor Lazio. (Clinton garnered 55 percent to Lazio's 44 percent.)

Even term limits—ordinarily a stake in the political heart—were almost side-stepped by Rudy. For a brief moment there was serious consideration to change the constitution of New York state allowing him to run again for mayor of the Big Apple. Fortunately, the New York pols were not ready for dictator Rudy.

Murray Rothbard used to say whenever a name suddenly becomes household, that he or she didn't drop down from the sky.

Rudolph Giuliani certainly didn't drop down from the sky. He came from Brooklyn.

Rudy was an ambitious lad who once considered entering the priesthood. His father, Harold, had a criminal record before Rudy was born.

In author Wayne Barrett's book, *Rudy!: An Investigative Biography of Rudolph Giuliani*, he says, "The father he celebrated so often was a pathological predator. His extended family harbored a junkie, a crooked cop, and a murky mob wing. He dissolved his first marriage with a lie so he could appear Catholic when he remarried. The very personal jewelry his first wife found in her bedroom wasn't hers." (Read the book for the answer to that and a lot more.)

In 1983 Rudy was appointed US Attorney for the Southern District of New York. His record 4,152 convictions with a mere 25 reversals is a testament to his zeal for the job.

Giuliani did not accumulate this glittering record on behalf of the citizens of the Southern District. He was motivated purely by political ambition.

As a prosecutor he employed ruthless tactics such as seizing prominent stockbrokers and traders from the floor of the exchanges and dragging them away in handcuffs with the television cameras already in place and rolling.

In his most famous case, against stock market innovator Michael Milken of Drexel Burnham, Giuliani used the threat of the Racketeering-Influenced and Corrupt Organization Act (RICO) statutes—which were so draconian that Milken had no choice but to make a deal with the federal government.

Prosecuting attorneys are never lovable, but Rudy Giuliani was despicable.

We all hope you recover from your recent surgery and that your personal life stays out of the gossip column on Page Six of the *New York Post*.

As far as I'm concerned, Rudy, I'd be relieved to see you relegated to that insignificant never-never land occupied by ex-New York city mayors.

November 5, 2001

I STILL HATE RUDY.
BUT AT LEAST I'M NOT ALONE

C riticizing Rudy Giuliani is dangerous, and I have the "hate-mail" to prove it.

My "I Hate Rudy Giuliani" piece was posted on LRC on November 5, 2001, Most of the initial e-mails shared my disgust with the aura of sainthood which glowed around the power-mad ex-NYC Mayor. "Benito" Giuliani didn't fool many of our crowd.

Several weeks went by, and the e-mails turned ugly. I was a "hater," an "ingrate." A few even compared me to the "terror-ists." How dare I attack this great American?

Who were these people? Lew Rockwell explained that they were not LRC regulars and that the article was being sucked up by search engines employed by Giulianiites seeking out infidels. Well, they found me.

Rudy had accumulated hordes of political enemies, but they were all muffled by the events of September 11. Every time he appeared on TV he became more self-assured. A first-rate actor growing into his role. Sure, Giuliani was arrogant, but the grim events which created him permitted the swagger.

When his term as Mayor of New York City neared its end, Rudy faced the prospect of being unemployed. There was a flurry of ill-conceived plans to: (1) eliminate the term limit restriction and allow him to run for Mayor again (it failed); (2) make Rudy the Czar in cleaning up and restoring the devastated area in lower Manhattan (it never happened); (3) find Rudy an important, cushy post in the Bush administration (not a chance). To hard-core GOP operatives, New York City Republi-cans, when the veneer is stripped away, are actually disaffected

Democrats and this brash Giuliani fellow was too ambitious to be trusted.

His last chance for political glory was the much anticipated race against Hillary for the US Senate seat. Rudy's bout with cancer made him drop out, but he never had a chance against la Clinton.

And that was the end of elective politics for Rudy Giuliani.

I'm sure there were many nights when Rudy dozed off amidst pleasant images of being the first Italian American in the White House. It was a shame that didn't work out. Well, maybe someday, but for now, it was time to get rich.

Giuliani Partners, a consulting firm, was born out of the tragedy and debris of the World Trade Center. Guess who's chairman and CEO? Rudy's corporate team includes many cronies from his corrupt administration. The company provides "preparedness and leadership" during crisis. Huh?

I wouldn't trust that crowd to wash my car.

The "Commodities Page" in the *Wall Street Journal* is usually as far as I get, but I do recall reading that Giuliani Partners had established alliances with Nextel and Ernst & Young and they have attracted major corporations as clients.

Maybe one of our Wall Street mavens could tell me exactly what it is these folks do for their clients. Whatever it is, I suspect the bucks are rolling in.

In the meanwhile, Rudy the Icon was collecting a glittering array of trophies:

- In 2001, Rudy Giuliani was *Time Magazine*'s "Person of the Year."
- In 2002, "Sir" Rudy was knighted by Queen Elizabeth.

- In 2003, a crowning glory. A made for TV movie. "Rudy: The Rudy Giuliani Story" starring actor James Woods as Rudy was viewed by millions. It met with mixed reviews.

- Rudy became one of the hottest and most expensive speakers on "the tour." Reportedly, his fee was $75,000.

There may be other instances in the nation's history when a relatively obscure figure skyrockets to fame and fortune almost overnight. Charles Lindbergh comes to mind, but there had never been anything quite like Rudy Giuliani.

In recent days, Rudy sort of faded from view. I don't know if he still rates invitations to the best parties, but if you look at *Vanity Fair* or *New York* magazine you'll probably find photos of Rudy and his new wife.

As far as I'm concerned, Rudy's revered status is just another unpleasant fact of life I've learned to live with. As usual, I'm on the wrong side of the issue.

And then it happened. Giuliani and his aides were called to testify before the Independent Commission investigating the September 11 attacks. The hearings were held on Rudy's turf, at the New School, just blocks from the site of the Twin Towers.

Rudy's former commissioners of the police, fire, and emergency management departments appeared before the panel on the first day. They didn't fare too well. Rudy was scheduled for the next day.

Many instances of neglect on the part of the Mayor's team were revealed in the questioning of Giuliani's department heads, but one tragic issue dominated the proceeding.

Had faulty communications been responsible for the horrible death of at least 121 firemen?

The doomed firemen were following orders, trekking up the North Tower's stairways in full gear. Exhausted, they stopped to rest between the 19th and 37th floors. Their last communication was the "order to evacuate."

Police helicopters were blaring the news that the North Tower was ready to collapse and for all to flee the building immediately. The police in the North Tower escaped just in time. The firefighters couldn't hear the bull-horns and they NEVER got that urgent message from their own superiors.

Every inch of the auditorium at the New School was occupied as Giuliani sat to face the panel. The only sound was the clicking of cameras. It was soon evident that there were some angry folks in the room. Initially they were silent, and their presence was known only because they occasionally flashed signs which read, "Lies."

The panel members were a dismal bunch. They are tired, used-up functionaries. Any integrity they might have once displayed was pounded out years ago.

Typically, everybody had to make an opening statement. Each exceeded the previous in extolling "America's Mayor." Rudy has become so accustomed to the adulation that he has learned to bask in low key.

Next, it was Rudy's turn. His recounting of that horrible day and his own survival is theatre at its best. Laurence Olivier could not do better. As Rudy concluded, the audience was barely breathing and the panel sat mesmerized.

God gave us Rudy Giuliani to direct us through that desperate time.

Watching C-Span at 3AM reveals much about a person's life style. The cats are usually frisky at that hour, but even they nod off when C-Span is on. Only the knowledge that Rudy was soon to be answering questions kept me conscious.

Finally, finally, the questions. More compliments, more adulation. Would somebody please ask a tough one? Then, I dozed and missed the question, but Rudy was in the middle of a response and I was wide awake. He said, "—those firefighters heard an evacuation order, but still did not leave the building. They were standing their ground to make sure civilians got out."

What did he say?

It was about that point in the hearings that the small group of dissenters started to shout their complaints. "You murdered my son," shrieked one woman. Everybody squirmed. As they pushed him out of the room, one bearded young man said,

"Remember, your government taught them how to fly." Nobody listened. With such views he would have been better off on the Internet.

Rudy and entourage briskly exited the room shortly after that outburst.

Rudy, Rudy, witnesses say that there were few civilians left to rescue at that point. Those poor firefighters should have walked down to safety. They didn't know. They hadn't been told. It was the negligence of your Fire Department that cost them their lives. This was confirmed by the oral testimony of over one-hundred witnesses.

Jim Dwyer of the *New York Times*, May 20 commented, "For all the power of his voice and stature, however, Mr. Giuliani's account must compete with a substantial and diverse body of evidence that flatly contradicts much of what he and his aides say happened that day, particularly on matters that could be seen as reflecting on the performance of his administration."

Is the Giuliani mythology near being punctured? I think so.

In his May 20 *Newsday* column, "Camera hog, not a hero," inveterate New Yorker Jimmy Breslin writes:

"He was a nowhere guy until the planes hit the World Trade Center buildings. He was a failed mayor, was Rudy Giuliani."

"He went on the television. He was good. What was he supposed to be, bad? He was talking to the world from a city of catastrophe. He went on television five or six times that day. He went on more the next day, and the day after that, and for all the days of the fall of 2001 and the television made him an international hero."

Nice prose, Jimmy, but where have you been for the past twenty-six months?

Breslin is a good guy and I'm confident that he will keep the heat on reminding New Yorkers that Giuliani is a creep through and through.

Once the Giuliani myth is shattered in New York, the rest of the world will fall in line.

May 24, 2004

WHO GETS THE CREDIT FOR AL GORE'S AGONY?

Everyone wants to take credit for, or put the blame on someone for Al Gore's agony.

"It was Nader, he was responsible," say some diehards. "He should be in the back seat of a Corvair."

Even Pat Buchanan brags that it was his 17,000 votes in Florida that did Gore in. Pat doesn't know that his name appeared on the ballot in southern Florida as Buchananberg, and the elderly voters in the area thought they were voting for a nice Jewish boy.

In Bruce Shapiro's article, "How the Drug War Cost Al Gore the Afro-American Votes in Florida" (Salon.com: November 9, 2000), he makes his case. My first reaction was that Shapiro was being satiric. I was wrong.

Let me save you the trouble of reading the piece. It seems that Florida law prohibits convicted felons from voting in elections. Since one-third of Florida's Afro-American males have suffered from "felony disenfranchisement," and are legally prohibited from voting, candidate Al Gore was the victim.

Truth be known, I, me, Burt, personally, was responsible for Gore's woes in Florida. On election eve, I called a friend in Boca Raton, and although I don't quite remember the message, every member of his poker group was so persuaded by my argument they switched their votes from Gore to Howard Phillips and his Constitution Party. Those votes tipped the scale.

Paul Gigot, upper echelon talking head, on the razor-thin difference in vote total, pronounced on Jim Lehrer's show on November 8: "The next time someone tells you that your vote doesn't count, remember the election in the year 2000," blah, blah, blah.

Former President Jimmy Carter, at a press conference on November 9, repeated the mantra, and we will hear it *ad nauseam*.

What garbage. How does the closeness of a political race add importance to the individual's vote? If we can find him, let's award a lottery prize to the fellow whose single vote determined the result of the election.

American elections are a referendum on indifference.

The remarkable dead-heat distribution of the one hundred million votes indicates how difficult it is to distinguish between the two parties.

Voting is like being part of "the wave" at a sporting event. No one will ever notice if you don't participate. But if more than 50 percent don't partake, the whole futile exercise disintegrates.

Third parties that truly threaten the two-party system are unacceptable. They are tolerated only when they are irrelevant. (The Libertarian Party's Harry Browne received 381,000 votes, typical of the parties' vote totals in presidential elections since 1984.)

When Ross Perot was spearheading the Reform Party, he exceeded the amount of influence that could be tolerated. That party has now been marginalized, and Perot has found peace, presumably back in the fold as a Republican supporting George W. Bush. (The Reform Party's Pat Buchanan received 441,000 votes.)

The Green Party is on the cusp of being regarded as either a mounting threat or irrelevant. We will know in the next two to four years. (The Green Party's Ralph Nader received about two-and-a-half million votes.)

When a third-party movement becomes a potential dagger in the heart of the established political order, all niceties are forgotten, and "contracts" are let out to solve the problem.

In 1968 American Independent Party candidate George Wallace won 14 percent of the vote and almost elected Hubert Humphrey over Richard Nixon.

Wallace's performance in the 1972 Democrat presidential primaries stunned the established order. He won the primaries in Tennessee, North Carolina, Florida, Maryland, and Michigan and was a close second in Pennsylvania and Indiana. Wallace was no longer winning just the southern states; he was a national candidate.

On May 15, 1972, George Wallace was gunned down and almost killed while campaigning in Maryland.

The sober leaders of the present two-party regime will not allow the "shock of voter irregularities" to exist too long. At this moment the Democrats are presenting two faces, one strident and aggressive, implying they will go all out to contest the vote in Florida. The other face, represented by Warren Christopher, is committed to order, continuity, "respect for the Constitution," and reassuring the world that this is an example of American democracy at its best. Translation: We are scared to death that our house of cards will be seen by all. Let's get back to business as usual as quickly as possible.

When the power elite decide on the identity of the next president, that will be it. Any lawsuits will fizzle and hysterical minority voices eventually muffled (see Waco). The losers will be reminded that, okay, you lost this time, but you'll be back in two or four years, so cool it. And here's some pocket money to tide you over until then.

The power elite message continues:

And to any of you rogue states that may be watching and listening, you had better know that American internal squabbling never diminishes our ability to unleash our military might. So, if you are considering any mischief, don't even think about it.

Sadly, neither Al Gore nor George W. Bush would dissent from this position.

November 10, 2000

WHO'S THE NEXT PRESIDENT? DEPENDS ON WHICH COURT YOU ASK

P resident "As Of Now" Bush has asked Attorney General Alan Dershowitz to look into reversing the pardons issued by Bill Clinton at the end of his presidency. Dershowitz, selected by Bush as an early gesture toward bipartisanship, growled that some of his best friends were among the pardoned.

Dershowitz was angered by Bush's recent Thanksgiving message to the American public.

The fiery Dershowitz said, "Those Indians at the first Thanksgiving dinner were forced to sit at the children's table and reparations are in order." He threatens to take the case all the way to the Israeli Supreme Court.

Another first: The Sixth US Federal District Court in Richmond, Virginia, will now be open 24 hours a day, seven days a week, holidays included. A court spokesman said, "Justice cannot be blind only during business hours."

Some of the Bush-Gore lawyers seemed puzzled by the statement. Others admitted not knowing what the Hell the guy was talking about, but opinions were unanimous that all day and night court proceedings are definitely a step in the right direction. (Sure, and Arthur Murray dance instructors would vote "yes" for all night ballrooms at taxpayer expense.)

One senior Gore barrister commented: "Midnight basketball has been a terrific success, so why not . . ." A noisy truck obliterated his last words so fill in the blank yourself.

Relations between Republicans and Democrats reached all-time lows again in the District of Colombia when young suit-and-tie conservatives held a massive sit-in at the Smithsonian Institute. This was clearly a retaliation for the skirmishes at Dulles Airport when a group of lads described as "Democrat thugs" occupied the Control Tower.

In the US Congress things are no better. There has been no civil exchange between the Demos and the Repubs since last year's riot, which ended only when high-pressure water hoses were aimed at the legislators. No future meetings are even planned.

It is rumored that patriot Bo Gritz has offered himself as an intermediary between the warring parties. A reporter reminded Bo that the Democrats kept H. Ross Perot hostage for seven days while he was attempting to intercede. Since then H. Ross has been followed by bands of demonstrators chanting "Perot must go."

The Swiss ambassador to the US has graciously offered to act as a buffer between the feuding parties. In addition, he will facilitate prisoner exchanges.

One problem that won't go away is how to address the 43rd president. In overturning a Washington, DC, Municipal Court opinion which required George W. Bush to be addressed as "President 'As of Now' Bush," the Appellate Court changed that to "President 'Certified By The Florida Secretary of State' Bush."

Both the Washington, DC, Municipal Court and the US Supreme Court were of the view that the term, "Grande Cojones" was undignified and they rejected the use of the expression when applied to either president.

Notwithstanding these momentous legal decisions, ex-Vice President Gore will only respond to staff and family when addressed as "President 'With More Popular Votes' Gore'."

The drive to lower the voting age to fourteen is gaining momentum. New York Senator Hillary Clinton suggested that if they are old enough to say "no" to drugs, they are old enough to vote. If they don't say "no," they are probably using drugs, and drug users must not be excluded from the voter rolls.

One Republican responded: "It won't be long before they'll be demanding prescription drug relief for teens, and we will all be paying for their anti-pimple medication."

All the while the lawyers keep on truckin', Attorney David Boies is seeking a court order based on a GSA regulation that would evict the Bush family from the White House. Boies cited as precedent a similar directive two years earlier that dispossessed President Strom Thurmond. (As per the US Constitution, Thurmond served as president for twenty days back in 2001, and US Marshals reported that the old fella refused to leave the White House, and put up quite a struggle, claiming the presidency as his birthright since 1948.)

DC GOSSIP

Friends report that Warren Christopher and James Baker have taken their three-year-old road show to eighty-seven different nations, and their next stop is Kabul, Afghanistan.

The Chrisotpher-Baker debate is identical to their early exchanges back in the election of 2000, and immediately puts the audience into a deep sleep.

The performance closes with the grotesque vision of two "alte kackers" wrestling over a butterfly ballot. Claims that the pair broke all tour attendance records set by the Harlem Globetrotters are viewed with some suspicion.

Bill O'Reilly from Fox TV's *O'Reilly Factor* has never approached his old grand style since a heroic guest calmly—as though performing a valued public service—stuffed a microphone into the talk show host's mouth.

From their headquarters in Washington, DC, C-SPAN announced the birth of C-SPAN 8. The new channel will devote its entire schedule to criminal court cases featuring defendants who are government officials. (Brian Lamb did not rule out the possibility of C-SPAN 9 in the future.)

Americans love Hollywood disaster movies about earthquakes, floods, and tornadoes. This summer's smash hit is a different type of disaster picture and it's a candidate for the 2003 Oscars. *The Devastating Destruction of the Process Whereby America's Leadership is Selected* or *Come See the Naked Power of Second-Rate People as They Lie and Cheat All in the Name of Democracy*. Superbly edited from hundreds of hours of tape from the 2000 presidential election, the film is 185 minutes in length.

Fans of the epic movie with the long title lovingly refer to it as "The Process is Dead, Fred."

"Dead, Fred II" is already in the works by these same prizewinning producers whose "Disaster at Waco" won wide acclaim.

December 13, 2000

I'M MAD AS HELL

W hen Patrick J. Buchanan finally decides he's had enough of presidential campaigning, he will surely be primed for a career as a master of public relations.

Since the release of his new book, *A Republic, Not An Empire*, Buchanan has had more exposure on cable TV than Lanny Davis, Arianna Huffington, and Alan Dershowitz put together. For Pat, every TV appearance was like walking through an oft-visited minefield, but he always emerged unscathed and one wag noted that Buchanan has no reverse gear.

Typical was an appearance on the Geraldo Rivera show. Pat and Dershowitz had equal time, separately, to present their case. Dershowitz, on first, predictably, spewed a stream of invective. The charges were familiar: Buchanan is an anti-Semite, a Hitler apologist, and a Holocaust denier. The always-venomous Dershowitz became especially agitated and shrill when he spoke of Buchanan's book and WWII revisionism.

"Moderator" Rivera could hardly conceal his blackjack when it was Pat's turn before the camera. The small group in my living room dug in awaiting Buchanan's retaliation—it never came. Suppressing a smile, Pat expressed wonder at the professor's apoplectic hate. He proceeded to control the balance of the show, answering those questions he chose to, deflecting the transparent barbs, making all his points, and only occasionally finding it necessary to defang Geraldo.

Even veteran Buchanan watchers, however, are surprised by the width and breadth of the present assault upon him. The cast of characters was much the same in 1990–91. Their hate campaign was ignited by Pat's passionate opposition to US involvement in the Persian Gulf. They lobbied CNN to dump Pat. They also exerted pressure to get newspapers to drop his syndicated column. Pat fought back, and although he had few public figures as allies, he survived.

Another anti-Buchanan skirmish occurred a year later when Pat challenged an incumbent Republican president. A mythology evolved over Buchanan's speech at the Republican convention in Houston. In addition to the usual charges, Pat was portrayed as a scowling and angry man. But he prevailed again, in 1996 scaring the hell out of the establishment by winning the New Hampshire primary. For a few days their worst nightmare was the possibility that Pat could beat Dole and win the presidency.

Now his charm and wit are grudgingly acknowledged. But they charge that he uses these skills to devious ends, seducing colleagues and concealing his anti-Semitism.

In 1990–91, the campaign against Buchanan was a coordinated effort by the ADL, and I am convinced that a similar orchestration exists today. All the usual suspects get regular press packets and memos, but they really aren't necessary. Each player knows the party line, and his obligation to advance it.

Aside from the usual villains—the *New York Times*, the *Washington Post*, the *Wall Street Journal*, the TV networks—the hitmen now launch their missiles from such Internet sites as Salon and Slate.

Editorial piles on editorial, and feature columnists, including the alleged conservatives, vilify Pat. "He's soft on Hitler," is the central theme, except for those who call him a second Hitler.

It isn't important to actually read Pat's book. You only have to read your instructions and repeat the lies.

In a huge op-ed in the October 25 *Wall Street Journal*, Norman Podhoretz made what was supposed to be the definitive attack on Pat. Podhoretz, editor-at-large of *Commentary* magazine, a senior fellow of the Hudson Institute, and godfather of the neocon wing of the warfare-welfare party makes the same tired old charges against Pat, adding the specious accusations drawn from Pat's book (which he apparently did not read).

But Podhoretz's piece is important because it provides a clue to the strategy Pat's enemies will employ in the days ahead. First, however, I want to expose some of Podhoretz's most glaring distortions:

To support his position that Pat is soft on Hitler, Podhoretz extracts a quote from an old column of Pat's describing the "Fuehrer as an individual of great courage, a soldier's soldier in the Great War." Crudgingly, Podhoretz quotes Pat's following statement that Hitler was also "a man who without compunction could commit murder and genocide."

There you have it. The evidence that Pat is soft on Hitler. Here, by the way, is more of the quote, from 1977:

> Those of us in childhood during the war years were introduced to Hitler only as a caricature. . . . Though Hitler was indeed racist and anti-Semitic to the core, a man who without compunction could commit murder and genocide, he was also an individual of great courage, a soldier's soldier in the Great War, a leader steeped in the history of Europe, who possessed oratorical powers that could awe even those who despised him. But Hitler's success was not based on his extraordinary gifts alone. His genius was an intuitive sense of the mushiness, the character flaws, the weakness masquerading as morality that was in the hearts of the statesmen who stood in his path.

Podhoretz's hit piece then moves on to the case of John Demjanjuk. Pat almost single-handedly held that it was a case of mistaken identity, and that Demjanjuk was not "Ivan the Ter-rible" from the Treblinka death camp. Finally, the Israeli Supreme Court exonerated this working-class Catholic grandfa-ther, and Pat was proven right in pursuing a noble cause.

But Podhoretz had a different view. He says, "But it turned out that if Mr. Demjanjuk had not been a guard at Treblinka, he had served in the same capacity at Sobibor, another death camp."

Sure he did, Poddy, but this smear couldn't be proven in court either.

Finally, Mr. Podhoretz cites John Muravchik, a contributor to *Commentary* magazine, and one of the pack-dogs constantly snipping at Buchanan. Muravchik wonders if "Buchanan was a dove on the Gulf Crisis just because of his animus against Israel."

Knowing Pat's fervent dislike of foreign wars renders Muravchik's musings ridiculous.

The bulk of Podhoretz's piece is a rambling tirade accusing Buchanan of anti-Semitism. I will not use this space to refute him, but respectfully refer readers to "Pat Buchanan and the Menace of Anti-Anti-Semitism" by Murray N. Rothbard (*Roth-bard-Rockwell Report* 1, no. 8 [December 1990]).

Now, to the party line according to Norm: most Republican Party hacks recognize that Pat Buchanan on the Reform Party ticket could cause certain doom for George W. Bush. That's not the way Norm sees it. With some help from William Kristol they submit the following wisdom:

> Mr. Buchanan's defection may help Mr. Bush. . . . Without the Buchanan albatross around his neck, Mr. Bush will be protected against the Democratic accusation that he is a

moderate fronting for the worst elements of the radical Right.

The word is out, and I predict they will be selling this mantra using the usual suspects as their pitchmen (the wholly owned Rush Limbaugh claimed this on his radio show on October 26).

These neocons are smart. The ugly campaign they orchestrate against Pat simply reveals how much they fear him. But that is no excuse. There are plenty of legitimate reasons to criticize Pat Buchanan, but these scurrilous charges against him should not go unchallenged.

June 13, 2000

I HATE 3RD PARTIES, BUT I'M INFECTED WITH 3RD PARTYITIS

I bragged to a friend, "I personally know most of the people running for president: Pat Buchanan, Harry Browne, Howard Phillips, and Joe Sobran, before he quit."

"Yeah, and you probably know most of the people voting for them," he observed.

Very funny.

Although hardly a card-carrying member of the Buchanan Brigade, Pat has been a pal ever since 1990. It's been a bumpy decade. The 1996 primaries provided the high point. Pat had swept the Republican New Hampshire and South Carolina primaries and was on a roll. Things were so hot that a friend seriously confided he wanted the US ambassadorship to the Vatican in the Buchanan administration.

Take your pick on low points but the press conference with the commie Fulani scraped the bottom.

Which leads to my present condition. One morning last winter I awakened to the dull pain of a disease long in remission. The dreaded virus was back: Third Party Itis (TPI).

Pat Buchanan was superbly cast as the Republican outsider. His intelligence, wit, and commitment to principle exposed the rotten Stupid Party for what it was. Rotten and stupid. But that is all changed now. Pat has entered the world of third party politics, and I am having a relapse.

Pat's decision to go third party released a flood of images I thought I had suppressed. My initial exposure to fringe and third party candidates was as a victim of direct-mail solicitations during the 1970s and 80s. In those days it was a ten-dollar check if the fundraiser pushed at least one appropriate conservative button.

It never occurred to me at the time, but never ever has one of my chosen candidates ever come close to winning.

In the early 1980s I received an emergency phone call on election eve. The Council candidate in a Southern California city had a "real chance." All that was needed was a last minute media blitz. This was before Fed-Ex, and my $100 went Western Union. "We can win it" was the last thing the caller said. The candidate received 8 percent of the vote. Were these people crooked or dumb? No, it is pure self-delusion. Roger MacBride the brilliant, flamboyant Libertarian Party presidential candidate in 1976 used his own DC-3 aircraft to campaign, hopping from airport to airport. As the crowds grew from a hand-full of well wishers to one hundred or more, MacBride actually believed there was a remote chance of victory.

Thus, what started as my innocent interest in third-party candidates led to years of third-party politics. Gradually and inexorably TPI sets in; reality becomes blurred, quality and shoddiness become indiscernible, and critical judgment is lost.

On Saturday, May 20, 2000, elections for Reform Party presidential delegates were held all over the state of California. The Buchanan campaign was well prepared, but it was unknown how much opposition the anti-Buchanan forces were going to mount.

I was on my way to San Jose. The drive to San Jose was California freeway at its worst. "Why am I doing this?" I implored the heavens. (Have you noticed how many solitary drivers hector to imaginary passengers?) I'm running as a Buchanan delegate, that's why I'm doing it. With full knowledge of my Third Party Itis medical history, and impaired judgment, the Buchanan campaign asked me to run and there I was.

All the major hotel chains are represented in San Jose, and there are several outstanding upscale sites the Reform Party might have used for the event. Guess where our meeting, followed by lunch, was scheduled? You've got it: Denny's. Its safe to say that in the realm of two-party politics so important an event would be at the Ritz-Carlton or the Marriott at least.

The Reform Party regulars at the San Jose elections were split into two groups. Some were neutral about Buchanan, others were for "anybody but Pat." Not only did we outnumber them, we "out-passioned" them as well. Victory was almost complete. Districts 14 through 17 were Buchanan's.

As for lunch, my hunger overcame the wisdom of delaying gratification, and I still shudder at the memory of the overcooked burger swimming in some sort of mayonnaise derivative. See what I mean about loss of judgment?

The Buchanan campaign still has big problems in California. Winning the delegates to the Reform Party national convention was one thing, but it was important that the state party, if not friendly to Pat, at least not be hostile to his candidacy.

The Reform Party state convention took place early this month, and it was a dismal event. The hotel in Los Angeles was a dump. Can you believe that my room's TV only received four channels? A bellman told me that the hotel had a disagreement with the cable company. Sounds to me like they didn't pay their bill.

The outcome of the weekend's agony was mixed. The Buchanan campaign lost several key votes, but survived a bit of treachery from the Fulani group when the convention voted down their insidious motion to essentially gag the Party's presidential candidate from dealing with "social issues." It's my guess that we won't have anything but hostility from the Fulani group from here on in and that is most likely a plus.

The really bad news was that the virulently anti-Pat elements of the party were emboldened by the results of the convention. We will learn more about all of this in the days ahead.

I've been to a dozen or so political conventions, several of the third-party variety, but the Reform Party's California state convention was as amateurish as anything I've ever encountered. The parliamentarian wasn't quite comfortable with Robert's Rules and on almost every vote the delegates were unsure if "Yes" really meant "No."

Years ago I was invited to address a third-party Central Committee group. I had difficulty locating the meeting room in the large downtown hotel. I found it, eased my way in, and sat in the rear listening to the rituals and procedures for fifteen minutes before I realized it was a Teamsters' local meeting. So much for the distinction between form and substance.

I must confess that when Pat finally left the Republicans for the Reform Party I had grave reservations. The GOP had returned Pat's loyalty, principle and grace with betrayal, lies, and plain old bad manners. They made it clear there was no place for him.

Pat is no third-party-type loser. He brings intellect, wit, and toughness to the debate. Pat Buchanan has no reverse gear. With luck, he can be included in the presidential debates. He may also expose the two-party stranglehold on ballot access, thereby making the electoral process more equitable.

Wait a second. The point of this essay was to discredit the third-party movement in this country. That is no giant task. But when all the evidence is weighed what third parties represent may be infinitely better than the corruption we presently live under.

June 13, 2000

Burt served on the Libertarian Party National Committee 1987–89, was treasurer of the Libertarian Party Presidential campaign in 1984, and chairman of the Ron Paul Presidential campaign, Libertarian Party 1988.

CONVENTIONS, DELEGATES, AND LIFE IN THE SWAMP

Delegates to political conventions rank amongst the lower forms of animal life. They are mindless adherents who fit Lenin's description of movement followers as "the swamp." They know nothing of the struggles around them, and are never part of the true decision process. They are viewed with contempt by the real party operatives, who keep them at arm's length except when soliciting their labor.

In real-world political conventions, the delegates, aside from the prestige they feel at winning the assignment, are rewarded with gifts, favors, celebrities, and—best of all—sumptuous parties.

All that is required of the delegate is that they follow orders and bring an ample supply of adulation to the combination revival meeting and rock concert they call a convention. In this environment, the delegate, like a moth to flame, seeks out every TV camera. Unfortunately, they are generally uglier than the population at large.

All of the above was true for the Reform Party delegates at the recent presidential nominating convention in Long Beach except that gifts, favors, celebrities, and sumptuous parties were missing. Still, the Buchanan delegates brought plenty of adulation for the candidate.

With hardly a whimper, the patient Buchanan delegates endured the entire first day of the convention jammed together, first in the vestibule outside the main hall and then in different rooms awaiting delegate certification. The air was foul as the air conditioner succumbed to the torrid heat outside. Without full comprehension, these worthies knew that their suffering was related to the presence of the "rival faction."

One sad soul described the ten hours as being in one of "Dante's lower circles of Hell."

As a Buchanan delegate from California, I marched in lockstep understanding the need for the painstaking care as the courts or the FEC were likely to review the proceedings.

Much of day two was devoted to the one-sided parliamentary struggle between the Buchananites and their triangle of enemies. Finally, with all secure, it was time for the convention program.

SNAPSHOTS AND SOUNDBITES

Prior to Buchanan's nomination, and the four "keynote" endorsers, the program could not have been more dismal. My personal low point was the appearance of "Granny D." Granny is the nonagenarian who trekked across the country promoting campaign finance reform.

That seemed safe enough, but she used her seventy minutes of prime time to harangue us all with a commie interpretation of the history of the reform and progressive movements in the US.

After forty-five minutes she began to extol the greatness of the evil Teddy Roosevelt, and how he smashed uncontrolled corporate power. I broke ranks.

"Put the commie back on the highway," I mumbled.

It got worse. She was mouthing every socialist platitude. By now, out of control, I rose, fist in the air, shouting: "Throw this old windbag out."

Just as I seemed to be gaining support from the California delegation, other delegates physically subdued me as the California state chairman muttered through clenched teeth, "Don't create a scene. The C-SPAN cameras are covering everything."

As they pinned me to the ground, I relished the headline that might have been: "Buchanan delegate beats up 90-year-old woman."

Overheard in the Pennsylvania delegation:

"Which one is Justin Raimondo?"

"He's standing to the right of the podium."

"Good lord, he looks like Madeline Albright."

"No, no, that's a convention clerk. Justin is the nice looking, slim fellow next to her."

Poor Justin. His anti-war, pro-Pat speech was a barnburner. As he neared the crescendo that would have pushed the delegates to frenzy, convention chairman Gerry Moan frog-marched him from the podium.

Why was Justin yanked? Theories abound, but my insider says that a KLA operative disguised as an ex-journalist issued the order.

In the hotel elevator, I found myself with a fellow delegate laden with "Go Pat Go" buttons and pitchfork.

Cowering in the elevator's corner was a Natural Law Party devotee clearly attempting to put the pitchfork in transcendental terms.

"Hah!" I shouted to the miserable, terrorized clump. "What do you say about Pat's bold move in selecting a black woman as his VP?"

"Your Buchanan is a repressed slave master," he hissed.

"Huh?" was my best response.

"He covets our black women. First Lenora Fulani, now Ezola Foster, and maybe Maxine Waters next."

And from the Buchanan Brigadier, the burning question: "If Pat dies, and she's president, where will her loyalties be if we have a crisis with an African country?"

"This is my floor fellas," I said, "See you later."

Kudos to Gerry Moan. He remained affable throughout the most difficult circumstances, and his impersonation of Jackie Gleason was the best I'd ever seen.

Two out of every three delegates seem to have a cellular phone. This explained how they stay informed, in contact with someone watching C-SPAN.

Finally, I am pleased to report that Pat was sensational. He looked rested and tanned (after all, he wasn't in the hall with us!). And he was never more eloquent. Ezola and her husband, both beautifully attired, will return elegance to Washington.

I am certain of these final snapshots, as I left the swamp on Saturday and watched the convention's last day on C-SPAN.

August 17, 2000

I Hate Doctors—
At Least, Most of Them

I HATE DOCTORS

*B*urt: "You've been my physician for over twenty-five years. You can't just dump me like you would a broken heart-lung machine."

Doc: "There's no room for sentiment in medicine, and frankly, your quaint right-wing viewpoints aren't as interesting as they once were. I'm turning your medical records over to young Dr. Kaloofka from my office."

Burt: "But Kaloofka doesn't speak English, and I've never heard of a doc, or anybody for that matter, who keeps a venomous giant lizard as an office pet."

Doc: "You're always making mountains out of millstones. As for Kaloofka, he has become a star with my female employees. They're all smiling a lot and humming ditties from the Pakistani hit parade."

Burt: "What about loyalty? It was because of you that I joined 'Californians Against Midwifery.' I haven't missed a meeting in two years, and although I have no idea why, they just elected me secretary/treasurer of the district. And what about those thousands of buttons I own that say 'Chiropractic Isn't Christian'?"

Doc: "Humphhhh." (He grumbles, undecipherable.)

Burt: "I could have sued you back in '97 when your lab mistakenly diagnosed me as having cholera."

Doc: "Most people would have seen humor in that."

Burt (voice choked with emotion): "Things aren't so funny when the county board of health puts you under quarantine, but the worst indignity was when you forgot me in an examination room. I spent that weekend locked in, with no clothes, a very cold bench, and nothing to read but the spring 1988 edition of 'Living The Good Life With A Partial Colon'."

Doc: "Sure, Blumert, you've been OK at times, but you came up empty when we asked for volunteers to firebomb the health food store that sold that profane book, *Good Health Equals No Doctors*."

(End of Transcription)

Being advised by my semi-retiring family physician that I was no longer his patient reminded me that, basically, I hate doctors.

Nothing personal: I also dislike lawyers and bureaucrats, major and minor, and anybody who has anything to do with the tax code.

Only "physicians" from the list above claim "victim status," however, and seek out conservative/libertarian thinkers to articulate their interests and link them with free-market principles. That's okay. We all do better in an environment free of government intrusion, but my physician friends think that they have "special" victim status and that their grieviences are unique.

A visit to any "hard-money" financial conference or freedom-oriented seminar will find docs well represented, shoulder-to-shoulder with the other freedom fighters. The docs are decent, well-intentioned guys who "talk a good game," but when it comes to their day-to-day practice of medicine, they thoroughly enjoy the benefits their State license affords them.

The socialist virus seems inexorable, and reversing that flow is difficult. If any group has the wherewithal to smash the evil trend toward socialized medicine, it would be the docs

themselves. Their AMA has enormous influence in every legislative body in the nation. Add to that the power inherent in
their medical associations at the state and county level, and
doctors can accomplish almost anything.

We have coddled doctors long enough. They can't keep
blaming government agencies, HMOs, and third-party payers
for all their deficiencies. It's widely perceived that patients
have low expectations when they have to arrange an appointment with a physician The patient finds indifference, rudeness,
and would have to visit the Department of Motor Vehicles to
find comparable attitudes.

Particularly objectionable is what happens when a medical
office employee becomes expert in every medical specialty. The
patient must convince this high priestess their condition warrants
an appointment with the doctor. Doctor friends insist that American medical care is the best in the world. It's also said that Americans are the freest people in the world. Neither statement provides total assurance.

The entire American medical delivery system can do better,
but it will take a sea change in the attitude of the average doc.

The four questions below present a hard cynical critique of
the status of the health care industry.

1. How would you like to be in a business where one-half
of your customers are addicted to chemicals but can't obtain
them without express permission from you?

2. How would you like to be in a business where the companies who produce the chemicals require your endorsement for the
success of their product? Payola becomes the way of life for every
physician. He is provided with free samples, junkets to resorts all
over the world, and other worldly pleasures beyond the imagina-
tion of the layman.

3. How would you like to be in a business where the moment some competitive force is evident, all guns are turned toward that threat? Competitors are marginalized and often face criminal charges with some level of government acting as enforcer.

4. How would you like to be in a business where substandard performance caused by drunkenness, laziness, or plain old criminality often escapes proper notice?

The great medical curmudgeon, Robert S. Mendelsohn, MD, author of *Confessions of a Medical Heretic* (New York: Warner Books, 1980), spent the latter years of his life goring medical sacred cows. He once pointed out that "Historically, when doctors have gone on strike, the mortality rate has dropped." Indeed, a friend and former medical editor remembers a doctors' strike in Israel that only ended when the undertakers picketed the medical association headquarters. Their business was being hurt!

January 5, 2000

I STILL HATE DOCTORS AND NOW THEY HATE ME

Life is a series of humiliations.

Maybe it's neurotic, but I have much stronger recollections of humiliations suffered—large and small, real or imagined—than I do of events that were celebratory.

For example, my only surviving memory from ages 0–5 was of a horrid moment at a Horn & Hardart Automat in New York City.

For those born after the war between Italy and Ethiopia, who know nothing of those American icons, let me provide some history: For much of the twentieth century, the Automat was America's largest restaurant chain, feeding 800,000 people a day.

Every Automat was cavernous and ornately bedecked with mirrors and marble—but there were no waiters.

The tunafish sandwiches and wedges of apple pie were housed in chrome-and-glass coin-operated little boxes. Each item was priced and the glass door sprung open when the proper number of coins was inserted. The last of the Automats, those magnificent "giant vending machines," closed in 1991. There is a thirty-five-foot section from the original Automat on display at the Smithsonian Institution.

It was magic land for a five year-old, and I was so proud when my mother entrusted me with two nickels to purchase my own slice of cherry pie. Unfortunately, the box was too high and I asked a man for help. I gave him my two nickels, he inserted them and peered down at me for a third as the price was fifteen cents.

It was a crisis too horrible to recall even now. The man was ugly and loud. He said that I was a dreadful little boy. What was my upbringing? He was a childhood dragon come to life. I was too frightened to cry and could only look helplessly to my mother back at our table.

It took days of mother-comforting to help me survive that humiliation.

Fast-forward a decade to my next major humiliation: I was fifteen, making my annual appearance at Aqueduct Racetrack with my father and his racetrack buddies.

It was the final race and we were betting on a long-shot filly named Bright Goldie. The odds on her were 45–1, and I decided to watch the race standing at the rail right on the finish line. The race ended in a virtual dead-heat. The stewards flashed "Photo" on the Tote Board but there was no doubt in my mind. Bright Goldie had won the race by an inch or two and I dashed upstairs to give my father and his friends the wondrous news.

I was Lazarus returning from the dead to tell all: "Our horse won, our horse won."

It took about ten minutes for the official results. Just as I said, Bright Goldie won, and she rewarded her backers by paying $97 for each $2 bet.

The fifteen minutes of excitement proved too much for this lad. (I was clutching a $5 win ticket in my hand.) Later, my father told me that I passed out cold when the official results actually flashed on the Tote Board.

I revived in just a few seconds, but the episode haunts me still, and provides solid evidence that I'm more at home with bad news than I am with good.

No list of humiliations can be complete without at least one instance of a lover's heart being shattered by a non-responding object. I was a college freshman, and she was a freckled-faced, brainy type with natural orange colored hair. I could barely breathe when I looked at her. She was kind to me in her fashion, but I had the feeling she was never quite certain of my name.

Yes, I was the one seen carrying her books around campus. I was an appendage, a sort of pet rock seeking any slight attention.

Finally, one day, fortune smiled and she invited me to brunch at her home that Sunday. I had four days to rehearse, four days to select the proper clothes. I memorized the list of the *New York Times* bestselling books and agonized whether or not to bring along a few poems she had inspired.

Sunday finally came and I took deep breaths before reaching for the door buzzer. From that point on it was all a blur. The eighty-five guests had already arrived and the party was at fever pitch.

My princess breezed by, handed me an apron, pointed to a room filled with dirty dishes, and said: "You're such a dear. We are desperate for help in the kitchen."

I never saw my Dulcinea again that day—but there was one indignity still to come: As I started to leave, her younger brother gave me a small tray of leftovers and said, "Blumert, you were great help today and I'm going to recommend you to friends." A $5 bill was neatly folded on the food tray.

I hated him then, and I was right: Today, he's a prominent commie professor at an Ivy League school.

As the years passed the humiliations become less frequent. But last year, I was devastated when my family phyician for twenty-five years summarily dismissed me as a patient. I had been loyal and recommended him to others when he was struggling to build his practice.

I was one of his first patients and comforted him during his malpractice suits. My reward—he dumped me (The sordid details of that epic humiliation are available in my article, "I Hate Doctors.")

The ingrate. He'll be begging me to come back as a patient, but if you must know, I've done just fine without him. Who needed him anyway? This is an age of medical specialty. The Internet provides unlimited access to data in the pursuit of good health. No waiting rooms, no surly receptionists, no crooked insurance companies.

And then three weeks ago the gods conspired against me and I was stricken with the flu. Every human who has walked the earth knows the agony caused by a bug that's trying to kill you.

Surely, there must be immediate help out there. I started my search at Walgreens.

After eleven purchases at the drug counter, colorful packages that promise to defeat coughs-chills-sore throat-runny nose-fever, I realized that all of these cold and flu medicines are essentially the same.

They are a fraud.

They drug you into an unpleasant stupor, but sleep is fitful and you'll probably make a mess of things if you are operating heavy equipment. With the passage of time the body will overcome both the drugs and the virus.

"I'm not going to use any of those head cold and flu remedies ever again.

Never," I moaned.

"Call a doctor!" my wife said.

"I don't have a doctor," I responded. "Don't you remember? He dumped me."

"Well, people tell me that there are now these new 'immediate-care' clinics all over the country."

After some *Yellow Pages* research, I selected the medical clinic named:

"WeReleva Your Feva. No appointments necessary. Physicians on Site 24 hours."

Somehow I felt a humiliating experience coming on.

I dragged myself in, coughing and sputtering. My face was pressed against the glass door waiting for them to turn the lock at opening time.

The receptionist, wearing a Florence Nightingale nurse's uniform, said, "You have an appointment?"

"Yes."

"How are you going to pay?"

"Cash."

"You mean a check cash, card cash, or cash-cash?"

"Cash. Cash. Cash."

"Please pay now. Getting money from an estate is never easy. By the way, if I catch your flu, you're in big trouble."

In the next sixty seconds I was weighed, blood pressure taken, temperature recorded, all without removing my jacket or unbuttoning a button.

I was put in the traditional examination room, only this one had bars on the window. The only thing to read was a crumpled magazine left behind by the last patient: "How to Live the Good Life With a Partial Colon, Part II."

Suddenly a huge figure blocked the doorway. There he was: the Doctor. He was wearing a white medical tunic studded with military medals on his chest.

"Hello, Doc," I wheezed. "I've got the flu."

"A few questions, first. Who is your primary physician?"

Well, it was clear he hadn't read my article, "I Hate Doctors"—so I explained: "My primary doctor dumped me."

"He dumped you. How come? What were the circumstances?"

"Well . . ."

"Have you considered that possibly it was because of you that he quit medicine?"

"No, I hadn't considered that."

"Think back: Why did he dump you?"

"Well, I was sick a couple of times."

"Sick or malingering?" he snarled.

"Look, all I'm here for is to have you listen to my chest and make sure I'm not getting pneumonia, so give me some real cough medicine with codeine and I'll be out of your hair."

It was clear the prescriptions were already written and he gave them to me.

"Fill those prescriptions at the pharmacy in the building. I get a cut."

In spite of the interrogation and strange bedside manner, he was my kind of a no-nonsense doc.

"Doc," I said. "You're my kind of doc, and I'd be proud to call you my family physician."

"Not so fast, Blumert," he said. "I'm not taking any new patients, and I'm not comfortable with your secessionist inclinations."

The same old feeling of rejection returned.

"What do I do? I need a primary physician."

He pulled out a yellowed, coffee-stained sheet with names. Some were crossed out with scribbled notations like insurance fraud, guilty of criminal negligence, and plain old embezzlement.

"Well, let's see who's available here. Ah, here's Dr. Goldfinger. He will be coming out of Detox this month. The two of you should get along just fine."

January 11, 2002

THE ANNUAL PHYSICAL EXAM
AND OTHER SCAMS

The dialogue was all too familiar:

Blumert: No, I don't need an appointment with Dr. Kaloofka (see: "I Hate Doctors"). All I do need is for you to call Walgreen's with a prescription for Vandoors, I don't recognize your voice, but I'm a long-time patient. Please check your files.

Voice from Hell (*V from H*): Yes, Mr. Blumert and as long as I have you on the phone, let's spend a minute bringing your file up-to-date. Here goes.

Are you still a proponent of Midwifery, Health Food stores, Chiropractic and other zany cultlike activities?

Are you still overweight and slovenly?

Blumert: Hold it! I don't have time for this nonsense. What else is in that file of yours?

V from H: Your file reveals that we have prescribed Vandoors 6 times over the past 8 years. Have you become addicted to Vandoors, Mr. Blumert? We are constantly on the alert for drug abuse. Have you considered seeking help?

Blumert: My dear Miss Who-ever-you-are, Vandoors is a skin ointment which combats warts. I no longer choose to speak to you. Would you kindly ask Dr. Kaloofka to come to the phone immediately.

V from H: Yes, I now see it on your chart. Warts. Tee hee, I've never heard of anybody having warts on—

Blumert: Enough! In less than 12 minutes I will be arriving at the doctor's office.

Have my file ready for me to pick up and if you are still around when I get there, it's likely I will strangle you with my bare hands.

V from H: Oh, don't be such a grouch. I was only trying to be friendly. I'll call Walgreen's right now and I hope you get rid of those warts. Tee hee. You must laugh out loud every time you think about them.

Blumert: Keep in mind that a physician has a privileged relationship with his patient. That extends to his dizzy receptionist as well. So, just forget about my warts.

V from H: OK, I'll only tell my husband, I promise. By the way, Dr. Kaloofka has you scheduled for your annual medical check-up on October 9. Remember, no food or water for one week prior to the exam.

Blumert (beaten): I'll be there.

EPILOUGE

Life is filled with petty indignities as above. To maintain sanity and longevity, one must build defenses: "Know your own worth," "Brush the cretins off," "Consider the source," "Don't be marginalized by midgets." (I just made that one up.)

So fortified, I only spent two days in bed after the confrontation with the V from H.

Friends and enemies alike are dazzled with such resiliency.

I must admit, thinking about my scheduled AMC-up, shortened my rehabilitation.

Why was I so submissive in agreeing to it? Is the procedure valid, or just another chunk of mythology that we inherit at birth?

Consumed with the challenge of the project, I set out to learn the origins of the AMC-up.

Predictably, there are competing theories as to how it all happened; I present them to you without bias.

THE ECONOMIC THEORY

It was the winter of 1913, in Troy, New York, and two young physicians were faced with closing down their shared medical practice for lack of patrons.

Dr. Cohen: I have no idea where the patients have gone. Could it be that they are just not getting sick, or maybe they're all broke and taking their ailments to the Free Clinic?

Dr. Kelly: Well, there's always a job in the US Army. With 3 or 4 wars on the horizon, they will be creating an abundance of patients for the indefinite future.

Dr. Cohen: No, there has to be a better way. Whenever my father's wholesale dress business was in trouble, he had a Sale. How can we get customers, oops, make that patients, to fill the Waiting Room? We need the medical equivalent of a Sale.

Dr. Kelly: I've got it! Our own patient base is the best source of business.

After my uncle bought his Model T Ford he was told to bring it back to the dealership for regular "check-ups." He originally paid $440 for the car, but has spent double that to keep it running. Some of the problems were discovered during those routine "check-ups."

The primitive Cohen-Kelly AMC-up program spread through the medical community like a prairie fire. Soon, Madison Avenue types were writing brilliant copy.

"You had better get an annual medical check-up, or you will die," was the essence of their message.

After all, it was a time when scientific progress was seen as inexorable. Every disease would be stamped out and life expectancy would be significantly extended.

It was not surprising that the concept of the AMC-up quickly became part of standard medical procedure.

(As a footnote: the two physicians, Cohen and Kelly, prospered. Later on, sadly, Dr. Kelly changed his name and drank himself to death. Cohen became an ambulance driver in the Spanish Civil War and was executed by a Franco firing squad when he refused to discard his red beret.)

THE BENEVOLENT (NON-PROFIT) ORIGINS OF THE AMC-UP

> Little is known about the disease Northern Puppick Fever, nor its cure. There is lore that it appeared in the Maine woods during the summer of 1914, killed and then disappeared forever. —*Hypochondriac's Medical Dictionary*

A young biologist had just exposed himself to the bite of a Warp Headed Beetle. He faced certain death if his theory was correct; The harmless looking little bug carried Northern Puppick Fever. Sadly, he was right.

Within seven hours the young man was dead, but there was the hint of a smile on his face and his dead eyes were frozen on a note in his hand.

We will never know the exact wording of the note, but old-timers I interviewed advised that the lumber company doctors, following the heroic biologist's instruction, instituted an AMC-up.

We don't know what it was they looked for, nor what they prescribed if they found it.

We do know that the AMC-up made Northern Puppick Fever disappear forever. And, monetary profit played no part in the drama.

Benevolence, as a motive to save lives by using AMC-ups, has also become part of medical ritual. Unfortunately, most of the non-profit research comes from Government laboratories, or those labs under contract to the state.

Granted, there are some really decent folks who advocate AMC-ups to keep people alive and healthy, but I'm perfectly comfortable with "Profit" as the driving force behind the Annual Medical Check-up.

The constant risk is that such a "check-up" becomes economically viable ONLY IF SOME DEFICIENCY IS REVEALED.

In another time, the guy who pumped gas often found that the hoses under your hood were frayed and, for safety sake, needed to be replaced.

As a consumer, there are times I'll buy the AMC-up, at other times not. As always, the consumer must maintain constant vigilance.

The concept of an "annual check-up" is a compelling merchandising concept. So compelling that I am creating Blumert's Annual Gold Check-up.

My Gold Check-up will scientifically analyze the individual's economic circumstance; it will explore his psychological make-up. Vital questions will be answered: Is it possible there is a genetic family link to gold? And, most important, how much brain damage has been caused by the pollution of the "war on gold"?

Once the Check-up is completed, the patient and Gold Dealer consult about the report's findings. Finally, the prognosis and the recommended prescription to achieve and maintain proper Gold health.

I have a strong premonition that every Annual Gold Check-up will indicate that the patient is woefully deficient and in need of some gold coins, NOW.

Please call our offices to schedule an appointment for your Annual Gold Check-up.

August 30, 2004

KEEP THAT KNIFE AWAY
FROM MY CHEST

This article is being written at Dr. Robert Cathcart's chelation facility in Los Altos, California. I sit in Lounge chair #4 and this is my 23rd session out of 30. Please forgive any typos as the IV is in my right arm and I'm writing left-handed. (Note: my pal and Lew's Tom Dorman also does chelation, but in Seattle.)

Having a cardiologist as a friend can be rather comforting. If you're dining together in a restaurant, and you keel over, there he is, your cardio-pal, kneeling over you-no teenage ambulance drivers-no strangers probing your vital parts. This is what friends are for.

Actually, I'm twice blessed: My cardiologist buddies are husband and wife. She heads up the Coronary Care Unit at San Francisco General Hospital, and he is a successful practicing cardiologist in San Mateo County.

I must admit—aside from the frustration of dealing with their neoconservative politics—there was a secure feeling when

I was with my "cardio-docs." It was like driving through the worst part of town in a Sherman tank.

That was until recently.

"You're overweight, you don't get sufficient exercise, blah, blah and more blah and it's time you quit those cigars," he said. "I'm scheduling you for the works—we will start with a stress test and then, blah, blah and more blah."

He's fatter, more sedentary than I and wears an awful hairpiece. As to the cigars, he never noticed that I stopped smoking years ago when those delicious Cubans plummeted in quality becoming as unsmokeable as the garbage from the Dominican Republic and other points in the Caribbean (For this sin alone, Castro should burn in hell.)

But I digress.

While he droned on, all I could think of was that dreaded "rite of passage." A straight line, without detour, starting with the stress-test, next an angiogram, leading almost inevitably to Open Heart Surgery.

"No," I said to myself, more out of fear than conviction. "I'm starting chelation therapy instead.

For those of you unfamiliar with chelation, I'll leave the detailed explanation to experts like our own Bill Sardi, but following is a short description from the Internet:

Chelation Therapy consists of slow-drip IV injections of EDTA (ethylenediamine tetraacetic acid) a synthetic amino acid, combined with aerobic exercise, special diet, and no smoking. The word refers to the alleged removal of plaque and calcium deposits from arteries and veins by EDTA.

I have scrupulously avoided my cardio-pals since I started chelation therapy four months ago. The instant I set foot in the world of anti-orthodoxy, my friendship with the cardio-docs was in jeopardy.

But I could only avoid Cardio-doc for so long—and the inevitable chance encounter occurred at the local sporting goods store. He was examining traps for large animals, and I was having small success finding waterproof boots that were truly waterproof.

The snippy clerk darkened my mood when she advised: "Why don't you forget about waterproof boots, stay home and just keep your feet dry." "Oh yeah'," I quickly retorted.

The deep voice of my soon to be ex-cardio pal boomed: "Well, Blumert, your chelation therapy certainly hasn't improved your wit."

What follows is the transcription of the last exchange between Blumert and the cardio-doc:

Cardio-doc: "You realize that the entire medical establishment views chelation as witchcraft. If there's any "leeching" of calcium that takes place, it will be from your skeleton, not from your arteries."

Blumert: "The medical establishment has been wrong before, and there's lots of testimony from thousands of folks who have been helped."

Cardio-doc: "It's all anecdotal, means nothing.

Blumert: "But I actually feel better."

Cardio-doc: "No, you don't feel better."

Blumert: "But I actually do."

Cardio-doc: "You only think you feel better. Anecdotal evidence doesn't count. Only double-blind research studies count."

Blumert: "Oh? Do they use double blind studies with open-heart surgery? Is there a control group?"

"Do you open everybody's chest but perform the surgery on only half the subjects?

"When do you tell the folks from the control group that their chest was opened but that no open-heart surgery was performed?

"What happens if years later the placebo group does better than the open-heart surgery group?

"How in heaven's name would you find subjects to participate in so absurd a study?"

Cardio-doc: "A typical, specious Blumert-libertarian argument."

Blumert (now on a roll): "Furthermore, isn't it sad the average working fellow cannot afford $100 per chelation session which totals a bit over $3,000, but a $40,000 open-heart surgical procedure is within almost everybody's reach. I'll respond to that myself.

"The insurance company does not accept chelation as a legitimate procedure, and therefore doesn't cover it, but there's not a health insurance policy that doesn't embrace every technique used in open-heart surgery."

Cardio-doc: "Hmff. That's because insurance companies recognize what is valid and what is not."

Blumert: "And that's the problem, isn't it?"

As the Cardio-doc left the sporting goods store he carried no large animal traps and I failed in my search for waterproof boots.

I wondered if he would ever talk to me again.

If chelation helps me, I'll happily share my experience with him. Poor guy, he has been immersed in heart surgery and the like all of his professional life. On most issues he thinks clearly, but when it comes to Medicine the roadblocks appear.

I'll wager that you know physicians just like him.

It's basic libertarian philosophy that the individual is free to seek out any path to good health without interference from regulatory agencies, governmental or private. (AMA.) This view is so entrenched that I have never heard any disagreement among libertarians.

In the struggle for liberty, I have shared the trenches with the folks from the world of alternative health-but this time I was not dealing with abstractions. My life is at stake.

Why is the establishment so venomous toward chelation?

The statistics are overwhelming that, at least, chelation doesn't hurt anybody, and if it delays some folks from rushing into surgery, what's wrong with that?

The war against chelation continues. A recent Canadian study indicated chelation was ineffectual, although the sampling was small and some chelation advocates questioned the procedures used in the study.

The worst news for physicians who use chelation in their practice came several weeks ago when they learned that their malpractice insurance was canceled. All sorts of theories explained the action of the carriers. Some suggested ugly motives on their part. Others were more understanding.

At this writing the Chelation Docs have been unable to find an alternative insurance carrier.

It's hard to predict what the immediate future holds for these courageous doctors.

February 20, 2002

SAVED FROM THE
SURGEON'S BLADE

Having rotator-cuff shoulder surgery isn't all bad. It puts you among an elite of macho types who come to the fraternity through power weightlifting, hurling a baseball in excess of 90 miles-an-hour, or missing too many right-hooks in the boxing ring.

Four years ago I earned my credential by pushing open the door to the men's room in my office building with my shoulder. The subsequent experience was a horror. constant, throbbing pain, sleepless nights, endless fog induced by pain pills, and the trauma of the surgery itself. One nurse likened it to a shotgun blast to the shoulder.

The subsequent physical therapy is conducted by people who seem sustained by the pain they inflict. And when all is done, the victim may recover 80 percent of his range of motion, but almost never without the distant, dull reminder of residual pain.

The nightmare had almost faded when late in February, racing up a stairway, I missed a step, lost my balance, and instinctively reached out to break my fall. I heard the same sickening sound, experienced the same dreadful, sharp pain, and knew beyond doubt that I had done it again, this time to the other shoulder.

My despair was profound. Knowing what was ahead of me, I could hardly face going through it again, especially now four years older. Yet this time, the pain was worse, the sleepless nights longer, and the pain pills less effective. Before I knew it, I was back on the same course, to the same hospital, the same operating table, the same surgeon, and probably that same shot-gun.

Enter Jim Foley, friend for 40 years, former Pan Am 747 captain now winding down his career with United. Jim never met a conspiracy theory he didn't adopt, a revisionist theory he found unreasonable, nor an alternative health procedure he did not accept. He urged me to call Dr. Tom Dorman before I "entered the surgical trap."

"Look," I said, "Tearing a rotator cuff is like breaking a bone. It's got to be repaired, and surgery is the only plausible approach."

Foley wasn't finished. Next I received a call from Dr. Art Robinson, brilliant biologist, former head of the Linus Pauling Institute, and another friend of many years. Art's message was a testimonial. He had faced and avoided disk surgery, and also begged that I visit Dr. Tom Dorman.

The next 36 hours were the worst. Jim Foley arranged a phone consultation with Dr. Dorman, and although my recollections were dim, my pessimism persisted. The doctor was kind and solicitous, asked me some pointed questions, and encouraged me to make the trek to Seattle.

The flight was a low point, as the change in air pressure made the pain more excruciating. I later learned I had the last seat on the last Sunday flight, intending to arrive early at Dr. Dorman's Tahoma Clinic Monday morning. I spent the dreadful night at the hotel sitting in a straight-backed chair so the throbbing was held to a minimum.

The next morning, on the way to Dr. Dorman's clinic, I wished I were back in San Francisco, headed for my inevitable destiny on the operating table.

I had spoken with Dr. Dorman several times through the years on shared political interests, never professionally. I knew a bit about him. He'd been born in Kenya of a British colonial family. Many of these folk left Africa when the Mau Mau's took over. Most scurried to South Africa or back to the UK. Tom's family, being Jewish, had the option of going to Israel. There he became a decorated paratrooper. Later, he studied medicine in Scotland, then settled in the US.

With his academic record, success in the US medical establishment was a lock, and Tom was headed for a metropolitan hospital or a chair at a major university. Nope, not Tom. The medical establishment was governed by too many charlatans, too heavy a bureaucracy, and too much deception.

Now, at 60, he's a medical maverick, scorned by the established order. Sound familiar?

Back to Blumert. The clinic Tom works out of is no plush, downtown facility. Tahoma Clinic is in Kent, Washington, a semi-industrial Seattle suburb. But there, Tom is free to practice his own brand of medicine.

I'd never met Tom Dorman face-to-face, but I was not surprised to find him meticulous in dress, manner, and speech, his clipped British colonial accent enchanting.

We chatted for a moment about our mutual libertarian bona fides, then moved to his office. His fingers deftly scanned my shoulder, and the muscles and tendons did not evade his touch.

"That's good," he commented almost to himself. "This won't take three visits. One should do it."

I listened with disbelief.

"Let's get to it," he said. The next five minutes were almost surreal. He pushed and probed around the unhappy shoulder until he found the spot he was looking for. First, a little air jet of anaesthetic, then an injection and about 30 seconds of discomfort before the magic elixir spread into the damaged area.

"Okay," he said, "the anaesthetic will allow pain-free movement, but that will be temporary. Tonight you will probably be in pain again until what I injected takes over. You should then start to feel better.

I tentatively rotated the shoulder and the pain was almost gone. What a relief, if only temporary.

"Doc, I also have a problem with my right elbow. I suppose it's a tennis elbow I earned by dragging around bags of silver coins through the years. What do you think?"

This time his fingers were a blur, the magic pain point quickly located, and the rapid-fire injection completed in an instant.

He then told me to call in a few days. "Hold it," I said. "What about torn rotator cuffs? What about the notion that they must be surgically repaired?

"Nonsense," he replied. "You have bursitis." He then proceeded to recite the anatomy of the shoulder and the implausibility that anything was torn or severed.

But what about those $40 million athletes and their torn rotator cuffs? "Well," he answered, "I supposed they are tended to by $2 million orthopedic surgeons."

"You mean," I shouted, "it's rotator-cuff mythology?"

"Good choice of words, Burt. Look, you know about the corruption and lies in government. It's no different in the government's approved medicine."

"What did you inject me with, Doc?" I think he said something about a cortisone equivalent, but frankly, my dears, I don't give a damn. As I write this, it's been weeks since my visit, the elbow is absolutely cured. Bags of silver coins, anyone?

My shoulder is almost normal. No more pills, no sleepless nights. Maybe I'll have to go back to Seattle if the pain returns, but I don't think so. One thing is for sure. I canceled my appointment with the operating room.

I only have one regret: When recounting these events to JoAnn Rothbard, she was very happy for me and said, "Murray would have loved this story." Murray, that great skeptic of establishment medicine, would indeed have loved it.

November 25, 2006

Dr. Thomas A. Dorman, Paracelsus Clinic: td@paracelsusclinic.com

DID HE SAY,
"A FOUR HOUR ERECTION?"

The Hollywood of my youth didn't contaminate their product with four-letter words.

It was the 1960s, and I was at the movies with my mother.

And there it was: THE dreaded four-letter word coming from the screen, resonating around the theatre.

I don't recall the film, but it was a horrid moment, THAT profane word in a movie, and my mother sitting right next to me.

Panicked, I felt like sliding under the seat—did she hear it? Maybe she heard it, but didn't know what the word meant. After all, this pure creature was my mother.

I admit it. I come from a different time. All aspects of sexuality were governed by, "Don't ask . . . don't tell . . . don't talk about it. Don't even think about it."

Not only were those of "deviant" sexuality confined to a closet, almost every male 11 to 17 had his own version of a closet.

My first sexual text was a dog-eared *National Geographic Magazine* featuring photos of bare-breasted tribal women, which passed from one sub-teen to another.

My parents would sooner discuss the insane uncle who lived in our attic than the specifics of procreation.

I don't recall the word "sex" uttered in a classroom until high-school biology, and then the reproduction they covered was confined mostly to the plants of the planet.

The bright kids, however, began to uncover wondrous excerpts about the taboo subject from "banned" books like *God's Little Acre* and Henry Miller's *Tropic of Cancer*, but those of us who grew up in the 30s and 40s were generally so ignorant on the subject that had it not been for the power of the human sex drive, the species might have died out—at least in my neighborhood.

By now, you've got the picture. I'm a prude, or worse. The so-called Sexual Revolution of the 1960s didn't even budge me. I remain unnerved by the way sex is dealt with in the schoolroom, and the boardroom. The only place it belongs is in the bedroom and even then, don't provide me with the details.

I squirm when I witness sexuality in film or theatre, especially when it's designed to shock or arouse. I'll admit to sharing an off-color joke now and then, but never with eroticism as the theme.

No, you won't find me on any picket lines. I state my position by flipping the dial or not buying a ticket—but I'll join you on the barricades if you're fighting government censorship.

In case you haven't noticed, there's a new assault on our sensibilities.

It all began with Viagra, and Bob Dole on network TV, often in prime time.

Most of us laughed, some were repelled, and others too uncomfortable to even discuss it. The Leno and Letterman writers had a field day, and I suspect that the supposedly staid Midwesterner Dole was the subject of a million jokes at water-coolers around the nation.

Soon the chuckles faded and the commercials became more graphic. Words we never read in print became "household" in TV sitcoms.

Here was the same old tactic: repeat the four-letter word often enough and it no longer shocks. Thoughts once private and personal become obscene. What was sacred becomes profane.

A desensitized herd is easier to corral, but don't get me started on that subject.

Back to Bob Dole, the new sex symbol, and the TV ads. They implied the nation was in the midst of an epidemic. Actually, two epidemics. "Male impotency" was the first, a problem solved by science. The consumer has the choice: chemicals requiring prescriptions or over-the-counter natural compounds.

The second "epidemic" is based on the "myth" that "size doesn't matter." In one TV ad, a deli clerk eyes a beautiful waitress, then turns to the camera, picks up a large salami, and tells you, the viewer, that size DOES matter and that just one dose a day will change your life. (Initially, their claims for "male enhancement" seemed based on hocus pocus, but lately, they, too, suggest that "science" plays a role in their remedy.)

The variety of brands fill a counter at Walgreens: Viagra, Vigorex, Cialis, Levitra, Enzyte, to name a few.

Enzyte produced a cartoon-like series of TV commercials featuring real people, including their own, "Bob." Since discovering the wonders of Enzyte, Bob has a grin frozen on his face. His matronly wife stands in the background of each episode gazing adoringly at the new Bob. His friends and associates are consumed with envy.

Cialis, the latest entry in the impotence drug market, runs the most graphic ads. Promoted by the biotech company ICOS and drug giant Eli Lilly, Cialis was late in coming to market. (Viagra had a five-year head start.)

The FDA requires that all negative side-effects for all drugs be listed in advertising. The listed side-effects for Cialis are predictable and boring: Headaches, upset stomach, nasal congestion, backache, muscle ache AND then comes the shocker: The voice over warns YOU about the possibility of suffering a FOUR-HOUR erection.

Although a rare event, the Voice advises, you'd better seek immediate medical attention.

"Did he say four-hour erections?" I asked my wife.

"Blumert, why don't you switch to C-Span? I always worry when you get interested in commercials."

It isn't often that I'm visited by my muse. She shows up so infrequently these days that I can hardly claim her as my own. I don't think she likes my politics.

But this time, she magically appeared and swept me away to the Emergency Room at the County Hospital. She was at my side through the following encounter.

(If Editor Rockwell deems this final scene too vulgar for LRC readers and my essay ends abruptly here, e-mail me and I'll forward the tasteless conclusion to you. If not, read on.)

Scene: Time: 2 a.m. Emergency Room, Mills Hospital, San Mateo.

ERD (Emergency Room Doc): "What seems to be your problem, Blumert? The Admissions Clerk says you are suffering the side effects of Cialis. Is that correct?"

Blumert: "Yes, Doc. I took one Cialis tablet 24 hours ago and I've got a pressing problem."

ERD: "Let's see, the PDA says the side effects could range from a headache to nasal congestion. Which symptom is yours?"

Blumert: "None of those, I fear. For the past 3 hours, I've had an . . . Doc, could you please ask the nurse to leave the room. Uh, well, since about 11 p.m. I've got an . . .

ERD: "Stop mumbling. You mean, 'an erection.' How interesting. I haven't seen that reaction to Cialis as yet. Face the table, please, and hold this tray. Let's take a look."

Blumert: "What are you doing with that fork, Doc?"

ERD: "Fork? I was having lunch when you came in and I was about to sample the coleslaw. Don't panic, please. Here, I'm putting the fork away."

Blumert: "What do I do? I have important people to meet with tomorrow. This could be an awful embarrassment."

ERD: "The way I size things up, Blumert, nobody would even notice. Go home and take a cold bath."

Humiliated, my muse and I slink away. That Doc was certainly unsympathetic and rude. I hope he needs to buy a gold coin some day.

July 14, 2004

GETTING OLD IS NO BARGAIN IN ANY CULTURE

I know I've had too much when the Thunderbird Industrial Red the host bought at $4 per gallon begins to taste like a rare French Bordeaux.

Like most cocktail receptions, the idle chatter around me was typical, but that all changed when the young woman smiled and said, with obvious respect and affection, "Mr. Blumert, I'm so pleased to see that you're still around."

When she realized her unfortunate choice of words, the poor thing was mortified and ready to die on the spot.

Those close by pretended they'd heard nothing, and I should have followed their lead, but not me. I had to save the day, "Well, I really died two years ago, but I haven't had the good sense to lay down."

Nobody laughed and I was astonished to see my wife able to roll her eyes with such intensity.

This was not the first occasion where my advancing years had caused discomfort for others.

There was the time I showed up a day early for a dinner party. (The hostess was very kind about the mix-up and insisted upon fixing me a ham and cheese sandwich.)

My wife says that I have worn the story out, retelling it to the same people at a hundred dinner parties ever since.

She exaggerates, and fails to mention that these folks are also ageing, that they don't remember much, and that they laugh each time I tell the story as though it were the first.

If you need hard evidence that not everybody is loving and patient with the aged, observe how abrupt and mean-spirited some family members become as Grandpa's hearing fails. (When I lost patience with my own father's refusal to use a hearing aid, he responded, "So you think I'm deaf, huh? Well, drop a coin and see who's first to hear it hit the floor.")

Some sociologists believe that you learn a great deal about a culture by examining their attitudes toward the aged. Some societies come out better than others, but, I assure you, the elderly have a tough time of it in EVERY culture.

It doesn't matter how lofty the accomplishments of a person's life, if they live long enough, eventually, they will encounter disrespect

Worse, live into your 90's and you run the risk of outright cruelty at the hands of the "low-level" types who comprise the work force in many "retirement" institutions.

Even those expensive, "Assisted Living Residences" that look like a country club hide dirty little secrets of cruelties visited upon helpless old folk.

All of which set me to thinking about how different societies in different times dealt with their old and sick.

In an earlier, more gracious time, nineteenth century American composer Stephen Foster (1826–1864) sentimentalized about, "The Old Folks at Home":

> Way down upon de Swanee ribber,
> Far, far away,
> Dere's wha my heart is turning ebber,
> Dere's wha de old folks stay.
> All up and down de whole creation,
> Sadly I roam,
> Still longing for de old plantation,
> And for de old folks at home.

Through the nineteenth century in America, the burden of caring for the elderly was a family matter. For those without family support, society looked to charity for assistance. The neighborhood church was usually the focal point for such help.

In the early years of the twentiethth century, in many American cities, the churches began to provide institutional support for the elderly. Almost every religious denomination had its version of a "Home For the Aged."

A close friend was a career social worker with Catholic Family Services in the San Francisco Bay area. He was one of those tireless professionals who genuinely helped real folks dealing with life's real problems.

One of Bill's fellow workers called him, "A priest without collar or credential serving those who didn't attend a regular church."

During the 1980s things changed. It seemed like the private charities were having "jurisdictional" problems with various government agencies. The "private sector" social workers did not have a chance and they were losing ground to the government "commissars" by the minute.

It wasn't much later that Bill quit social work. I recall his comment that, "when the elderly were designated as 'Senior CITIZENS', their lives were doomed to domination by the state, just as what happened to the 'citizens' during the French Revolution." (Everybody was called, "citizen," even as your head was lopped off.)

A visit to Google and the San Francisco phone books reveal that the Private Sector of charities, although shrunken, still exist and do good work, BUT the bloated leviathan of state agencies will smother them until they are extinct.

There are optimists out there who look to advances in science and medicine to alleviate the pain and misery of being old.

I wish I could share the view that the market, through science, will create "Golden Years" for the elderly, but I wouldn't bet a dime on it. Not as long as the bureaucrats infect the entire system.

Well, is there anywhere in the world where the old are revered and treated with respect? I don't think so.

The Chinese are supposed to dote on their aged. Maybe they did a few dynasties ago, but I fear they are just as callous with the aged as their occidental counterparts. At least that's the way it seems in San Francisco.

I doubt if anybody really believes that the Eskimos abandon their elderly on a chunk of ice. It's a heartless piece of mythology, but at the center of it, is there an underlying integrity?

After all, the folks they deposit on the ice are old, unproductive, sick, and not long for this world. It seems pointless to expend scarce resources on them. Resources that can be better used elsewhere. (Or so it seemed when I was a young Randian.)

"Your piece is a downer, Blumert," chided my wife. "People don't want to hear about getting old, getting sick and dying. Lighten up, or Rockwell will 'deep-six' it.

"Don't forget he wouldn't take your calls for three months after that article you did on 'The Inca Indians and Their Influence on Suicide in the West'."

Well, as I always say, "When reality is too grim, try fiction."

In the 1937 Frank Capra film, *Lost Horizon*, the world was introduced to Shangri-La.

Robert Conway, played by Ronald Colman, leads a group of plane crash survivors from certain death in the frigid mountains of Tibet to a perfect valley called Shangri-La.

Shangri-La is paradise, but eventually we learn that the place has its problems. I won't spoil the movie for you by telling everything, but I can say that *Lost Horizon* presents the best fictional example of a society dealing with ageing by putting it on "hold."

It just so happens that my favorite *Star Trek* episode, "The Menagerie," Episode 16, Season 1, takes a different approach. This Gene Roddenberry masterpiece solves the problem of ageing and other disasters through a combination of science and mysticism.

In "The Menagerie," former Enterprise Captain Christopher Pike is severely injured from exposure to delta rays. The Captain's mind is prisoner to his broken body.

Mr. Spock had served under Pike for many years and at the risk of being charged with mutiny, is determined to bring Pike to Talos 4, a planet off-limits to Federation spacecraft.

The Talosians, after losing a war several thousand years earlier, developed illusion and telepathy to a remarkable degree.

The plot is intricate, but Spock knows that the Talosians have the ability through illusion to put Captain Pike "back together."

The court martial committee exonerates Mr. Spock and Captain Pike is left on Talos, finally free of his disfigured body, to live a perfect life of illusion.

Good science fiction puts me in a reflective mood. What would a life of illusion on Talos be like, I wondered?

My reverie was penetrated by my wife's pronouncement that, "There are two people at the front door asking for Blumert. They look like Eskimos and are talking about a reservation you have somewhere in the Bering Sea. What's that all about? And, what shall I tell them?"

It's clear that I have enemies on the "Eskimo Ice-Floe Selection Committee." Tell them I've already booked the Motel 6 in Shangri-La and to buzz-off.

December 20, 2004

GOLD, GOLD, GOLD, GOLD
—AND MORE GOLD

THE *NEW YORKER* MAGAZINE SLAMS GOLD AND GOLD OWNERS

In a scurrilous article in *New Yorker* magazine (July 7, 2000) titled "Gold People: Will They Ever Be Rich Again?" author James Collins doesn't think so.

> Let's say that for some reason you decided back in 1980 that you wanted to lose money on your investments over the next 20 years. Succeeding in this would have been very difficult to do as it turns out. . . . There was, however, one investment that would have lost your money, causing not only financial distress but also shame and humiliation. That investment was gold.

Terrific. Reminding the reader that gold lost its luster as an investment, never matching those highs of 1980, is not the kind of investigative reporting that wins Pulitzer Prizes. The market realities are dismal enough for the gold investor. We don't need Collins, a former senior business editor at *Time* magazine, using distortions and/or deliberately slanted figures to make it appear worse.

Collins: ". . . On January 21, 1980, the price of gold on the New York Comex was $825.50. Today its price is about $280 per ounce. . . . In other words the value of an ounce of gold has fallen about 70 per cent."

Blumert: This is not unlike the fellow in a balloon who is lost. Spotting a farmer working below, our wayward balloonist shouts down: "Sir, I'm lost. Where am I?" The farmer, with clear voice, responds, "You're in a balloon."

The information may be correct but of no value. The likelihood of an investor buying gold, one time only, on January 21, 1980, is sixty-eight million to one. (Ok, I made this number up, but it seems about right.)

Why not arrange for our mythical gold investor to buy on January 21, 1976, when the yellow metal was $124 per ounce? In the year 2000 he would have been ahead 240 percent. Or, pick any other year that helps make your point.

When he describes the gold investor as suffering "shame and humiliation," it's evident Collins has constructed a hit piece, not a serious article.

Rather than deriding the gold investor, Collins would do better to provide his reader with an understanding of those critical events twenty years earlier, and their impact.

The winter of 1979–80 was not a good one for super-powers. While Soviet troops were being drawn and quartered in the mountains of Afghanistan, the daily parade of blindfolded embassy hostages by the Iranians provided the best evidence of a futile US foreign policy.

Back in the US of A, interest rates were approaching 20 percent and double-digit inflation was plaguing consumers and terrorizing politicians. The Dow Jones Industrial Average had failed several times to reach the magical level of 1000 and was languishing at about 800. Investor confidence was at low ebb.

From November 1, 1979, through January 21, 1980, reflecting the prevailing malaise, the price of gold soared from $372 per ounce to $825. In less than ninety days the "gold rush" made the front pages of newspapers around the world.

For Americans, holding gold was illegal from 1933 to 1974. In 1974 all restrictions on gold ownership were lifted, and it was amazing how quickly an efficient American gold market developed. To a large extent, brand new companies provided the consumer with quality products at low premium with instant liquidity. Gold sales reached fevered levels as the yellow metal filled its historic role as a "fever thermometer" reflecting the society's political and economic ills.

From its high of January 21, 1980, the gold price headed lower, and for the next two decades ranged between $250 and $350 an ounce on average. The rallies were infrequent. What happened?

One dark view believes there are conspiratorial forces working against gold. That the king doesn't like gold, never has, never will. That gold reveals truth, and that kings, along with prime ministers and presidents, can't handle too much of that. The evidence of a war on gold is very compelling, but that is a subject for another time.

Some credit former Federal Reserve Chairman Paul Volcker's monetary policy with de-emphasizing gold's role. Baloney. That's as arrogant as the Democrats and Republicans taking credit for the economic boom of the past decade. They are irrelevant.

The computer revolution is a pure American offspring. It has provided the boom along with the unprecedented strength of the US dollar against all currencies AND gold. As long as the dollar retains this dominant position, gold will remain lackluster.

Back to Collins, his relentless attack on the gold investor, and his distortions.

Collins: "In 1980, the Dow Jones Industrial Average was at 800. Today, it is around ten thousand five hundred."

Blumert: It's one thing to look at averages, another to speak of individual investments. Many of the companies that flourished in 1980 no longer exist.

I won't dwell upon some of the devastating losses we have seen recently on the NASDAQ. Stocks that were one $170 per share in March 2000, are $4 today. How many stock certificates printed in the last twenty years are worth nothing, zilch, zero, bupkis? I imagine they provide enough "shame and humiliation" to go around.

Collins: "Bonds bought in 1980 would have soared in value as interest rates came down."

Blumert: The economist, Dr. Franz Pick, once defined bonds as "certificates of guaranteed confiscation." I recall a holder of certain junk bonds who ultimately used them as wallpaper in his den.

Collins: "Paintings . . . UP . . . Comic books . . . UP . . . Snuff boxes, stamps, coins, manuscripts, majolica, it seems that no matter what you bought in 1980 your investment would have increased in value by the year 2000."

Blumert: Is that so? As a gold dealer who also has handled numismatics for forty years, I can attest, with absolute certainty, that collector coin prices have never come close to matching 1980 levels. My stamp dealer friends say it is pretty much the same in their world, and I would warrant comic books, toys, and manuscripts are similarly checkered in their performance.

Collins: "In the 1980s the one hundred and eighty-five hundred thousand-dollar home is nine hundred thousand in the year 2000."

Blumert: Real estate is the king of all investments, but bitterly disappointing to some. REITs (real estate investment trusts) left some investors nothing but lawsuits, and even when market values soar, many realize that finding a qualified buyer is not always an easy matter.

The Collins piece disintegrates into a narrative on the life and times of "goldbug" Michael Levinson. It's the sorry saga of the New York City boy, educated at Harvard, who becomes interested in gold, and makes a killing selling gold mining shares.

As the price of gold tumbles, then stagnates, Levinson loses his money, and is now the tragic figure, broke, a pariah to his customers but clinging to a belief system that is obsolete and irrelevant.

Actually, Levinson doesn't even qualify for the "goldbug" fraternity. Gold dealer/brokers, as professionals, do not have parity with the true "goldbug." Which now brings us to the real question. Why does Collins choose to do his article on gold at this time? The commodity is certainly not in the news, and could never earn any space in a current issue of *Time* magazine. The characters, would, at best, be "quaint" to the *New Yorker* readership.

I've got the answer. What's bugging Collins is that these people that he marginalizes are in fact a "cut above" and principled.

I have dealt with gold investors for over forty years. Their checks are always good; they honor every commitment, stay informed on current issues, and have a profound understanding of history.

They provide for their families, and they don't go broke. I can assure you that many, many of them have done very well with their gold investments.

Our present culture of totalitarian liberalism is hostile to any criticism of the regime. Whenever a group of people like the "goldbugs" rejects a key element of the modern state, such as managed "funny" money, it's no surprise that the senior editors from *Time* magazine and the *New Yorker* find the need to subject them to ridicule.

October 23, 2000

BUY WHEN THE BLOOD IS IN THE STREETS, UNLESS IT'S YOUR BLOOD

NEWSPAPER HEADLINES

"Nikkei Averages Reach 1985 Lows"

"Nasdaq Averages Break 2000. Down 65% From Highs In Just One Year"

"Dow Jones Industrial Average Breaks 10,000. Down More Than 600 Points in Last Few Days"

The voice on the other end of the line said: "You are calling the 'INVESTOR'S CRISIS AND DESPAIR HOTLINE.' All our grief counselors are occupied with desperate stock market investors like yourself. Be calm and breathe deeply while you wait, or "Press 'one' if you are at the end of your rope. Your call will be transferred to the Suicide Prevention Center.

"Be prepared to be put on hold.

"Press 'two' if you are calling because you can't get through to your broker. He is most likely on the line with one of our counselors.

"Press 'three' if you are seeking religious support. Once again, be patient, as most religious leaders are also on the line with our counselors.

"Press 'four' if you want to hear Handel's 'Dead March'.

"Press 'five' if you want to hear FDR's famous 'We have nothing to fear, but fear itself' speech.

"While you are waiting, think positive. Consider the following that may comfort you.

"If the DIJA and the Nasdaq continue to drop 2–3 percent per day, in 37 days all the averages will be zero and you'll have nothing more to worry about.

"To those of you calling about Foot-and-Mouth disease, please be advised that it does not apply to the bubble-headed stock market cheerleaders on TV."

"Blumert, we need you for another shift on the phones," pleaded the INVESTOR'S CRISIS AND DESPAIR Director.

"But, I've been on for thirty-six hours straight. Surely there are other grief counselors available?"

"None as comforting to the poor souls as you, Blumert. After all, as a precious metals dealer you have been party to the most dismal, gold bear market for more than twenty years."

"Losers need other losers. Lord knows, you are at the top of the list."

March 15, 2001

CELEBRATING THE
ANNIVERSARY OF A CRIME

The thirtieth anniversary of Richard Nixon's closing of the gold window was hardly mentioned in the financial press.

In one article posted on August 12 at Miningweb.com, a mining trade publication, Nixon's dastardly act is described by writer Tim Wood: The Executive Order "unplugged the U.S. dollar from its gold life support," bringing about "the longest period a gold standard has been absent from the international system."

In effect, Nixon's dictatorial Executive Order cancelled the dollar/gold exchange rate established seventy-seven years earlier, when foreign central banks were allowed to claim an ounce of American gold for US $35. By his single stroke, Tricky Dick cut any relationship the US dollar had to gold.

Mr. Wood pines for those good old days when (allegedly) the Fed respected gold: "A central bank exists for no other (or better) reason than to keep the national unit of account stable."

I'm a bit surprised Mr. Wood didn't apply even a bit of his tortured nostalgia to the earthshaking event that occurred on April 5, 1933, when gold was demonetized, and Americans lost the right to hold "real" money.

I'm sympathetic with Mr. Wood's depressed state, but there's another date in gold's history that should be celebrated: January 1, 1975, when all restrictions on owning gold were lifted.

Why no mention of April 5, 1933, and January 1, 1975?

I have a theory: Mr. Wood's reverence for gold is pragmatic. He is more concerned with enlightening central bankers and reminding them of their proper relationship to gold than the freedom of the individual.

If this sounds like the wisdom of Jude Wanniski, you are correct. Mr. Wood gives full credit to Wanniski and the other supply siders for his views on gold.

Mr. Wanniski is one of my heroes, and there is no more courageous commentator on the passing scene. He buckles to no pressure, but I disagree with his recommended path to a gold standard. The Fed cannot be trusted. But that debate is for another time.

For now, I thank Mr. Wood and, indirectly, Mr. Wanniski, for prompting me to reflect on my forty plus years as a gold dealer.

If ever there was a day of infamy, April 5, 1933, qualifies. For the first time, gold was demonetized and Americans were forced to surrender their gold coins to the government. You received a $20 bill in exchange for your $20 gold coin. Later that year, gold was revalued from $20.67 per ounce to $35. The citizen was first plundered, then humiliated, by the monster Roosevelt.

On January 1, 1975, the beleaguered US citizen had a bit of freedom restored when the draconian laws denying Americans the right to own and trade gold were eliminated. No, a gold standard was not restored, but January 1, 1975, was a day freedom lovers celebrate.

Back to 1971: Nixon's action was more than symbolic. It had real impact. And to conservatives of the day, the anguish caused by the closing of the gold window was dwarfed by the shock of wage and price controls simultaneously imposed by Executive Order. (Some contend that several key Southern Californian Nixon supporters never forgave him for that betrayal, and quietly swung their financial support to Ronald Reagan.)

In 1971, Nixon was preparing for his reelection campaign. He was tidying up potentially troublesome areas. Consumer and wholesale price indices were bubbling up although the increases were miniscule as compared with inflation rates nine years later. Nixon's brain trust believed controls would be politically palatable, and could head off future price increases long enough to ensure his reelection.

The closing of the gold window meant little to most Americans as citizens had been legally barred from holding the precious metal since 1933.

As part of his reelection campaign, Nixon also wanted to punish French President Charles DeGaulle. In compliance to federal direction, the US media caricaturized the elegant, aloof French hero as unappreciative. After all, American conscripts had saved the French from the Hun in two world wars. This comic opera general was greedily using American dollars to plunder our gold reserves. Putting this ingrate in his place would resonate well with US voters.

Where was the dissent? Well, there wasn't much.

The equity markets had little interest in the closing of the gold window, but wage and price controls set the stock market off to record-high percentile increases the day following the announcement. Only a few old-fashioned economists, like Murray Rothbard and Hans Senholz, shook their heads in disbelief. The failed ghost of controls had arisen once more.

And by 1971 most Americans had little first-hand memory of gold. The Depression and WW II were indelibly imprinted on their psyches and if they thought about gold at all, it was as a murky link to the hard times of the 1930s. Silver was a different story. The dimes, quarters, and half dollars minted almost continually from 1796 through 1964 were 90 percent silver. Most folks simply took it for granted that the coinage was silver.

Not one in a thousand reflected that one dollar's face value in silver coins contained 72 parts of a pure ounce and that at $1.29 an ounce, the price fixed by the Treasury Department, the intrinsic value was precisely one dollar. This magnificent reality went unnoticed.

That all came to an end several months after JFK's death in 1963. The new "LBJ" nonsilver, 10- and 25-cent sandwich coinage appeared on the scene amidst a barrage of propaganda.

The experts said the "sandwiches" would circulate side-by-side with the silver coins for eternity. Speculator-hoarders would find slim profit in pulling the silver coinage from circulation. This obvious deceit provided me with early evidence that public opinion was being manipulated and the manipulators knew the truth.

Shortly thereafter the US Treasury announced that August 16, 1968, would be the last day to redeem the $1, $5, and $10 silver certificates. In effect, the government had created an expiring option, and as the days passed, silver's time as money was passing as well. The silver coinage quickly disappeared, of course.

Your local coin shop was the place where you purchased or sold silver coinage, or liquidated your silver certificates. This activity honed the coin industry for the onslaught that was to soon follow in the gold market.

In 1962 US Treasury Department policy toward gold ownership was little changed since 1933. Gold for jewelry was legal. Gold coins dated 1932 and older could be legally held, but ONLY if physically in the US and as collectibles, not investments. All gold imports were forbidden, except by special license which was rarely granted.

So, a US $20 St. Gaudens gold piece was available in Switzerland for US $50, but, due to a shortage of supply in the US, it was worth $60 plus.

Hmmm. . . . US gold coins minted prior to 1933 were legal if already here? You couldn't legally bring them in. But, if you were able to get them here, there was a nice profit. Interesting. Sounds like an invitation to the bootlegger.

My company, Camino Coin, was founded in 1959. Although our primary business was numismatics, we soon were deeply involved in buying and selling precious metals. In Europe, these services were provided by banks.

US government policy was harsh, and the gold coin bootleggers reign existed through the early 1960s. The process was simple: the bootlegger purchased the US gold coins in Europe where most of them had resided since 1933, and had them shipped to Canada. So far, everything was legal. Getting the gold safely across the border was the problem.

Treasury Department enforcement against the smugglers was sporadic. Most of the gold coins arrived safely, but occasionally the feds would "send a message to the coin community" by making midnight raids and confiscating gold as if they were dealing with dangerous drugs.

In one instance, I saw the process close up. A smuggler carried gold coins from Canada to the state of Washington, packaged them, and mailed the parcel from a Seattle post office to a US dealer. (This fellow was selling them to me.) When the dealer's sister sought to pick them up at her California post office, the Secret Service confiscated the coins.

The dealer, desperate to recover his merchandise, argued that since the coins were mailed from Seattle, they were physically in the US, thereby not subject to confiscation. The government held that these coins were never "here," but rather in transit from Canada, hence, contraband. The case finally went to a US Circuit Court and the government prevailed.

Near the end of JFK's presidency, the Treasury Department modified its restrictions on gold coins minted 1932 and earlier. US and foreign coinage could now be legally imported by Americans. This led to an avalanche of European gold coins like the British Sovereign, the French and Swiss 20 Franc, and all the American gold coins coming into the US.

In 1973, with the government in disarray, and a president near impeachment, a small but energetic movement to eliminate all remaining restrictions on gold ownership won a shocking victory and for the first time in over forty years, Americans could freely own and trade gold without restriction.

The late, great coin dealer and conference entrepreneur James U. Blanchard III was the main force behind the struggle.

For the first time since 1932 gold coins, bars, and gold certificates could be freely imported. Items that, prior to January 1, 1974, were almost as dangerous to handle as heroin were part of everyday commerce.

But it took a while for a dealer to hold a Krugerrand or a Credit Suisse gold kilo bar in his hand without looking over his shoulder to see if a Secret Service agent was lurking in the shadows.

August 20, 2001

WHAT IS HAPPENING
IN THE GOLD MARKET?

Paul is our regular UPS man and he has been telling his wife that they should own some gold. Finally, with gold in the headlines, they made their decision and bought 5 ounces.

He picked up his order yesterday;

"Sure, the minute I buy something, you can bet the price goes down," poor Paul mumbled as he wrote his check.

I'd like to have an ounce of gold, or even a gram, for how many times I've heard that wail from clients throughout the decades.

The corollary, that the price immediately spikes higher as soon as we sell something, is the other side of the coin (if you'll excuse the expression).

Few investors have escaped the agony of these experiences. It's as if there were little gods who monitor such matters and they whack us every time we decide to buy or sell something.

The dramatic ups and downs of the price of gold in recent days has tested everybody.

Some new gold buyers are disheartened; others are in a state of shock. Even gold professionals have been emotionally wrung out by the schizophrenic price gyrations of the ancient yellow metal.

In case you missed it, here's a summary of the gold market over the past two weeks using prices from the London Metals Exchange as our source; On Dec. 2, the price of gold punctured $500 per ounce price for the first time in about twenty years.

For the next ten days the gold price spiked higher almost every trading day and the inter-day price edged close to $540 per ounce.

Over the last few days gold has dropped sharply, and tomorrow, Thursday, Dec 15, the price could very well drop below $500.*

Let's consider these numbers in some prospective:

From its highs of two weeks ago gold plunged about 6½ percent.

I suspect that when we examine the history of gold prices in the years ahead, this recent spasm will register as a mere blip on the chart.

The following figures tell us the real story. I'm using the price of gold for each January since the year 2000 to make my point:

        January, 2000 $310 per oz.
        January, 2001   275
        January, 2002   295
        January, 2003   375
        January, 2004   425
        January, 2005   431
        January, 2006   ??? (I predict the price next month will
                             be $500 +)

If you purchased gold recently and you're worried, phone me and I'll hold your hand.

If I'm more worried than you, you can hold mine.

---

*This article was written on Wednesday night, December 14. The price touched $500.80 early Thursday morning in London.

I can assure you of this:

When all other monies crumble into dust, the value of gold will endure.

December 17, 2005

Yes, There Are Risks When You Buy Gold

This speech was delivered at the Steve Sjuggerud Conference in Long Beach, California on Wednesday, January 28, 2004.

At breakfast a nice young man set aside his French toast to ask me, "Burt, how do I know if a coin dealer is reliable?"

I answered without hesitation. "To start with, make certain he has been in the business at least 43 years 7 months and 11 days—Make that 12 days."

You guessed it, that happens to be my tenure in the trade, and I admit my sassy response sounded self-serving. You don't need a novice practicing on you whether he is selling a Krugerrand, a Proof Seated Dollar or, anything for that matter.

Some years ago, I was seriously troubled by a potential tax problem. I foolishly mentioned the matter to my family attorney. As he listened to the details, his face drained of color, and I feared he would pass out. Irving was clearly the wrong lawyer for this problem,

If I need brain surgery, I want a doc who has handled so many cases that my particular tumor is almost boring.

Which gets to my subject matter for the day: "What risks does the first time gold buyer face?" And, the follow-up, larger question: "Is there a downside to owning gold?"

Answer: Yes, there are reasons NOT to buy and own gold. (These reasons apply to silver and platinum as well.)

Here are just a few:

- There is a risk in holding gold! All the crooks, those in government and those in the private sector all want to get their paws on your gold.

Some of my crusty old-timers are comfortable ONLY when they sit, shotgun in hand, on top of their coins.

- There is a cost to holding gold. Not only do you pay for Safety Deposit boxes, the gold owner is also "punished by losing interest" he might have received from other investments.

- Your government will start to regard you as peculiar. Buy a Treasury Bill, or a share of IBM, and you're a fine citizen, a patriot. But, buy an ounce of gold, and "there's something wrong with you."

You may be one of those "paranoid crazies" who owns guns and writes letters to his local newspaper.

Speaking of paranoia, I have been invited to join Paranoid's Anonymous, but they won't tell me where the meetings are.

- A high percentage of gold owners will never use banks to store valuables. They would rather hide things around the house.

Which leads to a new and scary risk. As we age, we are inclined to forget things—What was I talking about?

Oh yes, forgetting where you put things.

I have a pal, Kurt, who was barely in his 50s at the time. He owned seven or eight investment-grade diamonds, D color, flawless, VVS 1 or, however they grade those things. Kurt had paid over twelve thousand dollars for each.

Well, he couldn't recall where he'd hidden them. But, he wasn't worried. He was confident he would find them when he REALLY started to look. One day, he REALLY started to look, but didn't find them.

Panic set in and he compounded the problem by telling his wife about the missing stones. She took over the search, located a hypnotist who was renowned for delving into the subconscious, and poor Kurt was subject to three tortured sessions with a fat lady from Romania.

Result: No diamonds! (unless the hypnotist had them)— and although Kurt has no conscious recollection of the three evenings, to this day, whenever he smells garlic, his left hand gets numb.

A month later, Kurt wisely told his wife the white lie that he found the missing diamonds and sold them at a profit.

He confided that it all came back to him in a flash on New Year's Eve while watching an old Guy Lombardo video tape. Every male in sight was attired in a tux. That did it.

In searching for a place to hide his precious diamonds, what could be more plausible than placing them in the pocket of an old tuxedo that no longer fit?

He also remembered depositing a trunk full of old clothes in a giant Goodwill box at the local shopping center.

Lesson: If you hide something, better tell someone younger what it was you hid and where it was you hid it.

Some folks think that the greatest risk of all to the gold owner is confiscation. They use 1933 and the events that took place that year as their evidence.

I don't share the view that confiscation is that great a threat. The situation today is unlike 1933. Gold is not circulating money and those who own gold are regarded as wackos. Let them go unnoticed seems to be government strategy.

I'm not minimizing the threat government poses to assets and privacy. They can come and take your living room furniture, but I do not think confiscation would be their weapon.

Some who contend that there is safety in holding gold coins dated prior to 1933 haven't thought out the premise.

Can you imagine the absurdity of a bureaucrat standing at your front door with an eye loop examining your gold coin to see if it's legal or not?

Let's review what happened that fateful year. On April 6, 1933, a month after his inauguration, FDR demonetized gold. The $20 gold piece was no longer money. Well, since it wasn't money any longer, bring it to the bank, they said, and we'll give you a $20 bill for it.

That's called theft.

In January of 1934, The Gold Reserve Act changed the value of an ounce of gold from $20.67 to $35. Somebody almost doubled their money! Anybody we know?

Here's an interesting historical aside: Prohibition was just about coming to an end. It had been a disastrous, failed social experiment. Prohibition spawned the crime families, which endure to this day.

Other great American dynasties were enriched by Prohibition. Joseph Kennedy, the clan's patriarch, held the contracts with the Scotch Distillers. He could legally import the good booze to Canada, and, then, the bootleggers and rumrunners took over. Magically, the illicit hooch appeared off the coast of California destined for thirsty residents of San Francisco and points south.

The proceeds probably wound up back in Europe. The system was too good to scrap.

The UK demonetized gold in 1931. The handwriting was on the wall for the US. A million dollars was a lot of money in those days, but there were folks who could raise much more for a "sure thing."

A million dollars bought 50,000 $20 gold coins. It boggles the mind how many coins were legally "purchased" through the banks, sent to Canada and then on to Swiss banks.

To this day, over 70 years later, US gold coins are still available from European banks. That gives you some idea of how many left the US between 1931 and 1933.

I don't believe anybody was ever prosecuted for not turning in gold coins, nor for sending them out of the country.

Unfortunately, most poor schnook citizens turned their few gold coins in because they were told to do so.

Some months ago I wrote an article for LewRockwell.com describing why "The King Doesn't like Gold, He never Has, He Never Will."

Gold is synonymous with freedom, and most of the kings we see these days are hardly interested in expanding the freedom of their vassals.

We should regard anybody seeking the throne with suspicion.

Well, I've used all of my time telling you why gold is a problem to buy and to hold.

I never got around to telling you the danger you face if you DON'T own gold.

For now, all I can say is that NOBODY ever went to the Poor House buying gold.

January 30, 2004

IF YOU WANT TO MAKE GOD LAUGH, TELL HIM YOUR PLANS

The customer complaind. "But you quoted me $11 less on a Krugerrand yesterday." "It may only seem like yesterday," I reminded him, "but, in fact, you called last Wednesday, and the gold price is up 3 percent since."

"I hadn't noticed," he muttered.

The gold price did quite well in the month of April, but it went mostly unnoticed.

Market rallies come dressed in different clothes. This is especially true for the Gold Market, where rallies have visited infrequently over the past twenty years.

In late 2002 and early 2003, the price of gold behaved spectacularly. We witnessed a rip-roaring run-up in price. It was a Classic Type 1 Rally. For want of a better term, let's call it a "Blow-Off Rally."

It was as if Gold had a voice and was shouting to the world, "Hey, look at me. In just sixty days, my value has gone up more than $60. Almost every other area of investment has either collapsed or languished, but I have glowed.

"All you non-believers and naysayers should be falling on your knees seeking forgiveness."

Even the government mouthpiece financial press and the cable TV business shows—no friends to gold—could hardly ignore the "Blow-Off." Although they would choke before saying anything favorable, two things became apparent: they knew nothing about gold, but that didn't prevent them from being miserable watching gold climb against the world's paper currencies, particularly the US dollar.

During a Blow-Off Rally, the futures markets is an engine where highly leveraged positions lead to wild price fluctuations.

If these fluctuations become violent enough the gold story may make the front page of your morning newspaper, or the lead story at LRC. That didn't happen this time, but I predict it will in the not-too-distant future.

Such blow-offs are often followed by a significant retrenching, and the 2002–03 version was typical, surrendering 50 percent of what it had gained.

By contrast, the Type 2 market rally is subdued, even boring. Let's call it an "Unnoticed Rally." It certainly went unnoticed by my Krugerrand customer.

In an Unnoticed Rally, the financial press is able to maintain their indifference. Trading in the futures markets remains tepid. Nobody pays much attention to the modest price increases, and there is less volatility.

Market technicians might contend that such increases are more positive. They may be right.

In my apprentice years as a gold dealer, I held strong opinions on market direction and was happy to share those views, even with strangers on the street. After the passing of decades, and getting kicked in the teeth 1000 times, I have changed my ways.

I've stopped forecasting, and if you corner me today and ask tomorrow's gold price, you will note how adroit I am by turning the conversation to what Lew Rockwell is really like, or how modern medicine now deals with gall bladders.

In re-reading this short web-essay, I seem to have regressed. You can surely see a prediction or two above and the implication of higher gold prices based on April's performance.

By the time you read this, the gold market could be in a shambles, making my observations absurd. It's like bragging to friends that you haven't had a head cold in six months. Then, WHAM, here comes the burning throat, followed by the other horrible symptoms.

Uh oh. I better be careful. I must remember to keep in mind what a wise man once told me, "If you want to make God laugh, tell him your plans."

To this, I have added Blumert's Corollary: "There is a wholesome force in nature designed to humiliate those who predict markets."

The fool, having once predicted something correctly, keeps forecasting and eventually all who encounter him see him as the buffoon his wife sees. He never learns and those who follow his counsel are larger fools.

The more experienced prognosticator (see Talking Heads) frames his statements so that six months or six years later nothing can be learned from his words. If clever, he can take credit whether the market is, up, down, or unchanged.

I fear that I have invited the wrath of my own corollary and may be punished by lower gold prices.

It's like clicking on "Today's Gold Price" button at LRC and observing that gold is down $4 dollars that morning, but reading somewhere else on the web that gold's performance was lustrous yesterday in Europe and should be higher in New York.

Blumert's Corollary at work.

In the old days we were satisfied to get the price of gold once a week. Now, prices are stale in 30 seconds.

But, you can disregard any predictions I might have made.

May 7, 2003

THE "HARDLY NOTICED" RALLY OF GOLD

I've watched and listened to the "Cable Heads" as long as my supply of Rolaids allowed.

All they've talked about is the drop of the US Dollar against other currencies. Of course, that's a big story.

But what about the price of gold?

In the past 30 days (April 19–May 19), the price of gold has risen from $332 per ounce to $366—an increase of 10 percent—a significant change for a "money" commodity.

No surprise to me that the talking heads aren't covering gold.

In my last essay on the mysterious yellow metal, I discussed the different types of rallies.

There's the "Blow-Off" rally, where the price increases are accompanied by media coverage. The higher the price, the more prominent the coverage. I have lived through several Blow-off rallies where gold's story finally winds up in headlines on the front page.

I described the other type of rally as the "Unnoticed Rally." In that instance the price goes higher WITHOUT media focus, or, often, without any kind of focus.

The past months have brought us a classic "Unnoticed Rally."

When the talking heads discuss the drop of the US dollar, for example, their "take" is either: "It really doesn't matter" or "A cheaper US dollar is good for our exports."

Am I alone, or do you hear the same garbage I do?

Here's some additional jewels from the "Kable Kooks":

"Inflation continues to be a non-factor. The real concern is deflation."

"The equity markets have turned from the 'killer bear' to being under-valued."

"Yes, bond yields are the lowest seen in decades, but there are some attractive bonds with higher returns worth considering." (Junk bonds)

"Residential real estate is 'bubble-bursting proof'."

It's just as well that these "heads" don't have much to say about gold.

This gold rally is also going unnoticed by customers. There's very little buying on the part of the public. In fact, the opposite has happened, and we've seen a huge amount of selling with every $5 dollar increase in the price of gold.

Do these savvy sellers know something we don't know?

I don't think they're so savvy.

Which brings us to the "Question of the Day": When Should Gold Be Sold?

I asked one middle-aged-investor-type why he was selling. He admitted he didn't need the dough and wasn't guessing that the price of gold was going lower.

He sheepishly confided that the only reason he was selling was to take a profit on something. It had been a long time.

Here is my advice on when to sell gold: this counsel may be considered single minded or myopic.

Hold your gold, sell ONLY when you need the dollars.

When, for instance, you are buying a house, helping the kids, paying for your brain surgery.

Never sell gold to use the dollars for another investment UNLESS it's a business venture you know something about (preferably YOUR business).

And then we have those dramatic instances when you are forced to liquidate your gold.

For example, you're thirsty, I'm the only one with water, and it's going to cost you a gold coin per bucket.

Or, the LAST TRAIN is leaving the station and the price for a ticket is a gold coin.

I trust this message is clear.

When should you NOT be selling gold?

When the price goes up too high or down too low.

When someone tries to convince you that the bullion type gold coins you own = Bad and the collector type coins he wants to sell you = Good.

In fact, he will try to persuade you that the bullion type gold coins are so bad that the government will come and take them.

Sometimes people will sell just for "the action." Resist such temptations.

My granddaddy once advised me never to run after a trolley or a woman. There was always another one coming.

I have no idea what grandpa's wisdom has anything to do with the above, but the rhythm of his words seemed appropriate.

May 21, 2003

BEWARE THE CHARTIST: HE BRINGS YOU FALSE SCIENCE

"How come they didn't predict this?"
—*Overheard from an anonymous fellow as he
plunged off the Flat Iron Building,*
NYC, October 1929

I've always tried to be civil in the presence of Chartists.

I am also polite in the company of snake charmers and bungee jumpers, but if my daughter announced one day, "Daddy, I'm in love with Lancelot. He's a ————"(fill in the blank), I would immediately retain a top-notch team of de-programmers to bring the poor girl back to her senses.

Come to think of it, bungee jumpers don't inflict pain on others, and the world's no worse because of them. They are a spirited group and good for an occasional laugh, especially when their cord breaks.

As for snake charmers, what if we found ourselves overrun by venomous serpents as happened in Ireland once upon a time? The "charmers" could act as non-combatants until a St. Patrick came on the scene to wipe the critters out. (Unfortunately, the charmer's magic is useless against the most deadly of all snakes, The Political Viper.)

There's a certain unworldly aura that surrounds anyone who devotes his life to out-staring a snake.

These worthies must have a tough time earning a living, yet they too, do little harm while practicing their craft. The fact that snakes seem to tolerate them should be regarded as a plus.

Note, how I've already come to terms with having a bungee jumping fellow, or a snake charmer as a son-in-law, but my tolerance ends when it comes to Chartists.

Let me be clear. I am not talking about Chart Makers, diligent folks who map the crust and waterways of the planet. Nor am I degrading the Chartists, those English political reformers, active between 1838–48. (I think they were bad guys, but knowing our LRC readers, I'll find out soon enough.)

I'm talking about those arrogant snobs who promote the belief that the future performance of markets can be predicted from analyzing yesterday's lines and dots on a page.

This group is deadly dangerous: They leave empty bank accounts and broken spirits in their wake.

Look, if there are customers willing to pay the Gypsy lady to read tea leaves, that's OK with me. After all, she entertains her clients—but never presents herself as possessed with a body of scientific knowledge.

Even the Voodoo Priest who predicts the future by reading animal entrails, never confuses the source of his dark knowledge with human reason.

Of all the mystics, only the Chartist pretends a rational basis for his gobbledygook. The Chartist further elevates his status by including himself in a larger, even more virulent group that label themselves as "market-technicians."

Surely, one would think that the devastating losses suffered recently in the equity markets would have exposed these charlatans and their false religion. But, no, their followers are like zombies. Never questioning, and in constant search for that blip on the chart that pierces the shrouded future.

"You're just looking for trouble, Blumert," said my wife as she burned the toast. "You have friends who make their living as technicians. Worse yet, you must have dozens of customers who believe in that stuff. They'll be offended."

"If that's the price I must pay in the pursuit of Truth, so be it," I proclaimed.

"Pursuit of Truth? You've been annoyed ever since that fellow told you he didn't like the looks of the gold chart," she said while scraping the blackened toast.

"Is that so?" I muttered sardonically. "If he spent more time understanding the fundamentals, he would know that his gold chart was nonsense. He'd be better off predicting that you'll burn the toast again tomorrow."

November 18, 2003

CONFESSIONS OF A GOLD PUSHER

Gold is addictive. I've seen it a thousand times. The buyer innocently starts out with silver, and although studies claim silver is not
addictive, it leads to gold every time. Some even wind up experimenting with platinum.

—From Blumert's Public Service Announcement
"Gold is Bad," December 2003

Lew Rockwell takes great pride in not owning a TV set.
Bully for him—but he still wants to know what the "talking heads" are saying on Sunday's TV news shows.

Solution? Assign Blumert to watch and report.

My Sunday starts with orange juice and *Meet the Press*, followed by coffee at MSNBC with Chris Matthews. *Face the
Nation* is usually placid enough so that I can digest my lunch.

The day turns grimmer as Tony Snow at Fox rolls out one
fatuous, retired military creep after another, celebrating the glo-
ries of Empire and crowing how we are winning every war in
spite of minor setbacks.

Struggling to pay attention, my assignment mercifully ends
as Wolf "The Blitzer" drones on at CNN.

This was the dullest of News Sundays: Hillary Clinton giggled her way through thirty minutes with Tim Russert, denying
that she was a presidential candidate, and you will be relieved
to learn that Newt Gingrich, who also spent thirty minutes with
Russert, will no longer plague us as a politician. Newt pro-
claims he is now an historian, although he sounded more like a
"new age" economist.

The news this Sunday was not even worth a report to Editor Rockwell, and I was ready to switch to the Cooking Channel when a commercial caught my attention. You've probably heard it, too.

A mellifluous female voice representing the Philip Morris Company tells us that, "There is no such thing as a safe cigarette."

The low-tar and low-nicotine varieties are useless and the only "safe thing to do is to QUIT smoking."

She continues to shock us with her public service-type message: Phillip Morris provides a website loaded with antismoking pamphlets and tapes. The message was clear, "Let's stop the world from smoking." Aided and abetted by Phillip Morris.

I knew the tobacco companies were in trouble, but I did not realize it had come to this.

Then, it all became clear. A Gestapo-type fellow holds a gun at the announcer's head as she reads the antismoking commercial.

The Company succumbs to the violence, relying on that hearty group of nicotine addicts who will disregard these admonitions and continue to buy and puff so that the Company can pay billions of dollars in ransom through the coming decades.

In return, the tobacco companies are allowed to survive and will be immune to harmful death civil suits.

The politicians are also well aware that these "purveyors of death" collect hundreds of millions in "sin" taxes, thus fattening the coffers at every level of government.

This goose may be evil, but its eggs are pure gold.

A friend comments, "You're wrong about them holding a gun at her head, Blumert. There's no need to. The defiance is long gone. All that's left is resignation."

"It's like China during the 'Cultural Revolution,' where the victim dons a dunce cap and participates in his own condemnation."

"Funny you should mention China," I responded. "Today, China is slowly clawing its way to an open society, complete with freedom to smoke, while back here in the good old US of A, zombie-like-managers are telling their customers not to buy their product. They might as well be wearing dunce caps."

"I'm not trying to worry you, Blumert, but cigarettes and gold have much in common. The King's not so crazy about either. If you buy a share of IBM, you're a patriot. Buy an ounce of gold, and they figure something's wrong with you.

"They just might come down on your industry next. It happened in 1933, and I would give anything to see you in a dunce cap."

He may be right, and one day a whistle blower on *"60 Minutes"* will reveal how gold advocates conspire to spread their message. That they hold clandestine conferences at vacation area hotels, poison the minds of the young with a philosophy better suited to the sixteenth century, and undermine the stock market, the Fed, and the American dollar.

They are nothing but a cult.

Next, will be the clicking of jack-boots outside my office.

"We are questioning gold dealers. Where is Blumert?" the group leader asks.

"Put away your guns, fellas. I've been expecting you. I've prepared a statement titled, 'Gold is Bad.' You are free to use it. All I ask is a seat on the 'US Anti-Gold Commission' and tickets to the Super Bowl in New Orleans.

Text of Blumert's statement: GOLD IS BAD

There is ample evidence that gold brings out the basest of human qualities. Instead of spending their money for the benefit of society, gold owners are inclined to horde, and they become miserly.

Gold is addictive. I've seen it thousands of times. The buyer innocently starts out with silver, and although studies claim that silver is not addictive, it leads to gold every time. Some even wind up experimenting with platinum.

In summary, gold is bad. But, so are cigarettes, pork-chops, chocolate eclairs, and Sunday's news shows. What would we do without them?

December 10, 2003

THE KING DOESN'T LIKE GOLD, NEVER HAS, NEVER WILL— *UNLIKE MR. CHANG*

From the annual Freedom Futility Award ceremony.

"CSPAN is covering our event today, so those of you here in the audience, don't be caught napping if the camera scans you.

"I was only kidding, America, that was my little joke.

"Nominees for the award are passionate freedom fighters generally identified with organizations committed to hopeless causes.

"The winner of last year's Freedom Futility Award was the Libertarian Party, and true to their tradition, they have proudly worn the mantle of futility over the past twelve months.

"Now, ladies and gentlemen, we come to the exciting moment when this year's award recipient is revealed. Mr. Rockwell, the envelope please.

(Sound of envelope being torn open, slicing through the breathless silence.)

"And the winner is . . . the GATA Group."

To those unfamiliar with these unsung, yet futile heroes at GATA (Gold Anti-Trust Action Committee), let me briefly describe the evil they have "discovered," and the windmills they battle.

The GATA folks realized after getting kicked in the teeth thirty-seven times that the gold market does not behave as other markets. They deduced that a scheme to suppress the price of gold involved not only bullion trading banks, but also governments, particularly the US government. (Wonder of wonders.)

GATA believes that the gold price suppression will end when it is exposed, and to their credit, they have hammered away at getting the word out. They also advocate litigation and actually helped bring suit in US District Court in Boston, Howe vs. Bank for International Settlements, et al.

Occasionally, events overwhelm the conspiracy, and gold prices shoot higher. GATA is always quick to celebrate such victories, proclaiming that the tide of battle had turned.

Unfortunately, so far every victory has been short lived, the conspiracy persists, and gold loses the gains.

Does GATA deserve the Freedom Futility Award?

Yes.

The GATA folks seem blind to the history of gold: that the role of gold as a monetary commodity cannot be legislated away. From the beginning the "king" hated the yellow metal. He always did and always will. His power to influence the market is virtually without limit and the stream of negativism is constant: "Gold is a barbaric relic. It's a horrible investment. Why, buying and holding gold is downright unpatriotic."

Should the propaganda barrage fail, government can always employ the iron fist. "Restrict imports. Smash the market. Make it illegal again. Confiscate the citizen's gold," as the feds did in 1933.

Gold historically reveals the mischief the "king" has been up to, and as it is much easier to manipulate the price of gold than to remedy the mischief, the king is forever intervening in the gold market.

So, the GATA folks remain frustrated. They seem puzzled by the actions of the US government and its allies: "the banks, the brokerage houses, and the gold mining management" itself and the unwholesome influence they wield.

Let me remind the GATA gang how it used to be.

When I was a young gold dealer in the 1960s, severe restrictions existed on the holding of gold. Many of the products we handle today would have sent you to prison then. Markets were rigidly controlled and the gold police were always lurking.

Being a gold dealer at the time was not only dangerous but uncertainty prevailed. Gold coins dated 1932 or older were legal IF they were already in the US. You could bring them in from overseas only if you were granted a license—but licenses weren't being issued. An American couldn't buy a Krugerrand in Switzerland even if it were stored overseas.

A prestigious currency trading company in San Francisco was raided and the employees shackled and arrested because they had some Austrian gold coins of questionable legal status on display.

By the manner in which the press handled that event one would think that bales of heroin were the issue. To those who read about it in the papers, it seemed that these were real criminals.

This tyranny existed for over forty years (and GATA wrings its hands over the present day level of government intervention. Hmphh.)

Finally in 1974 restrictions were lifted, and all forms of gold, including bars, were legal to manufacture and to hold. (Some credit this exhilarating event to Nixon's near impeachment. I don't know about that, but surely the breakdown of government led to gold's legalization.)

So here we are. The good folks at GATA continue to whine on a daily basis.

If they think that government will ever be neutral toward the gold market, they are fools. It is equivalent to thinking the US government—or any government for that matter—would relinquish their ability to collect taxes.

To protect the corrupt stranglehold they impose on the economy, the insiders will violate every commandment. Intervening in the gold market is just a minor chore.

Will the price of gold ever go up? Yes.

Will the house of cards collapse? Yes.

Will the paper dollar be repudiated in the marketplace? Yes.

When?, you ask.

There will be a clear signal. The fat lady will finally sing when there is a hemorrhage of dollars leaving the US. That will be your indicator.

Where will those dollars go? Nobody knows—but it won't take many of the greenbacks seeking refuge in precious metals to cause an explosion in price.

By the way, as the gold price increases, the king's intervention will become more desperate. Remember , the king doesn't like gold, never has, never will.

The last small rally that gold enjoyed carried it to $306 per ounce (it has since fallen back to $290). One of the reasons given for the run-up was that new money was pouring into gold from Japan and China.

We don't get much reliable information about those markets but I've experienced very strong inclination among Asians toward gold.

Which reminds me of my favorite Chinese customer, Mr. Chang.

I don't remember when he first became a customer but it had to be a decade before 1974. He barely spoke English, and I'm not even sure he was legally in the US. He worked in food service at United Airlines, and his wardrobe was Shanghai c.1930.

We didn't have much in common. His English was primitive and my Chinese non-existent.

The only thing we shared was his interest in gold and my desire to sell it to him. In those days we were prohibited from selling anything that could be considered a bullion coin. That didn't matter to Mr. Chang.

There was only one coin he would buy and that was the US $20 Liberty Head coin. He was familiar with it from China and to him the Liberty $20 gold coin was gold and gold was the Liberty $20 gold coin. Any other gold item might as well be counterfeit.

Through the years I saw him almost monthly. He brought his paycheck, would negotiate price, and then decide how many coins he wanted. (The $20 Liberty cost about $50 each.) I would give him change against his check.

Originally, I was amused that he came with his own balance scale. It was made of bamboo with a plate at one end and a weighted rock at the other. It was designed to balance the $20 Liberty. If a coin failed, it was either shaved or counterfeit.

After about a decade I became annoyed with his scale. "Mr. Chang, when in heaven's name will you trust me and not need a scale?"

He considered the scale just part of doing business, but he got my message and was embarrassed. Although his scale was present for the next purchase, I never saw it again after that.

In those days it wasn't easy getting information about the gold price. There was no US market and the London AM and PM fixings were sometimes available on the radio but it often required seeking the financial pages of the *Wall Street Journal* to learn the value of an ounce of gold.

Mr. Chang followed the price very closely. He would call almost daily, and ask, "Wuddah prica London gol?"

Upon getting the information he would respond: "Very thank you," and that was that. There was never any doubt about it. It was Mr. Chang on the phone.

Then we didn't hear from Mr. Chang for months.

"Has anyone heard from Mr. Chang," I asked? I was sure he was ill or worse.

Then one day there he was. "Wuddah prica London gol?"

I had answered his call and asked, "Mr Chang, have you been ill? We've missed hearing from you."

Dead silence.

How in heaven's name did I know it was him, he wondered. Gold dealers are amazing, with wondrous perceptions. I guess he believed that every customer said, "Very thank you."

Mr. Chang retired. I don't know if he had social security checks coming in, but his gold coins provided for his retirement. He came in as regularly as when he was a buyer. Only this time with one or two gold coins to sell. As he came in the front door, I noted he had coins in his hand, wrapped in tissue paper. He pretended he might be buying to keep me honest, but of course I knew that was not the case.

Then we learned from one of his old Chinese cronies that Mr. Chang had passed on. In fact he had gifted several coins to the friend who gave us the sad news. We dearly missed Mr. Chang, although "Very thank you" had become a part of the language in our office.

Some year or two later a young Chinese woman, whom I later learned was Mr. Chang's grand niece, came in. She was an accountant and evidently had found Mr. Chang's check stubs with Chinese characters on them breaking down how he had spent each check.

She was convinced there were gold coins some place and wondered if we were actually storing them. It was clear that she was not part of Mr. Chang's inner circle.

She left rude and angered.

As if rehearsed, my employees looked at me and in unison we all said: "Very thank you."

March 11, 2002

BARRY BONDS COMMITTED
THE UNFORGIVEABLE SIN

STERIODS, SCHMEROIDS:
NO ASTERISKS FOR BARRY, PLEASE

A s a kid growing up in the frigid northeast, winter seemed without end. Any small sign of spring was dashed by the inevitable "surprise" snowstorm in early March. But there was one infallible symbol of spring's inevitability,

"Baseball's Spring Training camps open in Florida," blared the sport's pages.

The headlines were reinforced with photographs of over-weight pitchers and catchers descending upon sun-drenched fields. (They always came first.)

Baseball is a metaphor for renewal, for hope and optimism. As the fresh season nears, even last year's losers start without a blemish, tied for first place. After all, look what the Boston Red Sox did last year.

To most New Yorkers in the 1940s and 50s, Florida was a mysterious paradise, with palm trees yet. The flocks of "snow-birds" migrating south was a decade or two away and Arizona had not yet been discovered by baseball's moguls as a spring training alternative to southern Florida.

To most easterners Arizona was a place they sent you if you had trouble breathing.

Fans from small market cities like Milwaukee and Kansas City may never see their teams in a playoff, but, for those few weeks before the games start to count, they shed the loser's mask and dare to believe this will be their year.

Such is the joy of baseball in the spring.

But not this year.

STERIODS

Major League Baseball initiated a steroid testing program last week. Nobody showed much enthusiasm. The Player's Union has always been wary of any such testing, and the owners' primary concern remains "counting the house."

Commissioner "Bud" Selig seemed near nausea at the press conference announcing Baseball's great need to cleanse the game of "performance enhancing" drugs. This was the party line, and Selig was faithful to the script,

Everybody knows what's going on here. This is a media generated fraud.

Baseball has no steroid problem!

Blumert's Beautiful Wife (BBW) "Did I hear right? You'll get 10,000 angry e-mails on that one. Why do I suspect that Barry Bonds has something to do with all of this?"

As I patiently explained to my dear wife: steroids can have a critical impact on people who are "jerking and lifting 500 pounds," or, racing 100 yards in less than 10 seconds. To such folks a jolt of steroid juice could make a difference.

Those 300-pound behemoths that put on body armor for three hours every Sunday and are called "Linemen," can also be beneficiaries of a visit from the friendly "vitamin" dealer.

But not Major League baseball players. They would never benefit from the use of steroids over a 162-game season. Baseball is a slow, measured game. Things can get excruciatingly tense, but rarely is there need for an explosion of effort that would be abetted by a stab of steroids in the butt.

The media people know this. If they are appalled, yet fascinated by the use of steroids, let them spend their time monitoring Track and Field. They can compete for Pulitzer prizes every 4 years at the Olympics where there are enough "dopers" to go around.

Allow me to dwell a moment on that great American, the "sports writer." Most were nerds at college, jealous of the "jocks" they would later report about, hating them all the while. By temperament, they would be better suited writing obituaries.

My wife was right about one thing, Barry Bonds is the real target of the media's attack on steroids and baseball. We know the media despises Bonds (see "The Mortality of Baseball Players— Even Barry Bonds" and "The Unforgiveable Sin: The Superstar the Media Hates") and this was their grand opportunity to mortally wound him.

"Bonds is a 'cheater' and an asterisk should be placed next to every one of his records," whine the media pygmies. Some of Bonds's more vociferous critics would have his name expunged from the Record Book entirely.

Bonds has remained indifferent to the years of image-hammering the media has conducted. He's done little off the baseball diamond to win friends and influence others. A charmer he's not.

This may explain why people who should know better have succumbed to the media's scurrilous attack on Barry's accomplishments.

One absurd example is that steroids have enlarged Barry's head by several hat sizes. You mean there are muscles on the skin side of the skull?

Maybe Bonds knew the "clear" he rubbed on his knees was an illicit substance; maybe not, but 2005 is his 20th year in the Major Leagues. For those who have been suckered by the media and would give credit to chemicals for his assault on Baseball's hallowed records, I submit this brief overview of his career; what follows are Bonds' production for his first 15 years and the last 5 (steroid years?):

	FIRST 15 YEARS	LAST 5 YEARS
BASES HITS	2010	720
STOLEN BASES	460	46
BASES ON BALLS	1430	872
HOME RUNS	445	258
STRIKE OUTS	1112	316
ALL STAR	9	4
MVP	3	4
GOLDEN GLOVE	8	0

To the non- or casual baseball fan they may be just numbers, but to those of us weaned on baseball statistics, these are the "stats" of a super superstar.

Is Barry Bonds the best baseball player ever? I don't know, but it's the sort of debate that links the generations. Don't let the loathsome media poison the well.

March 8, 2005

THE UNFORGIVEABLE SIN:
THE SUPERSTAR THE MEDIA HATES

W hen a prominent athlete hits the front page these days, it's usually a sordid tale involving murder and mayhem.

One athlete savagely dismembers his wife, another sullen footballer hires an amoral thug to murder a pregnant girlfriend, and on Super Bowl weekend in Atlanta, an NFL poster boy takes part in a bloody confrontation that leaves two dead.

It was very different when the *San Francisco Chronicle* featured baseball star Barry Bonds on their front page on June 1, 2001. But the only violence in this story was Barry Bonds bruising baseballs during his record-breaking barrage of home runs in the month of May.

Baseball was forever changed by the mighty Babe Ruth—from a bucolic game played on a cow field with a dead "ball" to a struggle dominated by the "home run"—an American metaphor for success.

Bonds, in his sixteenth year in the major leagues as a superstar, was never identified as a home run slugger in the mold of the great Babe or modern bashers like Mark McGwire and Sammy Sosa. In his early years, Bonds was a lithe figure, emphasizing speed and defensive skills.

When Bonds struck his 500th career home run earlier this season, the baseball establishment seemed surprised. How had this interloper entered the legendary domain inhabited by only seventeen baseball immortals? The event was well covered by the media, but Bonds membership in the exclusive 500-career home run club seemed more honorary than earned.

Then came the month of May—and Barry's shower of home runs. Almost one per game. Unbelievable.

No longer the slender figure, Bonds, mature, solid, but clearly not shaped by steroids, has become a *bona fide* slugging home-run hitter. He is currently on pace to break all existing single-season records for homers.

Bonds is a baseball aristocrat. His father, Bobby Bonds, was a proven major leaguer with impact of his own upon the record book. It is also widely known that Willie Mays, whom baseball experts rate as one of the three best players ever, is Barry's godfather.

While growing up, Barry might have had difficulty identifying with Mays, an icon from another time and place, but Mays's accomplishments were part of Bonds's family lore.

Barry attended Serra High, a fine Catholic school in San Mateo, a prosperous suburb in Northern California. Arizona State was selected for his college "education" as the school had an outstanding baseball program with a pipeline to the big leagues.

Baseball, more than any other sport, has a reverence for statistics. During Bonds's sixteen-year major league career, he has accumulated an impressive array of records and approaches many more. This tornado of statistics makes it impossible for the baseball establishment to deny him superstar status, although some writers consider him an intruder into hallowed territory.

What is it about Barry Bonds that the sports media cannot countenance?

What's wrong with Barry?

If he were guilty of domestic violence or had succumbed to drugs, and then became contrite and begged forgiveness, would he be embraced by the media?

I don't think so.

There is one sin the media can never forgive. One sin which drives them into an unrelenting crusade against the perpetrator. This is the sin committed by the star athlete who doesn't like the media.

Barry learned early in his career how duplicitous the sports reporter could be. With a smile, Barry's honest comments were solicited and then perverted. Barry would learn that some reporters were snakes and he suffered their venom repeatedly. It was self-defense for him to withdraw, become defensive and aloof.

In one instance, some years ago at Candlestick Park, he hit a soft fly ball along the left field foul line. Barry guessed that the ball would fall untouched in foul territory and did not "hustle" by running it out. When the ball fell fair, some fans booed. In an interview about the incident, Bonds explained that after years of wear and tear, he has learned to ration his energies to avoid injuries, thereby extending his career.

Barry's response was perfectly plausible, but by the time the story was recycled, he emerged as lackadaisical and uninterested.

Even ESPN baseball expert Peter Gammons shocked a TV baseball panel when he compared Bonds to the legendary Ted Williams, the greatest hitter of all time. The other sports panelists seemed offended with Gammons' assessment, and poor Peter backed off his observation by pointing out that what Bonds shared with Williams was their mutual dislike of the media and vice versa.

I fear this deep-rooted dislike of Bonds will endure whatever his final baseball accomplishments. It's possible, I suppose, that Barry will acquire theatrical grace and be transformed into a media darling. After all, Mark McGwire converted from a surly, unresponsive interview to a lovable American hulk while pursuing his remarkable 70-home run year.

Will this happen to Barry? I don't think so.

The criticisms of Bond continue like a mantra: Barry is not a team player, they say. He never performs well under the pressure of post-season play. He doesn't exhibit the fervor of a Pete Rose, for example. And finally, that Bonds's home-run accomplishments are due to the era of the "juiced" baseball.

Phew. Where do I begin refuting these phony allegations?

It is true that Bonds is a reserved fellow and not a chum to his teammates. But in the manner in which he plays the game he is the consummate team professional and earns respect, particularly from young players. Bonds stays in excellent physical condition, and now at age 37, works harder at it than ever before.

He leads by example and is acknowledged as one of the all time great defensive players. He is a consistent Golden Glover, a rare quality for a home-run slugger.

As to Barry's disappointing post-season statistics, it is interesting that Willie Mays's World Series performances are almost identical to Barry's, yet where is the criticism of Mays? This is additional evidence of the media bias against Barry.

Regarding Bonds's attitude, in his sixteen-year history, it is well known he often plays "hurt." Never before has a slugging superstar stolen 500 bases, risking injury on every hard contact with the ground while at the same time dodging the spikes of enemy infielders. Another rare quality for a home run slugger.

Over sixteen seasons Barry played an average of almost 150 games per year. Even in the year 2000 when he underwent major arm surgery, he amazed the doctors with his recovery, playing the last third of the Giants championship season.

The "juiced" baseball charge is ridiculous. Sure, there's lots of homers hit these days, but Bonds struck his in the difficult home field confines of Candlestick Park. The new Pac Bell

Park may also prove to be more favorable to pitchers. Even Barry's harshest critic would acknowledge that he would have collected over 600 career home runs by now had he played his home games in any other major league park.

The fans either love him or hate him, but nobody goes to the john or the fridge when Barry Bonds is due up. At the ball park business stops at the concession stands when Barry is at bat. He remains the most dangerous hitter in baseball.

Barry, I'm rooting for you to hit 71 home runs this year, although everybody knows how impossible a goal that could be.

Most important, don't let the media creeps get under your skin. You are true baseball royalty, and they are unworthy plugs.

April 29, 2004

THE MORTALITY OF BASEBALL PLAYERS, EVEN BARRY BONDS

MEMO TO EDITOR ROCKWELL
AND OTHER BASEBALL FANS:

L et me shift your attention for a moment from the Red Sox vs. the Yankees, the finest teams money can buy, to the Left Coast and the incomparable Barry Bonds.

I know you read all about Bonds's heroics in Box Scores the following morning, but the media bias dulls his accomplishments.

Let me bring you up to date.

For the first twenty games of the 2004 season Bonds:

- Leads the league in batting: .500
- Leads the league in HR: 9
- Leads the league in Bases on Balls: 30 (this statistic is ominous)

These astonishing numbers are consistent with Barry's shattering of records the past three seasons. Here are those highlights:

- In 2001 Bonds hit 73 Home Runs (a record that will NEVER be broken)
- He won the League's Most Valuable Player Award (MVP)
- In 2002 Barry won the Batting Title by hitting a glittering .370
- During the World Series, he batted .471, hit 4 HR and was walked 13 times.
- Bonds' performance during the 2002 playoffs dispelled any theories about his "choking" in big games.
- He won the MVP.
- In 2003 Barry Bonds hit his 600th HR and won his 3rd consecutive MVP. This was his 6th MVP. For this, Barry Bonds stands alone in baseball history.

"Steroids, Steroids," the hateful chorus chants.

Listen, steroids might enable a body-builder to win the Strongman Competition on ESPN by schlepping a 6-ton truck up a hill, but a carload of steroids wouldn't improve bat speed, nor the ability to hit a baseball launched at 95 mph. As baseball afficionado Joe Sobran points out, hitting a sphere moving at that speed with a cylinder is the greatest achievement in sports.

As the Spring Training Camps opened the media insects couldn't wait to see how "withdrawal" would affect the steroid juice-heads. Several well known "sluggers" were visibly depleted of muscle mass.

Not Barry.

He has consistently denied the use of steroids. Even those snakes hired to do nothing but study Bonds's anatomy, and expose him as a fraud, found the same magnificently conditioned athlete they see every year.

Whatever the future reveals about Bonds and his relationship with some of the questionable characters who push enhancers, none of that can tarnish Bonds's place in baseball's pantheon.

In some sports super-stardom can be earned through one superlative effort, or a glorious series of accomplishments like California swimmer Mark Spitz winning seven gold medals in swimming at the 1972 Olympics.

There are other winners who don't require validation by the Record Book.

On May 6, 1954, Dr. Roger Bannister became enshrined in Track and Field history as the first to run a sub-four minute mile, a feat then believed impossible.

Even Mohammad Ali's dazzling boxing career can be distilled in just a handful of three minute rounds, his greatness measured in milliseconds as he proved to be more lethal than his opponent.

One of Ali's primary credentials as a legendary pugilist was his epic, bloody war, the "Thrilla in Manila" with arch rival Joe Frazier. The drama, the violence, the action, all took place in less than forty-five minutes.

Statistics were not necessary.

Seven-footer Wilt Chamberlain, arguably the best basketball player who ever shot a hoop, is remembered for one quirky night in April, 1962 when he scored one-hundred points in an NBA game. (Some were more impressed with Wilt's claim in his 1991 biography, *A View From the Top*, that he bedded ten thousand different women. Another group of admirers contend that the statistics here were understated.)

But baseball is different.

There are no shortcuts in baseball. No quick way in. The only passport to immortality is the revered "Record Book." Every hit, every error, every injury is recorded. The athlete's place in baseball history is uncovered beneath an avalanche of statistics.

As Barry Bonds enters the final years of his career, not only has he been rewriting the Record Book every time he comes to bat, he has altered the way the game is played.

Rival managers walk Bonds rather than give him a chance to beat them. Barry has broken all of Ruth's Base on Ball records and it is certain Bonds will break his own record in the current 2004 season.

It is hard to imagine that as recent as 2001 there were baseball writers who questioned Bonds's credentials as a Superstar.

In May 2001. I wrote a piece for LRC proving the case for Barry Bonds's greatness and indicting the media for allowing their bias of Bonds to cloud their objectivity. They hated him because he hated them.

And Barry keeps rolling on—

Two weeks ago he surpassed Willie Mays's Home Run Career total. Only Babe Ruth and Hank Aaron remain in his crosshairs. If Barry's home run production continues he will pass the "Babe" in 2005 and exceed Aaron in 2006.

Some respected baseball writers contend that Barry could hit over .400 this year, a feat unattained since 1941 by Ted Williams. (Williams was also despised by the media.)

Barry will be 40 this summer. In recent games, I've sensed a change. I'm not talking about his skills diminishing. For the first month of this season his bat had never been quicker and the pitchers never in greater fear, but I realized that even Barry Bonds was mortal.

When I was a kid, I actually saw Babe Ruth in uniform. He was near the end of his life, making an appearance at Ebbets Field in Brooklyn. Can you imagine a seven-year-old seeing the great legend Babe Ruth? It's an image that never fades.

Hall of Famer, New York Giant first baseman Mel Ott was my idol. I watched him play at the Polo Grounds in New York City. I still have my Mel Ott jersey. (Not for sale, thank you.)

Willie Mays in about my age, and we sort of "grew up together." He never lost his boyish charm.

Often, in those half-awake moments before drifting into sleep, I would re-run Willie Mays's unique baseball exploits of that day's game. I never met Willie, but he was a companion for over twenty years.

(I said above that Bonds is the greatest player ever. If you put my back to the wall, and ply me with four ounces of wine I'll admit that Willie Mays shares the mantle of the "Greatest Ever" with his godson, Barry.)

At forty most baseball players are set out to pasture. The legs go first, they say, and then the reflexes.

Bonds takes more games off these days, and his feet must be giving him trouble. He never complains. By the way, Harold Reynolds, the brilliant ESPN baseball analyst, pointed out that because Bonds is issued so many walks, he spends more time on base than anyone in the game. Unlike every other major leaguer, Barry does not get his share of rest time in the cool shade of the dugout.

Barry Bonds is driven by challenge, to be a winner and finally wear that World Series Ring. To rewrite every record in the book, with Ruth and Aaron as his targets.

What happens when the challenges are gone? When the aches and pains that visit the forty-year-old athlete finally subdue him?

The original purpose of this memo was to alert Editor Rockwell and other baseball fans that we are witness to the best baseball player EVER. It was my hope that he would be around at least through the year 2006. If that were true we would have many opportunities to see him perform.

Now I'm not so sure. I have become pessimistic about Barry's immediate future in the game.

I fear that the constant refusal to pitch to him, to walk him twice a game, is beginning to wear him down. This has never happened to any other player in the history of the game.

If I'm right, it's extra URGENT that you get to see Bonds on the field soon.

If you go to the ballpark, get there early and watch Barry take batting practice. See him when the Giants visit your hometown team, watch Barry on tv, or better yet, come to San Francisco. I'll help you get a ticket.

There will never be another like him.

April 29, 2004

BAM, WHACK, POW

In a startling piece of investigative journalism, Jack Newfield (*New York Post*, 20 March 2000) reveals that the so-called "sport of boxing" is corrupt. Reeling from that shock, the reader braces himself for the next revelation: the New York State Athletic Commission (supposedly boxing's watchdog) is a "cesspool of patronage and incompetence."

This hard-hitting expose is what Pulitzer Prizes are made of, and it's rumored Newfield's next explosive piece will disclose that New York City has a traffic problem.

Boxing has also drawn the attention of political heavyweights. Senator John McCain (R-AZ), before he adopted campaign finance reform as his mantra, was urging federal guidelines to govern the sport. There was even a movement afoot to make McCain US Boxing Czar.

Listen, you bozos, leave boxing alone.

There is a refreshing quality about the world of boxing and the commissions that govern it: corruption is pure and unadulterated.

The road to ascendancy in the world of boxing has no moral detours. For those who rise to the top, a stretch at Sing Sing is more valued than an Ivy League degree (and the alumni connections more useful). A murder indictment is equivalent to a graduate degree (see the bio of impresario Don King).

There is no waste of resources in locating members for the athletic commission. The marketplace assigns a dollar value on each appointment and the only concern is that the bills are unmarked.

As with every facet of the sport, money drives the engine. However, when money isn't enough to get the desired result, violence is employed quickly and efficiently (usually outside the ring).

Hypocrisy is unknown in the world of boxing. Who cares about the stumble-bums the state agency is supposed to be protecting? Victims-schmictims. "Let's get ready to rumble," as the man says.

To the charge that boxing is just as phony as wrestling, I submit that that observation is rubbish. Wrestling makes a mockery of such noble American traditions as fixing the outcome, and where boxing involves true violence, wrestling simulates it with ketchup and break-away chairs.

Actually, the New York State Athletic Commission should be a model for all government agencies. No political correctness, no transparent efforts to appear judicious, and a disdain for the art of subtlety.

And, by the way, the taxpayers manage to get a few laughs for their money.

March 22, 2000

SEABISCUIT REVISIONISM

*B*lumert's *Wife* (B.W.): "Could somebody please tell me why, at 6 o'clock in the morning, we're rushing to see a movie?"

Blumert: "Rockwell wants me to review *Seabiscuit*, so we better step on it if we want good seats at the 7:00 a.m. showing.

B.W.: "The 7:00 a.m. showing?"

Blumert: "It's the Senior's Sunrise Special, and a ticket is only $3.50. I'm sure I'll get reimbursed."

B.W.: "Don't forget to keep the ticket stub, and, if you want, I'll sign an affidavit swearing you shelled out the $3.50."

Blumert: "Don't be sarcastic. Rockwell's been on an economy kick lately. Since the beginning of the year we've been washing the cancellation marks off postage stamps so we could use them again.

"And, this morning, I got a parcel from Auburn containing a Tee Shirt Stencil kit, including instructions. By putting the LRC logos on myself, LRC saves 85-cents per tee shirt. So far, I've ruined seven shirts, but I'm getting the hang of it.

"Anyway, if Rockwell doesn't reimburse my $3.50, I'll get Medicare to pay. Seniors have entitlements, you know."

B.W.: "Why in heaven's name does Rockwell even want a movie review from you?"

Blumert: "Murray Rothbard was Mr. First Nighter, and he did great movie reviews for the old *Rothbard-Rockwell Report*. I'm just carrying on that tradition."

B.W.: "So now, I suppose, you're Mr. First Thing in the Morninger? I remember one tasteless movie review you submitted to Rockwell that he not only rejected, but afterward, would not take your phone calls for six months."

Blumert: "What was so tasteless in my reviewing, *Charlie Chan Gets Circumcised*? Recently, all the Charlie Chan movies have been virtually banned as politically incorrect. I was just an early victim."

B.W.: "Well, Rush Limbaugh was talking about the Seabiscuit movie and how the horse did so much to heal the damage of the Great Depression by lifting people's spirits."

Blumert: "What sentimental goop! It's just like giving that commie FDR credit for getting the country out of the Depression. All Roosevelt did was prolong the hard times and move us to socialism. Yes, I said FDR was a commie. And Seabiscuit was a commie horse."

B.W.: "Don't blame the poor horse. Seabiscuit was a champion, wasn't he?"

Blumert: "Champion? He doesn't rate in the top 50. Don't even mention Seabiscuit with the true great thoroughbreds.

"Here's my Top Ten:

1. Man o' War; Won 21 of 22 races
2. Citation; Triple Crown Winner
3. Secretariat; Triple Crown Winner
4. Affirmed; Triple Crown Winner
5. Count Fleet; Triple Crown Winner
6. Native Dancer; Won 21 of 22 races and
7. Genuine Risk; The greatest filly of all
8. Whirlaway; Triple Crown Winner
9. John Henry, a "true" Cinderella horse who got better with age.
10. Kelso: Five Time Horse of the Year.

"As to Seabiscuit's great Match Race victory over War Admiral, that was more hype than history. War Admiral, a Triple Crown Winner, was severely injured in the Belmont Stakes, the last of the Triple Crown races.

"It was feared he would never race again, but the courageous colt defied the veterinarians and continued competing.

The War Admiral beaten by Seabiscuit in the Match race, however, was not the same champion who won the Triple Crown.

"Seabiscuit was a nice, gritty colt and a boon to California racing. After all, horse racing had been illegal in the Golden State for twenty-five years at the time Seabiscuit was racing.

"The Eastern aristocratic owners who scrupulously studied and improved the bloodlines of their magnificent thoroughbreds had every reason to be contemptuous of any California horse at that time.

"They weren't being elitist or arrogant. The 'Sport of Kings' is dominated by history and bloodlines. It would take California many years to build reservoirs in both areas. (To this day, California-bred horses rarely achieve the status of those bred in Kentucky, New York, or Ireland.)

"The magic of Seabiscuit is the magic of Laura Hillenbrand. Her best-selling book, *Seabiscuit*, is beautifully crafted, and she weaves her characters seamlessly from Coast-to-Coast, with an important stop in Tijuana, Mexico.

"Unfortunately, she did not write a reference book for the Sport of Kings. She took a myth and made it into a mile.

"Laura Hillenbrand could have spun just as riveting a tale had she focused her creativity on some plug equine on its way to the glue factory."

B.W.: "It sounds as though you're not going to like the movie. In fact, it seems to me you just wrote your review."

Blumert: "Well, at least I don't have to worry about getting reimbursed the $3.50 from Rockwell. Let's have breakfast."

EDITOR'S NOTE: Eventually, Blumert did see the movie. Even though a witness observed him shedding a tear during one touching scene, he stands by the views expressed above.

August 2, 2003

THEY ARE COMING TO GET ME (OR AM I PARANOID?)

IF I DON'T SHOW UP AT MY
OFFICE TOMORROW, YOU'LL KNOW
THEY GOT ME

Political Correctness (PC) is so potent that it can never be measured by the polls (who'd ask? who'd tell?), is scrupulously avoided by TV's talking heads, and scares the hell out of academics. An effort to dissent on the following of many "hot" subjects would quickly reveal that PC reigns supreme. Winston Churchill and Abraham Lincoln are heroes. The invasion of the South and WWII were "good wars," and that's it. Case closed. Nor does death provide relief for villains. T.S. Eliot and H.L. Mencken, for example, are forever branded as purveyors of hate. But if there's a "How To Successfully Employ Political Correctness" manual, the key chapter must be devoted to the Holocaust. Consider the extraordinary success in disseminating the prevailing Holocaust message, and the impact. How did this come to pass?

In a remarkable new book, *The Holocaust in American Life* by Peter Novick (New York: Houghton Mifflin), the author, himself a Jew, traces the history of the Holocaust. During WWII, policy makers feared that America's participation would be credited to pressures from American Jews on behalf of their Eastern European cousins. All victims were considered together. Even by the mid-1960s the Jewish victims of the war were still just one group among 50–60 million others. After the 1967 Mideast War, and through the 1970s, however, things changed. Novick observes that "the Holocaust, as we speak of it today, was largely a retrospective construction, something that would not have been recognizable to most people at the time." Indeed, the Holocaust has become atrophied by political correctness. Jewish groups, spearheaded by the Anti-Defamation League, have successfully relegated the Holocaust to "holy" status beyond analysis or discussion. If you listen to them, it was the seminal event of World War II.

There is something akin to medieval mysticism at work here. Jew and Gentile alike must swear a blood oath to the Holocaust. The very word "Holocaust" has been sanctified and withdrawn from general use. The Armenians better keep their hands off it and find some other term. Holocaust "churches" in the form of museums and monuments are required in every major city around the world.

If the religious metaphor is valid, how does "Holocaustism" deal with nonbelievers and agnostics? The dreaded twin charges of "Holocaust-denial" and Anti-Semitism are a death sentence for career and reputation. In some countries today Holocaust anti-blasphemy laws lead to jail for heretics. A Swiss newspaper publisher was just sentenced to three years in prison for an editorial, while the freedom of the press groups are terrified into silence.

There are pressures for similar laws in our own country, to abolish freedom of speech and the press in this area. Most distressing, political correctness permeates ever-expanding domains. To any complacent readers, I issue the following red alert. If you are a revisionist, conspiracy buff, member of a religious sect, an anti-anti-gun controller, a home schooler, a pro-lifer, an anarchist, one who is out of the "mainstream," or simply make a political fool of yourself publicly, you are on borrowed time. And if your message is cogent, and you are winning adherents, especially watch out! Neither your livelihood nor social standing is safe. And it may get worse. The bounds of allowable debate are narrowing. The tentacles of political correctness pollute the schoolroom, the boardroom, and the bedroom. "Truth" comes only from the *New York Times*, the *Washington Post*, the *Wall Street Journal*, network TV, cable TV, the weekly magazines, and Sunday morning's pulpit in mainstream congregations. The PC message may be delivered in a more subtle fashion through TV commercials or rammed down our throats via court decisions, legislative enactments, or executive branch edicts. Hollywood prepares the final package. The web is the last hope for free expression, and even that delicious miracle of inventiveness is under the gun. The hointious nature of the web encourages the assassins of freedom to seek legislation making the web's discordant product a possible hate crime. Only the First Amendment saves the US from the path followed by Germany, Canada, France, and Switzerland, where the accusation of hate crimes is a constant fear, and where mere words can land you in the slammer.

As a proud American Jew, I ask the Jewish leadership: how can you countenance a policy that creates genuine doubt and fear among writers, academics, political activists, and plain people? Your policy may lead to less public expression of bias and "hatred," but at what price?

Jews for centuries have been victims in societies where uttering the wrong word or failing to comply with dogma meant danger. How can you sponsor programs that make Jews the oppressors?

However you define Anti-Semitism, the accomplishments and prosperity of the American Jewish community are without question. Second-class citizens we are not. There are ample laws to protect Americans against violence and real violation of our genuine rights. We need no hate crimes legislation nor vigilantism in the name of Political Correctness, let alone terror tactics to prevent feelings from being hurt.

May 11, 2000

HERE'S THE PROOF— THEY'RE OUT TO GET ME

I can't stand trouble. Friends credit me with patience, serenity, and level headedness, all ingredients needed to throttle trouble. But, it's all an act.

Trouble comes in the form of angry people. It hardly matters what made them angry, or that their anger isn't even directed at me, it's simply being around "trouble" that unnerves me.

Mind you, I lead a fairly normal life. Yes, I hate trouble, but I also hate alligators, and I have managed to conceal both idiosyncrasies from friends, family, and co-workers.

My wife knows the truth: "If you hate 'trouble' so much, why do you hang around with Lew Rockwell?"

She has asked that question hundreds of times and my answer is always the same, "Look, it's not Lew's fault, it's those @#$%&*. . . ."

This time it started innocently enough.

Through the years, I have convinced Lew that the gold and silver consumer has a tough time finding reliable venders. I keep him abreast of industry horror stories and recently we launched "Burt's Gold Page." Our initial purpose was to provide LRC readers with up-to-the-minute market quotes.

A few days later we added a chart indicating Camino Coin's, my company's, selling prices. These prices allow a decent profit for Camino, yet are significantly cheaper than other gold and silver prices seen on the Internet.

Finally, this week we offered LRC readers a few "Special Introductory" coin deals.

Yes, the prices were at wholesale levels. What better way to get the LRC reader's attention?

There was nothing innovative here. There are other old-line companies like Camino that offer the consumer good value, buying and selling, though they are not as visible as the high-profile, high-pressure, fancy-brochured firms.

Burt's Gold Page was well received, and business was brisk from Day 1. Several important hard-money websites linked to the gold page at LRC, and we began to get phone calls from non-LRC people.

And then, it began to happen. "We got trouble, right here in River City," sang Robert Preston in *Music Man*. It was a familiar feeling: "We got trouble, right here at LRC."

First thing Monday morning, I received three angry phone calls from folks rudely attacking our company and the "phony" prices we had posted.

On the first call I tried responding, but it was clear that reason wasn't going to prevail. One creepy guy actually placed a bogus order for 100 ounces of gold.

In my forty-plus years in the business, all this was a first.

I don't know what prompted me to visit the hard-money web sites that had linked to LRC and our gold page. But you guessed it. All traces of any link to LRC were gone. An old friend at a big wholesaler explained: "You have caused no end of trouble with your prices. All the big boys are upset, especially the ones with lots of high-priced telephone salesmen."

Oh well. My wife suggests that I secretly love "trouble." That much of the trouble I credit to Lew Rockwell I bring upon myself.

What does she know? She better not make any trouble.

January 20, 2003

BLUMERT INTERCEPTS A WHITE HOUSE MEMO

Note: I cannot reveal how this interesting missive came into my hands.

To: the Board of Governors of the Federal Reserve System
From: Karl Rove, the White House
Date: July 19, 2002

Gentlemen:

The President was very supportive during his recent visit to Wall Street. Well, from here on in there won't be any more of this "Mr. Nice Guy" stuff. President Bush has lost patience with the dismal performance of the equity markets and now demands that this situation be reversed immediately.

Burton S. Blumert — 221

Given the success of his War on Terrorism, the President is formulating an Equity Protection Board (EPB) that will seek out and destroy all enemies of the equity markets. Ralph Nader and Patrick Buchanan are possible choices for the agency's Czar. The prosecutor will be, of course, Rudy "Benito" Giuliani.

Effective Monday Morning, July 21, 2002:

1. Brokerage firms will be prohibited from dealing in short sales and any violators will be dealt with as felons. Any corporate official who sells his own company's shares will face lethal injection.

2. "Bad-Mouthing"—speaking negatively about any aspect of the equity markets—will be considered lewd behavior and the perpetrator will be subject to fines and imprisonment.

3. At the start of the business day in every financial institution, all present will recite a short pledge of loyalty to the government and the equity markets. (No reference to God will be included.)

4. Any customer who seeks to sell a stock must provide documentation that he faces some emergency. A panel comprised of a physician, a mortician, a man of the cloth, and a bookie will judge if the need is sufficient.

5. All media outlets will be required to devote at least 25 percent of their time and space to positive articles and pronouncements about the stock markets. Since this is War, all public figures and celebrities will be required to travel the nation appealing to people's patriotism under the slogan, "Your Country and Your Stock Market Need You." A plan to extend this program overseas, headed up by Tom Hanks, in the spirit of WWII, is under study. Until a better name for the project is conceived, it will be called the USO.

6. In every public school across the nation children will buy stock, even if only a few cents worth each week. They will

be exposed to this act of patriotism from the first grade and if the little ones feel that their parents are not sufficiently enthusiastic about the program, teachers will encourage them to report any such deviant thinking. Indeed, they should all be enrolled in the Youth Division of TIPS.

7. Throughout the business week, at every opportunity, corporate leaders will be humiliated and serious consideration is being given to publicly executing one per week. Your nominations are welcome.

Your government has already fired the first volley in this War. Yesterday, whilst most citizens spent their Sunday relaxing, this Administration was rolling out the "giants" to appear on the network and cable news shows. Dazzling performances by talking head Neil Cavuto, CEO of the New York Stock Exchange Richard Grasso, Congressman Dick Armey, and others made the selling of securities today by anybody very unlikely.

Your government also took decisive action so that the market makers in Asia and Europe get the message loud and clear. Collapsing equity markets will not be tolerated. The US Sixth Fleet raised anchors for Japan and American troops began military maneuvers in Germany.

Market stability is this government's primary goal, but be assured that no bank, brokerage house, or other financial institution will be allowed to fail. Nor will your jobs or any government program be in jeopardy.

July 23, 2002

MY PALESTINIAN PALS

S an Francisco's Arab-operated grocery stores are living on borrowed time.

They're located in dismal, dangerous sectors of town much like their Korean and Indian counterparts in other American cities.

These Mideast flavored, family operated businesses sprang up like desert flowers following a rain shortly after the immigration floodgates were thrown open in the1960s. Most came from Palestine and they measured success in two ways: How soon can I bring a family member to join me in San Francisco? And, when can I have my own store?

These little bastions of free enterprise survived in the most hostile environment, often in the middle of a battleground. In those days, before Starbucks and Krispy Kreme, there weren't many American merchants anxious to commit economic suicide by locating in the ghetto.

These hardworking Palestinians, toughened by decades of danger back home, would be amused by the observation that what they do is brave, or that they were satisfying a market need by serving a community shunned by others.

But these bubbly, intrepid folks are facing more danger now than ever before.

I can't remember the first time I sold a Palestinian a coin, but it was more than thirty years ago and a gold dealer could not ask for a more ideal customer. They are totally suspicious of paper money and always pay in cash. Once the dealer gains their trust they remain eternally loyal.

Unlike most customers, they are not frightened when gold prices drop, viewing cheaper gold as a buying opportunity. And they make life easy for the gold dealer since there's only one gold item they favor.

"How much is the COIN today?" they ask on the phone.

The COIN is a British gold sovereign. To those unfamiliar with "the coin," it contains a bit less than one-quarter ounce pure gold, and was produced in seven different mints on five continents. The gold sovereign reflects the span and wealth of the British Empire from the late nineteenth century through the1930s. It was the closest to a true international currency the world had ever experienced.

It is obvious that Palestine under the British Mandate—an island of freedom and free enterprise as compared to rule by Istanbul or Tel Aviv—led its citizens to a love affair with the gold sovereign that becomes more entrenched with time.

The women, colorfully attired in billowing silk dresses and head scarves, do all the gold buying. Cash is secreted in every fold and hem and it's amazing how much paper money could be concealed in one garment.

I don't know how they run their grocery stores, but it's a safe guess that the women wind up with all the proceeds at the end of the day.

I haven't mentioned the one tedious aspect of dealing with my Palestinians. Negotiating the price of "the coin" is an agony that is part of every transaction. Late one Friday afternoon, Mary, one of my favorites, called, agitated, with the usual question about price.

The dialogue went like this:

Burt: "Mary, it's too late. It's Friday, it's three o'clock now and you won't get here until four and since our dealings are always slow, I'll never get home. Why don't you come in Monday when we have more time?"

Mary: "No, it can't be Monday. We have family here from Cleveland and they're going home tonight. I promise we will buy fast so you can enjoy your weekend."

Burt: "All right—but I want you to promise that we will get it done quickly with no bargaining. You know my prices are always fair, so no haggling this one time. OK?"

Mary: "I promise, I promise."

True to her word, Mary arrived breathlessly, in record time from San Francisco to our shop in San Mateo. As usual she was accompanied by her array of family members. I sat the entire crowd down in my office, and proceeded to exact a pledge from every family member present, from grandpa, to Mary's six-year-old nephew to her husband, his two brothers, and the guests from Cleveland.

"Does everybody agree that there will be no negotiation, that you'll trust my fair pricing and that we will get out of here quickly?" I went around the room until I obtained everybody's reassurance, even the six-year-old's.

"Okay," I said to Mary. "How many coins do you want today?"

She said, "60."

"Terrific," I said, pulling several tubes of gold sovereigns from my desk drawer. "Mary, the price today is $82 each."

Dead silence around the room.

Mary, as if struck in the solar plexus, gasped, "But you sold some coins to a friend of mine this morning at $80 each."

Bolting out of my chair, I shouted: "Everybody out! You gave me your pledge, no negotiating! Out! Out!"

Stunned, and in a state of shock at my outburst, my little bevy of Palestinians staggered out of the office. I had never seen them so forlorn.

Standing in the hallway, I reopened negotiations, and we proceeded to establish the price at $81 per coin, and my group, now restored, went happily on their way.

Even before 9/11, I detected a change in my Palestinians. Although there is hardly a week that passes without one of their stores being hit, crime figures in San Francisco are somewhat improved and spending a night in an Arab grocery store isn't as hazardous as it used to be.

7-Eleven, and other chain-operated convenience stores, succumbing to political pressures began opening stores where they had previously feared to tread, thus providing new stiff competition.

Worse is the coming of the food marts that are part of the current generation of giant, 24-hour gas stations. The ghetto customer has far more choice and feels less confined. The day of the neighborhood Arab store seems past—but 9/11 may provide the final death knell for these little dots of Middle Eastern culture in San Francisco.

My Palestinian pals always seemed to be returning from or planning their next trip to Jerusalem or Amman. It is as if they have two homes. They go back and forth with regularity, and if air travel has become an annoyance for the rest of us, can you imagine the problems these Mideast commuters face?

One fellow I know cancelled plans to attend his brother's wedding in Cleveland. I started to suggest a strategy he might use to overcome the airport bureaucracy.

"Carry the wedding invitation with you and show it to every airport employee in sight," I said. He smiled, thanked me for my advice and asked, "Would you look forward to traveling if you looked like me?"

Such problems aren't exactly new. Another of my Palestinian favorites, Eddie, had an experience that he laughs about to this day although the incident reeks of tragedy.

Eddie had prospered in San Francisco. He had his very own grocery store, and it was time to visit his family in Jordan and proudly show-off his success. He bought a brand new red convertible, making arrangements to ship it by freighter to the Port of Eilat on the Red Sea. He would then drive to Jerusalem to visit friends before making his grand entrance in Jordan.

Those were his great plans. After all he was rich and carried a US passport.

Everything went smoothly. His red convertible survived the long voyage without a scratch, and he enjoyed every minute of the drive to Jerusalem. He kept imagining the faces of his family in Jordan as they saw him pull up in his red beauty.

Poor Eddie could not have predicted the Yom Kippur War. All hell broke loose hours after he checked into his hotel in Jerusalem and he was confined to his room, along with most of the other guests.

For days the war raged about them and the hotel was actually hit by an errant shell. When it was over, an Israeli Army Major told him his car had been commandeered, and that he would find it in some parking area on the edge of town.

His pride and joy was a total wreck. There was no appeal or remedy open to Eddie. To the Israelis he was just an Arab to be looted despite his US passport. To the Jordanians he was suspiciously viewed as an American. Finally, he got permission to leave Jerusalem and headed for Jordan.

I don't recall whether the bridge across the Jordan was out, or if he was barred from using it, but poor Eddie, trousers rolled up, had to wade across the River Jordan. An Israeli youngster carried his heavy baggage to the edge on that side, with an Arab kid waiting to help him with the bags on the other side but there was no help in between.

Loaded down, Eddie stopped in the middle of the River Jordan, looked around, considered his circumstance and started to cry. But it wasn't Eddie's nature to cry too long.

In recounting the story he admits that the tears soon turned to laughter when he realized how ridiculous he must have looked.

My Palestinians haven't been calling much lately asking the price of the COIN. Their future doesn't look too bright, but they have survived horrible oppression in and around Israel, and, maybe, just maybe they will persevere.

Meanwhile, I fear I've lost some terrific gold customers.

May 28, 2002

LRC HAS MADE THE BIG TIME, BUT, LEW ROCKWELL MAY BE EXILED TO CHINA

What a wild ride for LewRockwell.com! Between Thursday morning, April 5, and Saturday night, April 7, Eric Garris, our webmaster, tells me, a record 248,000 hits on our website. This is almost double any comparable period in our eighteen-month history.

More astonishing were the 600+ emails directed to Editor Lew Rockwell, six times more than anything previously seen for a single article.

If this wasn't enough to swamp our webmaster, add the additional new visitors and fresh emails linked from Yahoo, Antiwar.com, WorldNetDaily, and Free Republic.

What was the cause of this avalanche? The answer is in three little words: "China Is Right," the title of Lew's courageous article about the collision of the US and Chinese aircraft, and the events which followed. (If you missed it go to http://www.lewrockwell.com/rockwell/chinaisright.html)

Fearlessly, point by point, Lew refutes the US government's version of the event He reminds the reader of the history of the US as an international meddler, and warns of the danger of a new cold-war belligerency.

Frankly, although I expected some heat, I was surprised by the degree of vituperation and vulgarity that typified the incoming e-mails. If you'd like a breakdown, 90 percent were incoherently critical, 5 percent coherently critical, 3 percent mixed, and 2 percent supportive. It was like a drunken Saturday night at a veterans' convention, and about as thoughtful (though a few Korean War vets, like me, agreed with Lew).

Most of the hostile emails urged Lew to move to "Red China." My favorite told him to "go back to Austria." We both could have done without the death threats. But I guess you can't be a warmonger without wanting to kill people.

It all reminds me of the nasty climate created by the government propaganda machine during Bush the First's Desert Storm: the bipartisan unanimity, and the media's total acceptance of every government press release. Few questioned the "smart bombs" that found open windows, the characterization of Saddam's military capability as "first class," or the claimed

Iraqi "atrocities" in Kuwait. Fewer still realized the genocide being put into place, which continues to this day.

Those who questioned the bloody exercise were demonized as dreaded isolationists. Tax audits were the least thing to fear. Dissenting was dangerous stuff.

Months later, the mythology of Desert Storm began to erode. Little pieces of truth emerged: the smart bombs were dumb, Iraqi troops who had surrendered were gunned down or buried alive in the sand, and in the war's aftermath, evidence of the horrendous damage US policy inflicted on the Iraqi civilian population became overwhelming.

Let us hope that today's confrontation with China is no new Desert Storm in the making, or second cold war. The latter is ideal from the standpoint of the military-industrial complex, since they think they could tax and run us indefinitely, without any casualties. But the huge amount of trade with China, giving some established interests a pro-peace bias, may prevent this.

Indeed, there is some evidence that George W. Bush and Colin Powell may represent a new and less confrontational American foreign policy. We pray that this will be the case. If not, well, we have LewRockwell.com.

April 9, 2001

HELLO PG&E—
ARE YOU STILL IN BUSINESS?

April 6, 2001: Pacific Gas & Electric, California's largest utility voluntarily filed for Chapter Eleven federal bankruptcy protection despite months of effort by state officials to bail out the cash-starved company.

April 8, 2001: It was learned that $50 million in bonuses was distributed to PG&E executives the day prior to its declaration of bankruptcy.

—MSNBC News

PG&E: This is PG&E Customer Service. Your call will be answered in the order received. Since you are the last caller, we will get around to you last.

Blumert: Hold it, what's going on here? You're not a recording.

PG&E: I am too a recording.

Blumert: You're not.

PG&E: Am too.

Blumert: This is ridiculous. Why in heaven's name would anybody pretend to be a recording?

PG&E (suppressing a sob): Well, if you must know, they came and repossessed our telephone answering equipment yesterday.

Blumert: That's very touching, but I have a serious problem.

PG&E: You have a problem? Well, it's not exactly rosy at this end, buddy. We've all been on medication since April 6, but for all the good it will do you, go ahead and tell me your problem if it makes you feel better.

Blumert: My complaint is with the STING RAY ENERGY SAVER that you recommend and that I foolishly purchased. Here's how you advertised it along with my last electric bill:

> The dire energy crisis we face has been caused by unscrupulous suppliers of natural gas and electricity who, without conscience, have been charging us market price. This calls for a dramatic response. To fight back we recommend a terrific new product, the STING RAY.
>
> The STING RAY is installed on electric switches in your home or business zapping the user with 5000 volts when he flips the switch on. This is a certain reminder to conserve energy.
>
> The price of the STING RAY is only $85 and PG&E will send you a $20 rebate check.

PG&E: What's to complain? The STING RAY has been responsible for some families lowering their energy use by 50 percent.

Blumert: With a STING RAY installed on all electrical switches, it's a sure thing that most families will be huddled in the dark wrapped in blankets during the winter or sweating profusely with nothing but a garden hose to cool them in the summer's heat.

PG&E: Patriotic Americans! The STING RAY is a winner.

Blumert: Sounds like you'll only be satisfied when we are back in the Stone Age, but my real problem is with the $20 rebate check PG&E offered.

PG&E: So quit worrying about the check. You'll get it, you'll get it.

Blumert: My worry is I already got it and my problem is that it bounced.

PG&E: Bounced shmounched. Get with the times.

Blumert: You're not much help, but maybe I can get some useful information out of you.

Tomorrow I'm going to the baseball game at Pac Bell Park, and I'm concerned that there will be a power outage in the middle of the game. A nightmare, forty thousand people groping in the dark.

PG&E (musing): To think, we used to be bigger than Ma Bell. It's interesting that Pac Bell Park hasn't paid their April electric bill as yet. Hmmmmmm . . .

Blumert: Uh oh! Sounds to me like you've got some mischief planned for the ballpark, and that you are going to hit them with a "random blackout" at tomorrow night's game.

PG&E: Look, buster, this is war. Don't try to squeeze any classified information out of me.

Blumert: War? Seems to me you have a bunker mentality. Unfortunately, the only casualties are the customers.

PG&E: Who told you we were in a bunker? As we speak, we are in a crossfire between two armies, the Gray Davis Brigade and the George W. Federalists.

Blumert: What's the war all about?

PG&E (choking with emotion): The loser gets PG&E.

Blumert: You're depressing me. I think I'd rather have Tony Soprano running things. At least my garbage is picked up with no problems.

PG&E: Listen, Blumert, you sound like someone we can trust. There's a small group of us here resurrecting the company from the ashes. We call it Phoenix Gas & Electric, and we already have signed up thirty customers.

Can we count on you?

Blumert: Well, I haven't made a correct decision in years so I might as well join you.

PG&E: Terrific. The Phoenix Gas & Electric service man will be at your home to hook you up next week. He will be there sometime between 8 a.m. on Monday and midnight on Sunday. You have to be there when he comes.

Blumert: Lotsa luck, fellas, but it sounds like the old PG&E to me.

MAY 21, 2001

MEMO TO ABE FOXMAN: "ABE, I'M ONLY KIDDING"

There's never a scintilla of doubt about their mission at the Anti-Defamation League (ADL), but wouldn't it be refreshing if once, just once, something like the following exchange took place in their war-room:

Senior Staff Member (SSM): "Mr. Foxman, I have disheartening news. We have scoured all segments of the media worldwide, including the Internet and we can't find one instance of anti-Semitism anywhere during the past 60 days."

Abe: "Impossible! We have three fund-raising letters to get out and the bills must be paid. Get on it. What about the NY Knicks basketball team getting rid of Isaiah Goldberg? That incident reeks of anti-Semitism."

SSM: "Goldberg was only 5'4" and the fact that he had committed to memory the statistics of every team in the NBA was of no value during an actual game. The Knicks signing Goldberg was another failed example of affirmative action, and it was the Jewish fans who actually led the campaign to have the team dump him."

Abe: "What about those virulent statements coming from Malaysia attacking Jews? Let's play that up. Surely we can find some atrocity photos that will fit into an effective fundraising piece."

SSM: "Frankly, sir, anti-Semitism in that part of the world seems to be a non-issue. First, there are so few Jews living there, and the differences between Jew and Gentile is lost on most Asians. I just don't see our donors getting worked up enough to mail in checks on that story."

Abe: "You fellows are laughable. Anti-Semitism is suffocating all of us and you blithely go about your lives not finding anything. What about some of those leads to anti-Semitism I gave you last month?"

SSM: "We struck out, sir. Your wife's assessment that Martha Stewart seems like a nice Jewish lady, and that the shoddy treatment given her smacks of anti-Semitism is of no value, since she's not Jewish.

"Need I remind you of the embarrassment we suffered when you suggested that the Pope was guilty of an anti-Semitic cabal when he appointed eight new Cardinals and not one was Jewish? We still get nasty mail on that one."

Abe: "I was misquoted—but I still feel that all the churches could show a bit more tolerance in their hiring practices. It wouldn't kill them to have a few Jews around each church to provide a different perspective."

SSM: "One other thing, Mr. Foxman, the entire ADL staff is fed up with picketing Mel Gibson's movie. None of us share your concern that, at the close of the film, the entire audience would storm the closest video store to buy and then burn all Woody Allen movies. The only movement I witnessed were people moving closer to their faith."

Abe: "I'm glad you were so touched by the Gibson film, but if you don't find me some juicy anti-Semitic material soon you'll be back slicing corned beef in the kosher deli."

March 19, 2004

Are You a Threat to Liberty? Take the Blumert Test and Other Impertenent Essays

In Defense of Y2K Extremists

She said in her soft sunbelt drawl, "I want to talk to the owner of Camino Coin." "This is Burt Blumert. How may I help?"

"Gary North made me buy gold coins from you people. He said that if I didn't I would be in big trouble due to Y2K It happened under false pretenses."

On the defensive, I responded, "Well, I suppose many of us were caught-up with the Y2K scare, but you should feel relieved that our worst fears weren't realized."

"I want my money back," she said. "I never opened the box the gold came in."

The computer screen revealed her purchase in July 1999. "Mrs. Bartlett, you bought 61 one-ounce and 100 tenth-ounce gold eagles. You paid $277 each for the big ones and $31.50 each for the small ones. Today I can repurchase the one-ouncers for $286 and the tenth-ouncers for $29.50. If you sell today, you'll be ahead about $450."

That information didn't give her as much satisfaction as it did me and she asked, "What about the silly wind-up radio and flashlight that I got as a bonus?"

"Aren't those remarkable," I added hopefully. "And they are so well made, from South Africa, you know. I use the radio every morning. Sometimes it's the only exercise I get."

Without as much as a chuckle, she charged, "My pastor says that Gary North is a false prophet and should be punished."

"You know, Mrs. Bartlett, Gary North wasn't alone in alarming the public about Y2K. There were dozens of Congressional hearings about the horrors of Y2K and people like US Senators Bennett and Dodd caused me sleepless nights watching C-SPAN tapes."

By this time I sensed Mrs. Bartlett was in her own zone, and she said, "My son ridiculed me for buying the gold. I actually bought it for him. He called this morning sarcastically asking if the electric power was on. I was so embarrased."

As one long identified with losing causes, I commiserated. "It wasn't only the right-wingers who issued emergency instructions about Y2K. The American Red Cross, FEMA, and most power companies urged hunkering down with dried food, candles, and bottled water."

I didn't seem to be making much progress and she in an accusatory voice said: "Well, you ought to be ashamed of yourself. Imagine profiting on such a phony thing as Y2K."

In my best Jack Webb-John Wayne impersonation, I responded, "Ma'am, I'm just a humble old gold dealer who tries to treat the customer fairly whether their fears are real or imagined. We sell insurance, and as with most insurance policies, you're better off if there's no pay-out.

"Mrs. Bartlett, if you're looking for the real profiteers, seek out those computer programmers who created the problem and later reaped the harvest by solving the mischief they gave birth to."

The tide was turning and she stammered, "Well, Gary North and his ilk ought to apologize for what they've done."

I was now on the offensive. "Gary North and the other Y2K extremists were pikers. Most of their 'victims' were older folks intimidated by revolutionary technology they did not understand. That it contained the seeds of its own destruction seemed appropriate. Where are the critics of corporate America who spent billions on a nonproblem? And what about our lovable government? Where is its apology for all the taxpayer dollars it wasted on an imaginary project?"

A computer friend tells me that the Y2K scare gave corporate America an opportunity to repair the minor problem caused by the two-digit date, but also enabled them to upgrade hardware and revitalize software, in short tooling-up for the revolution in progress. In a way, "the right-wing Y2K extremists" accomplished the same for middle America.

The Y2K scare motivated people to improve their emergency preparedness. If it abetted people's suspicion of basic institutions like banks, insurance companies, and government itself, what's wrong with that?

My customer decided not to sell her gold coins and I direct the following postscript to her and others like her:

Most of the Y2K extremists were genuine in their concerns. The establishment, as usual, has taken this opportunity to savagely attack them. But remember, the media have no affection nor sympathy for you. To them you are aliens who live in "flyover country." So don't be embarrassed. The elites, in the end, were far more gullible than you.

January 8, 2000

POOR BURT—HE'S IN THE MARKET FOR A HOME HAIRCUT KIT

Many American males were brought up listening intently to their barber's opinions on any and every subject. Later in life the barber holds more sway than a barkeep. When encountering the former, there is sobriety, no solid wood bar counter providing a buffer zone, and the constant reminder that the sharp steel instrument in his hand could terminate life.

Conversation overheard at Antonino's Coiffiere, formerly Tony's Barbershop.

Customer (*Burt*): "Hello, Tony, 'the usual,' but not too short on the sides."

Tony: "The name is Antonino, and we don't do 'the usual' anymore. You're scheduled for a protein wash and a fashion cut followed by a blow-dry. Then a pedicure, and if Madame Arlene is available, she will reveal your future with the Tarot cards."

Burt: "Has Madame Arlene predicted that I may be out of here? All I wanted was a haircut, not a weekend at Elizabeth Arden's spa. Tony, sorry, Antonino, remember the old days—for auld lang syne—just a haircut one last time."

Antonino (brushing away a tear): "I must admit your plea is very touching. Ok, this one time only, just a haircut, but you mustn't tell anybody, and I trust you have shampooed within recent memory."

Burt: "I bathe once a week whether I need it or not, and it would be nice if we could skip the 'Antonino'."

Tony: "All right, but you still must pass the Politically Correct screening quiz we instituted when we became a Coiffiere.

Please answer the three questions on the white card my son handed you when he took your jacket."

Burt: "I can't believe I'm a willing participant to this, and you might suggest to your son that he shouldn't be eating a pizza slice and handling the customer's garment at the same time, but here are my answers to your dumb questions:

"1. The death penalty for wearing Confederate Flag under shorts must be reversed unless what's at issue is the defendant's poor taste or lack of color coordination.

"2. Although I have affection and sympathy for those vigilantes who overpowered the defense force and occupied California's power utilities, they must abide by the Geneva Convention when dealing with the PG&E employees they took prisoner.

"3. Yes, I am still of the 'Jewish persuasion' as you put it. It was just a week ago Thursday that we were at my nephew's Bar Mitzvah and you made a fool of yourself over-indulging and telling the young women that you were a retired Israeli fighter pilot. And, there was nothing funny about using your yarmulke to wrap the piece of honey-cake you were taking home. Do you suppose I can get my haircut now?"

Tony (scissors flashing): "You guys haven't been laughing very much since George W. Bush selected his cabinet without appointing one Jew. Your commitment to losing causes is so well-known, Blumert, it occurred to me this 'insult' might have put you in search of some other religious 'preference'."

Burt (ever mindful of flashing scissors): "Although I should know better, I am puzzled by Jewish folks who express outrage, some directly, others in an oblique manner suggesting that Jews shouldn't need such recognition given their success in many areas. In either instance, they don't like George Dubya. In fact, they hate him.

244 — Bagels, Barry Bonds, and Rotten Politicians

"There are no Armenian-Americans in the Cabinet. No Italian-Americans and so on. If every American ethnic sub-division were represented, the Cabinet would number 834 people.

"Do you want a foolproof way of measuring George Dubya's presidency? When Left/Liberal media stars, often Jewish, begin to recognize his merit (see George Dubya's education proposals and the Left's enthusiastic response), it's time to give up any hope that Dubya would give more than lip-service to true conservatism. Sounds to me like another lost cause. Remember, I am the expert in that area."

Tony: "Blumert, you're a downer."

Burt: "Haircut is great, Tony, and I'll see you in the usual 7 weeks."

Antonino:" Sorry, as I told you before, we won't be doing the 'usual' anymore."

Burt: "Well, Antonino, if I ever decide on lipo-suction, I'll call for an appointment."

January 30, 2000

CALIFORNIA'S FOUR SEASONS: FIRE, FLOOD, DROUGHT, AND EARTHQUAKE

Those folks who regard snow and ice as a dire threat to life and limb and flee to tropical, southern Florida never lose the imprint of the seasons. They are simply on a prolonged holiday. Well, more like a permanent sabbatical.

In case you hadn't noticed, Californians view the world through a cockeyed lens. We don't deny the traditional four seasons; we simply substitute our own version.

To most Americans, November 1st is a reminder that brittle cold nights and frigid winds are just around the corner. The first snow flurries never fail to bring a smile, and they reaffirm the seasonal nature of life.

This year in California, November blew in with blistering heat and fire-breeding winds, confirming that we do have seasons like every place else. The problem is that California's four seasons do not come with ordered sequence. Flood, Drought, Fire, and Earthquake seem to be scripted by Hollywood.

I will never forget that wondrous day when the offices of the San Mateo County Drought Commission were almost swept out to sea by a flash flood resulting from two inches of rain that fell in less than an hour.

Drought and flood are never out of mind in California. Both political parties are held captive by the giant farming interests and the cost and availability of water is a constant, even if under-publicized political issue.

California's citizens are under official directive to either be ready for the next flood, or not to flush too often. We are required to attend prayer meetings imploring the Creator to grace the farmer with good weather and good markets. (I have yet to hear any farmer show the slightest concern for gold dealers, or the gold market.)

Most of California's thirty-five million live in the counties near San Francisco and Los Angeles. The closest these folks get to agri-business is a visit to the Farmer's Market. I forgot to mention that of the estimated thirty-five million in the state, nine million are immigrants. (The breakdown of those who are "documented vs. undocumented" seems to be unknown. What is known is that the word "illegal," as applied to immigrants, will probably soon be illegal.)

Look, people who live south of the border come to California for wages. They recognize the opportunities. Start as a dishwasher and in six months you'll own a car. If you close your ears to lawyers about "rights," you'll be opening your own restaurant in just a few years.

The bad joke about Mexico's lousy Olympic team says it all; Any Mexican who could vault over seven feet, swim swiftly, or "out run a speeding bullet," had already crossed the border into the US.

The great appeal of California for American immigrants is the weather. There is nothing more democratic than a temperate climate. I've told this before, but Murray Rothbard had difficulty identifying the street "crazies" in California. In New York City, the marginal folks wore things like WWII battle gear with vinyl table coverings as overcoats.

In California EVERYBODY wears short-sleeved shirts. It takes a few moments of conversation to determine that rendezvousing on Mt. Wilson with a spacecraft leaving for another galaxy holds little appeal. Anyway, you quickly decide that you have enough friends.

But, Californians are just like other Americans. They know that November means the holidays will soon be upon us. The experts say that California is overdue for a 7+ quake. If we get one of those in the next sixty days, I may not get the opportunity to wish all of you out there in LRC land a wonderful and joyous Christmas and good health for the New Year.

Well, it looks like I just did.

November 4, 2003

SERIAL KILLERS OF AMERICA, UNITE

A LETTER TO THE EDITOR
COPIED TO BURT BLUMERT

Dear Editor:

O ur membership has deep contempt for police at every level of government, particularly those who investigate homicides. This group of bozos are at the bottom-of-the-barrel, the least intelligent, most corrupt and laziest law enforcement agents of all.

Actually, our 1,100 dues paying members survive and flourish because of police ineptitude. Amused, we watch the clumsy manner in which most murder case investigations are handled. Even more ludicrous are the transparent efforts to cover-up shoddy work.

For too long, we have lived with the "Dr. Richard Kimble" defense murder strategy. Predictably, the police and defense lawyers, in lockstep, have picked up this absurd premise. It matters not how the murder was accomplished, or who the victim was. Every murderer shouts:

"It was a one-armed man who did it."

Those unfortunate souls who have lost an arm to disease, have had it severed in an accident (shark bite), or war; even those cheated of an arm by nature, found themselves in constant danger.

It wasn't only people who looked like David Janssen, and years later, Harrison Ford, who were beating them up and dragging them into police stations. The fact that they could only "half" fight back made the one-armed fellow an easy victim.

It wasn't until the failure of a TV remake of *The Fugitive* that the "Richard Kimble" defense fell out of favor.

Without the "one-armed man" defense, the police continued to stumble along as usual, doggedly pursuing the wrong people and letting obvious murderers go free.

We at the *National Association of Serial Killers* are accustomed to this inefficiency, but some current developments greatly trouble our membership.

In a recent case in Massachusetts, a well-known allergist, as guilty as he was splattered by his murdered wife's blood, showcased the new defense:

"A serial killer did it."

The Washington, DC police blundering along in the Chandra Levy missing intern case are all set to pick up the mantra:

"It was a serial killer who did it."

In a cabal, which includes murderers, their lawyers, and the police, we detect a dangerous trend. Every murderer will soon be pointing to the hapless serial killer.

We are outraged by this new development.

Our members, the authentic serial killers, resent being identified with these run-of-the-mill murder cases.

The true serial killer should not be confused with amateurs.

- The serial killer is meticulous and rarely gets caught.

- Serial killers almost never murder friends or family.

- Serial killers often plant clues to help the inept police (to make the chase more exciting).

- Unlike their mundane, passion-driven counterparts, the serial killer is generally erudite and literate.

Mr. Editor, we implore you, please don't get caught up with this new tactic on the part of the police establishment to cover-up their own inadequacies by blaming members of our association.

Stop scapegoating. Stop maligning us. Don't sully the great history of serial killers.

The Association of One-Armed Americans join in this protest.

Sincerely yours,
Hannibal "the Ripper" Bundy
(Be advised, this is not my real name)
Executive Director
The National Association of Serial Killers

July 14, 2001

DON'T SEND ME TO DIXIE
IF I CAN'T GET EGG ROLLS

Make sure your hotel room is on a lower floor and remember to carry a rope ladder in your suitcase. The Cape Fear Hotel in Wilmington, North Carolina, serves a terrific pot roast special on Wednesdays— but don't waste your time looking for egg rolls because you won't find many Chinese restaurants.

—Advice from the district manager to his replacement

 $\mathbf{N}$ o egg rolls?

How could any human being survive without Chinese food at least twice a month?

It was the 1950s and this New York City boy was in culture shock. I was the replacement. The territory covered twenty-seven smallish to medium-sized cities in the "Old South."* God was surely testing me.

Like most Yankees, my knowledge of the South was based on bad Hollywood movies. In the Air Force, I encountered dozens of Southern lads who were the backbone of the enlisted corps, but, frankly, they were rural redneck types and only reinforced my bias.

By contrast, friends who served in the US Army met unwilling draftees—not volunteers—and discovered a cross-section of literate, young Southern men who had grace and breeding.

Remember, this was the Old South, post-WWII. The Holiday Inn and other national motel chains were only beginning to compete with the downtown hotels. McDonald's and Burger King were in the future and Won Ton soup was a treat experienced only by world travelers (folks who had been to Atlanta or New Orleans qualified).

Once culture shock was over and I established a routine, my attitude about the South changed—these folks were special. Never before, nor since have I experienced such cordiality, but I became uncomfortable accepting invitations to dine at people's homes and finding good restaurant food remained an elusive and difficult exercise.

After a few repeat visits to one of my cities, I might discover a culinary treasure. In "dry" counties, it was often the bootlegger who would point me to a family-operated restaurant where the ingredients were fresh and the slant was decidedly Southern.

---

*I call it the Old South to diffentiate that great region from what my fellow Northern Californians mean by the South: Los Angeles.

My favorite was a nameless restaurant on the outskirts of Lexington, Kentucky. It was located in a faded building that had once been a fine residence. The black chef introduced me to fare I had never experienced. Spectacular barbecue: succulent cuts of beef, pork, and chicken covered by mysterious piquant sauces, complemented by superb fried okra, leading to addictions I carry to this day.

But in most instances the weary traveler dined upon overcooked food in the hotel's dining room. And let me remind you: there were few Chinese restaurants.

During my six years in the Old South, it all began to change. Downtown was becoming shabby. Regional shopping centers were sprouting in the suburbs and as auto sales boomed, motels were attracting Americans as they sped along the new interstate highway systems. Even the seasoned business travelers— downtown hotel regulars—were tempted to try one of the flashy new motels.

Many of my Southern friends were troubled by the changes taking place—thanks to the federal highway program, federal school planning, and other unconstitutional interventions into the states—and they could not know of the disruption that was ahead in the 1960s. I never gave much thought to any of it, but by the time I was about to leave the South, Chinese restaurants could be found both downtown and in the suburbs in all of my cities.

The Chinese restaurant has universal appeal. From Kabul, Afghanistan, to Mombassa, Kenya, from Odessa in the Ukraine to Odessa in Texas to Zurich, Switzerland, satisfied diners savor Bird's Nest soup and become adept with chopsticks.

How is it that Chinese cuisine successfully cuts across all borders and cultures? The answer is simple: Most Chinese restaurants maintain an unusually high standard and the food is generally cooked when ordered, ensuring freshness. Aside from providing simply delicious food, there are other reasons why Chinese restaurants flourish the world over.

- They are almost always open for business. Local holidays do not mean closing down. They remain a haven for hungry patrons.

- Customers are almost never turned away for failing to book an advance reservation. Occasionally an upscale Manhattan or Beverly Hills location refuses a customer, but this is not typical. If the house is full, the enterprising owner/manager will set up a table in the kitchen, or squeeze one in the corridor near the restrooms.

- The Chinese restaurateur gives totally balanced service to all his customers. (The only exception is what appears to be a special menu of exotic dishes for his Chinese clients. The Caucasian observing these feasts from an adjoining table never knows for sure.)

- Chinese cuisine has zero tolerance for animal rights groups. The only qualification for what is prepared by the chef is that it fits in the wok and will taste good.

- Yet the Chinese chef demonstrates enormous tolerance when, for example, although perplexed by the vegetarian, he still manages to create magnificent dishes that satisfy even those idiosyncratic customers.

- In most places, Chinese food affords excellent value for the consumer's dollar.

- And although it is not a prime consideration for the kitchen, Chinese food is nutritious and low in calories while delighting the taste buds with unique flavors.

- It remains a custom in many Chinese restaurants around the world that the patron examines the fish or fowl before it's cooked thus, once again guaranteeing fresh fare.

- Almost every Chinese restaurant is family operated and this is particularly appealing to many consumers in this age of absentee and/or indifferent management.

Those years spent in the Old South had a significant influence on my value system and view of the world. I learned good manners, respect for tradition, and began to question, for the first time, the mythology presented as history in my government school education.

Oh, by the way, in case you're puzzled by my predecessor's admonition to make sure my hotel room was on a lower floor and to always travel with a rope ladder, he was referring to a custom handed down by travelling salesmen from an earlier time. The rope ladder allowed escape from a hotel engulfed in flames, but obviously could only be utilized from a lower floor. He was an old-fashioned fellow and for some unexplained reason, hated Chinese food.

April 16, 2001

WERE MONICA AND CHANDRA SPIES? ADVICE TO POLITICIANS— STICK TO SKINNY SHIKSAS

In a fascinating piece of analytical gossip, *New York Post* Page Six reporter Rod Dreher points out the "eerie similarities" between the Monica Lewinsky and Chandra Levy scandals.

Aside from the sexual intrigue with powerful Democratic politicians, Dreher's July 5th column catalogued other amazing parallels:

- Both women were bosomy Jewish-American Princesses from California.

- Both have physician fathers whose specialty is oncology.

- Both were "interns" rubbing elbows with the rich and powerful.

- Even the DC lawyers we now see crawling out from under their rocks are the same ones we observed in l'Affair Lewinsky.

Sherman H. Skolnick, longtime controversial, investigative muckraker, in his July 8 *Skolnick's Reports*, goes even further, adding a sinister twist to the mystery.

Skolnick is convinced that Monica was "a creature of renegade units of Israeli intelligence, the Mossad." He goes on to suggest that Chandra Ann Levy may have been similarly involved, that is, that she was also "a creature of renegade units of the Mossad, but not authorized as such by the state of Israel government."

He continues: "Like Monica, the reputed purpose of Chandra was to infiltrate. To use her womanly wiles to find out things."

One of Monica's missions, according to Skolnick, after she was tossed out of the White House by Hillary and mysteriously assigned to a high position at the Pentagon, was to mingle with important US military leaders and report back to a faction at Mossad headquarters their degree of loyalty to Clinton, a vital matter during and following the impeachment crisis.

Chandra, according to Skolnick, was in a perfect position to glean information from Congressman Condit regarding super-secret data on Tim McVeigh. Skolnick tells us that Condit, as a senior member of the House Permanent Select Committee on Intelligence, was privy to all the actual, complete details of the Oklahoma City bombing.

If one buys the Skolnick thesis, Chandra Levy may not have been a suicide or murder victim, but was spirited away to Israel.

In spite of some good judicial investigation he performed years ago in Illinois, Skolnick is regarded by many as "on the fringe." Frankly, I find his views of Mossad involvement with the interns a bit wacky. But the mere notion of Chandra as an Israeli agent is so enticing that I would give $100 of Lew Rockwell's money to have been there at her debriefing.

It probably went something like this:

Mossad Agent: Before we start, please tell me what kind of a name is Chandra? Nice Jewish-American girls have names like Tracy, Kimberly, or Tiffany. What's with Chandra?

Chandra: For a time my father had a practice near Watts, but I don't hear you complaining about the name Monica.

Mossad Agent: Never mind. You did nice work with the Congressman, but you seemed indifferent, and aside from your accounts of the sex, your reports were boring us to tears.

Chandra: Well, who wouldn't be bored? I was in Modesto while Miss Chubby is the queen of society in Manhattan. She goes to Le Cirque for dinner and I get Bob's Big Boy in Stockton for a burger.

Mossad Agent: Would you please forget about Monica.

Chandra: Sure, the slut gets to hear the "Three Tenors": Pavarotti, Carreras, and Domingo in concert at Carnegie Hall, and I get to listen to the best recordings of Johnny Cash, Merle Haggard, and Ferlin Husky at the American Legion Hall in downtown Modesto.

Mossad Agent: I'm getting fed up with this Monica business. Would you please . . .

Chandra: While the fat bitch was a judge at an elegant Women's Wear Daily fashion show at the Plaza Hotel in New York City, I was on my knees measuring the performance of Stanislaus County's best jumping frogs.

Chandra (now out of control): The slut jets in Air Force One to a Nato conference in Brussels, and I'm one of the Queen's Maids sitting on the backseat of a 1976 Chevy convertible at the San Joaquin Valley Walnut Festival in 100-degree temperatures.

Mossad Agent: Enough already. Let's get on to your next assignment. You will be serving coffee in the downtown Cairo Starbucks. It will be arranged to have Yasir Arafat as one of your customers. As you are pouring his double decaf latte, you will lean forward so he can see down your blouse.

Our intelligence advises that he will seize the moment and you'll be whisked to the bridal suite at the Cairo Hilton in no time at all.

Chandra: Sure, and I suppose Miss Bloated America gets assigned to Hollywood to seduce Russell Crowe.

July 10, 2001

ARE YOU A THREAT TO LIBERTY?: TAKE THE BLUMERT TEST

I remember reading somewhere that the average American male thinks about sex every thirty seconds.

During my first months in the US Air Force, back in Korean War days, the Jewish chaplain addressed our small group and advised that it wasn't going to be easy. We would be reminded of our "Jewishness" almost every waking hour. He was right. It was occasionally negative, but mostly good-natured bantering, and every airman, regardless of background, got his share.

There were times when the mental sexual imagery whirred along like a continuous motion picture rather than a clip every thirty seconds, and "Jewishness" ebbed and flowed with time and location. Most often, it was the folks encountered that brought it to the fore.

WEISS, SOBRAN, AND ME

Frankly, I hadn't been thinking about sex or Jewishness for quite a while until I read Philip Weiss's "Jews in Bush's Cabinet? Don't Hold Your Breath" (*New York Observer*, 22 December 2001) and Joseph Sobran's "An Anniversary" (*Sobran's*, December 2001).

Mr. Weiss, the consummate New Yorker, has written frequently on the subject of Jews and their place in American society. In earlier pieces, he appropriately concluded that anti-Semitism in America is a ghost. But in this present article, he removes all inhibitions and proudly acknowledges that Jews have changed America.

In earlier times Weiss would have been dismayed at George W.'s failure to appoint any Jews to his cabinet. Not now. Weiss is so confident of Jewish potency, he says, "Remaking the American power structure without Jews is like remaking sports without blacks."

Weiss details with pride Jewish influence in the civil rights movement, feminism, the media, popular culture, and law and finance. He tops off his sermonet by arguing that "the greatly diminished influence of the church on public mores wouldn't have happened without secularized Jews gaining cultural power."

Whew!

This is not a social agenda shared by most Americans, or by all Jews for that matter. Where are the dissenters?

Well, Weiss accomplished one thing; he got me focusing on my Jewishness full-time. What the heck. Since I am now part of America's power structure, I decided to enjoy it and bully my way around.

Unfortunately, when I started swaggering at my home or office as a sort of Jewish superman, nobody was impressed. In fact, everybody listened less than usual, and I had to commiserate with poor Rodney Dangerfield, who laments that "he don't get no respect."

Joe Sobran is a dear friend and unique talent. LRC readers recognize him as one of America's most brilliant essayists. In his "An Anniversary" piece, Joe wrestles with the issue that has bedeviled him. He states his respect for the ability and culture of Jews, but is convinced that they represent goals profoundly different from those of most Americans, since this is "still more or less a Christian country."

All Joe asks is that any exchange on the subject be open. He insists, "I reserve the right to talk about [the differences between Jews and Christians] and take it into my calculations without being called a bigot."

Joe can count on me to go to the barricades with him on this point, but he, like Weiss, has me focusing once again on my Jewishness.

THE LONE EAGLE

The anniversary of Joe's title involves Charles A. Lindbergh. His extremely dangerous solo flight across the Atlantic earned him the mantle of America's greatest hero. He was an icon, the leading anti-interventionist of his time, and the star spokesman for the America First Committee, the two million-member organization committed to keeping us out of WWII.

Interestingly, September 11th, 2001, marked the sixtieth anniversary of Lindbergh's famous speech in Des Moines, Iowa. He implored Americans not to succumb to the influence of "the British, the Jewish, or the Roosevelt administration," who were promoting our entry into WWII.

Lindbergh was vilified by the media and FDR for these remarks, and labeled an anti-Semite. The mythology of his anti-Semitism continues to reach beyond the grave. The smear against Lindbergh is an outrage: any objective evaluation of the man, his beliefs, and accomplishments shatters the lie. And as Joe notes, no one ever claims that these three groups were not pushing for war.

Joe, as usual, makes a rousing case, but in my view he becomes a bit one-dimensional in evaluating American Jews in today's society.

Like Lindbergh, Joe Sobran has been constantly maligned and I recognize his frustration when he observes:

"Even Jews who neither believe nor practice their ancestral religion have been formed by it and are conscious of belonging to an ancient nation, compared with which the United States of America is a very recent (and probably temporary) upstart."

Joe, that's an overstatement and I think you are wrong. I detect a hint of something akin to Original Sin. Yes, there are plenty of Jewish bad guys who by their actions or worldview threaten our American heritage and way of life. And they are powerful.

But, there are also Jews, religious or not, who are passionate about what America stands for, Jews who weep at the erosion of American values and struggle to stem that erosion.

I'm sort of tired being judged by some folks on only one aspect of what I am. "Blumert's a Jew." Sorry, that single word standing alone is not a true indicator as to whether or not I am a threat to your liberty.

We need more data. Have no fear. I have devised a foolproof test.

THE TEST

What follows is a broad formula designed to reveal an individual's "Potential for Evil" (PFE), and I offer it to society at no cost. Here's my methodology: I use five basic components to measure an individual's PFE.

1. Occupation. In almost every instance, what a person does for a living is the dominant factor in determining his PFE.

2. National origin. As always in history, this is vital in determining PFE.

3. Religion. It's an even more passionate measure of PFE.

4. Affiliations. Those interests that a person has aside from his occupation and religion also reveals his PFE.

5. Geographic section of the US a person comes from.

Below I have assigned scientific value numbers reflecting the Potential for Evil. They range from 0 to 10. 0 is terrific, and 10 is bad news. Remember, the higher the number the greater the danger.

OCCUPATION

Politician 10	Academic 05
Media 10	Sales 04
Lawyer 09	Physician 04
Accountant 07	Dentist 04
Lobbyist 07	Engineer 03
Government Employee 06	Travel 03
Military (Officer) 06	Blue Collar 03
Entertainment 06	Artist 03
Veteran 06	Military (Enlisted) 02
Retail 05	Farmer 02
Finance 05	High Tech 02
Non-Profit 05	Pilot 02
Corporate 05	

RELIGION

Jewish 10	Hindu 04
Muslim 10	Sects/Cults 04
Mormon 06	Protestant 02
Catholic 04	Davidian 01

GEOGRAPHIC

Mid-Atlantic 07	Midwest Flyover 03
New England 06	Dixie 02
Far West 04	

NATIONAL ORIGIN

Africa 08	East Asia 05
Mid-East 06	Latin 04
West Asia 06	Eastern Europe/Russia 03
American Indian 06	Southern Europe 03
UK 06	Western Europe 02
Canada 06	

AFFILIATIONS

Political Activist 10	Environmentalist 08
Pro-War Organization	Free Market/Freedom
Activist 10	Organization Activist 02
Legal Activist (ACLU) 09	Local Volunteer 02

Here are two hypothetical examples:

A Jewish (10) lawyer (8) whose ancestors came from Russia (3) and is a Sierra Club activist (8) reared in Boston (6). Score: 36. Watch out! This guy could be radioactive.

A Lutheran (02) with German roots (02), a software programmer (02) who contributes to the Mises Institute (02) reared in Mobile, Alabama (02). Score: 10. The sort of fellow who should be guiding a troop of Boy Scouts.

Our own Lew Rockwell is Catholic (04), with ancestors from the UK (06), reared in New England (06), employed by a nonprofit (05), and affiliated with the Mises Institute and the Center for Libertarian Studies (02). Score: 25

Even worse, I am Jewish (10), my ancestors come from Eastern Europe (03), I am in finance (05), my affiliations are the Mises Institute and CLS (02), but I was forged in New York City (07). Score: 27.

Clearly an appeal mechanism is necessary. If you—like Lew and me—believe your PFE is too high, that you have overcome your background, and that you are not a threat to liberty, request a waiver. You'll have to answer a few telling questions, however.

For example:

Who is H.L. Mencken?

What constitutes a just war?

Are you a regular visitor to LRC?

Well, add up your own score and see how you rate

SCORES

25 or more: You may be the stuff tyrants are made of.

20–24: Don't expect people to feel comfortable turning their backs to you.

15–19: People can be comfortable lending you their new car.

14 or less: You are a potential mate for the cherished child of an LRC reader.

December 29, 2001

FIVE PEOPLE IN THE WORLD
UNDERSTAND GOLD AND THEY
HAVE SIX DIFFERENT OPINIONS

MAINTAINING YOUR SANITY
WHEN GOLD DROPS $45

During an earlier lifetime I spent several years as assistant to Morris Colliers, an elegant Southern gentleman who kept an inventory of charming aphorisms and proverbs that he smoothly produced in a blink.

"If you hang by the neck long enough, you'll get used to it," was one of the old gent's favorites and it got stuck in my consciousness as well,

My wife says that watching the gold market during the month of April was like, "hanging by the neck" and, she claims, "That's what reminded you guys of the proverb."

There's much wisdom in the "hanging by the neck," maxim, but there are some serious exceptions.

For instance, you're in a commercial airliner and it hits an air pocket. It falls 3,000 feet before the pilot regains control. He announces that the plane is encountering "heavy turbulence." To me, that translates, "This plane is about to crash."

You can fly hundred times a year for fifty years and never get accustomed to one of those moments of shear terror in the sky.

It may not quite match the drama of nose-diving in a Boeing 767, but the gold buyer, too, never "gets accustomed" to as sharp a break in the gold price as we experienced in April.

It's a different kind of scary, but it's scary nevertheless.

While it's still fresh in our minds let's take a look what happened to gold in April, 2004.

The month started out with the price of gold at about $430. On the last day of April, gold was approximately $385.

A drop of $45 per ounce, 10.37 percent! That's a significant hit, and the volume of phone calls at Camino Coin increased as prices went lower. The first wave of questions were reasonable.

"Doesn't gold usually shoot straight up when there are wars and strife?"

"How come the price of oil is at highs, but not gold?"

Some callers seemed angry. It was as if gold had betrayed them. Others, suggested that their original decision to buy gold might have been ill advised.

In every instance, to a man, they wanted to talk. It was not long before their fears and panic became evident.

"How much lower do you think the gold can drop?"

(I never answer that one.)

"What about selling now and buying back at the bottom?"

(I had never even heard that one before last Friday.)

"Maybe I should have bought Krugerrands instead of St. Gaudens?" or

"Maybe I should have bought St. Gaudens instead of Krugerrands?"

Where I had the time I went back to basics:

- Why they should own gold?
- Who are the enemies of gold and why?
- Which gold items are the best to hold?
- When do you sell gold?

"Blumert, you sound like you're at the pulpit giving a sermon." observed George Resch, my long time associate at Camino Coin.

I started thinking. (Very dangerous) What's wrong with a sermon directed to the disappointed gold buyer? Show them the brighter side. Reveal the history. Explain that fiat money is immoral.

George Resch was right. I was sermonizing and, most of the callers admitted that they felt better after our visit. I felt better too. Returning to "basics" does it every time.

If you have read this far, you have been "sermonized" as well. But, any sermon to be judged as valuable, must close with "hell and brimstone."

1. If you are a novice playing with Precious Metals in the Futures Market, you shouldn't be there, GET OUT NOW.! See "The Risks You Run When You Own Gold, and the Danger You Face If You Don't."

2. Some newcomers succumb to the trap of "getting even." As gold goes lower, they get belligerent. "They're not going to shake me out of the market! Buy me two hundred ounces. If it goes lower, I'll buy more." See "The 'Hardly Noticed' Rally in the Gold Market."

3. A long term commitment to any market requires mental gymnastics. "Yes, the gold is down 10 percent, but look at the losses in other markets," See "Why in Heaven's Name Isn't Gold Moving Higher?"

Even though you never get used to a market breaking down like it did in April, living through it does help build scar tissue which makes it easier to handle next time.

I was discussing this complicated dilemma with long-time customer, Prospector Mike, who, when faced with a dismal precious metals market, closes the door of his den, goes to the calculator, adds up his total ounces of gold, silver, and platinum and then basks in the fact that, "it's all paid for."

Needless to say, old Prospector Mike could be a Poster Boy for the Sound Mental Health Society.

May 7, 2004

THE POWER OF AN EIGHT DOLLAR RISE IN THE PRICE OF GOLD

(I write this article defying Blumert's 7th Law, which warns that the moment that you report a favorable move in a market, it will be violently reversed, often with 24 hours.)

God is good; truth and justice prevail; the bad guys are in disarray; and the pollen count is at summer's low.

Everything is falling into place.

Oh yes, did I mention that the price of gold was up $8 today?

I was two weeks late submitting copy for "Burt's Gold Page." When pressured by Editor Rockwell, I explained that I couldn't find my pen. His withering glance was the one he reserves for neocons.

I just found my pen—Gold is up $8.

Those of us who comment about the gold market suffer "writer's block" just like other writers. I suspect that this $8 rally will dissolve all blockages and articles telling us WHY it all happened will inundate us.

I enjoy fiction, and look forward to the varied opinions.

What I cannot countenance are those who actually CLAIM responsibility for the rally. These bozos believe what they tell you, but should be kept under house arrest.

They seem oblivious to just how tiny is the pro-gold constituency. They should know that everybody else is against.

This rally is "catch-up." The weakness of the US dollar against other currencies and the disastrous results of insane economic and political policies can no longer be suppressed.

The level of fear may increase, but it is at the expense of US prestige. Mandating prestige may work for a while, but eventually, market forces prevail and that's why gold was up $8 today.

The world is witness to ruthless empire building reminiscent of Britain in the nineteenth century. With one major difference; the Brits did it with style.

Picture David Niven, in starched uniform and pith helmet, oblivious to the 130 degree temperature, calmly doing-in the Fuzzy Wuzzies.

There are some great movies depicting English presence in Africa, India, and North America. *Gunga Din, Four Feathers,* and in recent days, *The Patriot.* I think I'll do an article about this genre of film.

One prediction I feel safe in making—there will be no future movie classics dealing with the war on Iraq.

December 16, 2006

LOUISE ALLOWED ME TO MAKE MY LETTER TO HER PUBLIC

I thought you might like to see my response to a lady with limited assets who was considering buying gold for the first time.

Hello again Louise.

If you want a dismal view of the world, talk to a gold dealer. The sad truth is that he is usually right, although his timing on when events unfurl may be a bit off.

These are difficult times and we are all getting poorer. And things are not going to improve any time soon.

Aren't you delighted to hear this good news?

In the old days, if you inherited $10,000 but didn't feel comfortable with stocks, bonds, real estate, etc., you kept the money in a savings account and although there wasn't much return, you were neutral.

When you needed your $10,000 it was there, buying power pretty much in tact.

Today, if you hold dollars in a money market, or savings account, there's no neutrality! The risk in holding dollars is insidious. The fact that the account book continues to show $10,000, gives false security.

As to buying gold, it never fails that after you place your first order, the price will drop the very next day. (If it doesn't happen on the first order, don't get smug, it will happen soon enough.)

So, pick your poison. Lose the value of your money without fanfare by holding dollars, or buy some gold and learn to live with the ups and downs.

The inexorable flow of history contains the answer; at some point in the future, the dollar will be dust and gold will glisten.

Here's another way to view it; Gold is often thought of as "insurance." If you insure your car, your violin, or your life, you don't want to collect on that policy.

You pay the premiums, but when it's done, all you have is a vague recollection of something called "peace of mind."

Not so with gold! Gold is the ONLY insurance where YOU hold the premium.

If you view it this way, holding gold is a "no lose" situation.

OK, these time-tested rationalizations should help you survive, without pain, every time the price of gold gyrates.

There will always be ugly days in the gold market, when the market seems to be saying, "gold is garbage."

If one of those days puts you in a panic, call me and I promise to hold your hand.

If I'm more worried than you, then you'll hold my hand.

Burt

March 20, 2003

I LISTENED TO WHAT I WAS SAYING AND GOT SCARED

Generally speaking, nobody pays any attention to me. My wife never listens, and my employees have learned to nod and smile at appropriate times—but they don't listen either.

When I talk to some customers, their eyes glaze over after 90 seconds, and often, one will doze off.

None of this deters me, however, as I no longer gauge success by the level of impact on the listener. I grade myself after each customer encounter.

("I was pretty good even if he didn't react to anything," I said. "How could I know the fellow spoke no English? I guess I'll have to brush up on my Cantonese," I muttered to myself.)

That was the start of a difficult day and the following actually happened. A new customer called with a challenge. He never really gave me a chance to present my views (another non-listener). I hope he reads what follows:

New Customer: "What would Camino Coin's price be for 20 ounces each American Eagles, Canadian Maples, and Krugerrands? I want the order prepaid and insured. Please fax me the net price and if you are low dealer, you've got the order."

Burt: "Sir, how many dealers will I be competing against?"

New Customer: "Let's see, you're the 6th or 7th and I'm calling one more."

I worked up some competitive prices and sent him a fax. A 60-ounce gold order is nothing to sneeze at.

I haven't heard from him yet, so I presume somebody beat my numbers. Being competitive is one thing, but if a dealer is always the cheapest, he could be courting disaster.

I agree with the New Customer that price is very important, but there are other things the buyer might want to consider:

(1) Who is he dealing with on the phone? Is it a commission salesman? Whom does he talk with if there's a problem? Most dealers don't want to rip anybody off. It's when a problem comes up that you find out what kind of folks you're dealing with.

(2) How does the company handle a lost shipment? Yes, all parcels are insured, but this is still a toughie. There's no standard industry policy I know of, but the customer can judge the dealership by their demeanor when it becomes clear the coins are lost.

(3) What is company policy regarding payment? Do they require "good-funds?" If a personal check is OK, how long before merchandise is shipped?

(4) Does the company maintain an inventory, or are all shipments coming from a 3rd party? (There is nothing necessarily wrong with 3rd party fulfillment, but the buyer should know it.)

(5) What is the company's buy-back policy?

(6) Is the company concerned with "Privacy Issues"? (This is a tough one to deal with by phone, but while chatting, you can get some feeling for the dealership's sensitivity to your privacy.)

(7) Are they on your "wave-length"? Have they heard of Ron Paul or Harry Browne? The salesman doesn't need to be a supporter of the Mises Institute—it wouldn't hurt—but he should have some comprehension of "sound-money."

(8) Are these fellows selling me bullion coins today at competitive prices only to get me in their file to pressure me over rare coins next time? Also, are they trading or selling my name to someone else?

Is this asking too many questions? Hell, no.

Let's see, 60 ounces of gold, that's about $22,000. You used to be able to buy a house for that. To the smaller buyer, one ounce of gold is a big deal.

Don't ask these questions after the fact.

Now that I'm on a roll, and you may still be listening, here are some other pearls. Actually, they are more like "No-No's."

When buying bullion gold, do not buy medallions (privately minted). Only a government can issue coins (money). I am not being a statist here. All I'm concerned with is liquidity for the customer. Coins have it, medallions don't.

Avoid any new government issues, even bullion coins. For example, the US Mint was considering a pure gold American coin to replace the 22-carat Eagle. If they do and it's as nice as it sounds, let the new item establish itself in the marketplace before you buy one. Liquidity again.

Avoid any proof or mints sets produced by any mint, especially the US Mint. These items are over-priced and can usually be bought a year or so later in the "after-market" for less than the original issue price.

Don't get suckered by special series of coins or medallions. I have a pal who loves antique automobiles and purchased a series of 100 medallions honoring these junkers. With what they cost him, he might have bought a real Mercedes.

When selecting a coin dealer, his reputation should always be top priority. But be sure you have the right dealer for the right occasion. You may have a terrific coin shop in your neighborhood, but he may not be the right fellow to sell you 10 Krugerrands. Division of labor.

Finally, never do any business by phone—unless you initiate the call.

Wait a sec: I think I already told you that last week. My apologies. Now I know why people stop listening.

February 21, 2003

NEW GOLD BUYERS BETTER READ THIS!

After a glittering rally, the gold market sputtered this week and took an ugly turn.

"The minute I buy something, the price always goes down," a new gold buyer complained.

In less than 24 months the price of an ounce of gold went from $253 to $380, an amazing increase of about 50 percent. In the last few trading days, the price fell sharply to $353—a drop of 8 percent.

Some of the yellow metal's new fans and some old ones as well were stunned. Everything pointed to "onward and upward" for the gold price. The increases were so plausible: the weakness of the US Dollar, the collapsing equity markets all over the world and the sickening plunge to war.

How could the price of gold come down so sharply, so quickly?

Gary North tried to explain people's reaction to market disappointments with what he called "The Confirmation Blues." It goes something like this:

In order to purchase their first ounce of gold, the new customer has to overcome a lifetime of convention. This requires a fresh view of history; adopting new gurus, a revamping of their family's attitude toward savings. And, the recognition that failed government policy is usually the root of many of the problems.

When the new customer purchases that ounce of gold he is voting, "No." No, to stocks and bonds. No, to paper money, No, to just about everything.

There's an element of courage here and the new buyer NEEDS the market to confirm that he made the right decision. If the market goes up, all doubts disappear. The sharper the increase, the greater the confirmation.

Sadly, it doesn't always work out that way. Instead of going up and confirming, the price drops, leading to "The Confirmation Blues." It's not just losing dollars, it's an attack on self-worth.

One could suffer the Confirmation Blues in any investment area, but because gold is so counter cultural, so "out of the main stream," suffering the Gold Confirmation Blues is the most virulent form of the virus.

There is no easy antidote to the Blues. If the market is slow to recover, eventually the pain dulls. "If you hang by the neck long enough you get used to it," to quote Southern wisdom. Better yet, when the price goes up about 5 percent over cost, immunity builds. Bouts with the Blues became less frequent and painful.

In the meanwhile, I respectfully offer some band-aids to help you deal with the Blues. (I generally charge $4 an hour for this counseling, but, I waive the hourly fee for LRC readers.)

As an aside, a customer I had known for years asked if I would appraise a box of foreign coins and at what cost. My response was the little joke about $4 an hour. To which he responded, "It won't take an hour." I told him not to worry, that I would pro-rate.

I guess he was telling me the value of my time.

1. Don't watch the price every minute.

2. Keep in mind that the King doesn't like gold, never has, never will. Remember that the King is a powerful enemy to the gold market and lower gold prices can often be placed at his door. (See my article "The King Doesn't Like Gold.")

3. In the US gold is traded at the Comex, a futures market. This means that all trades are heavily leveraged. It doesn't matter what the commodity, technical factors like "open interest" and "short squeezes" become key elements in price changes. When trading is leveraged, the buyer of 100 ounces of gold, for example, puts up a fraction of the total value. This leads to speculation and exaggerated price moves both up and down.

4. Don't panic. Well, panic if you must, but don't sell anything while you're panicked.

5. Keep in mind that you have bought "insurance" with your gold. In a way, if gold is a fever thermometer telling us how sick we are, we don't need $1,000 an ounce gold. This kind of thinking leads to sound mental health.

If all of the above fails and the gold price really worries you, call me and I will hold your hand. Unless I'm more worried than you. Then you can hold my hand.

March 7, 2001

How Many Drachma Do I Get for a Reagan?

Please don't tell me this government doesn't know how to bury a President.

There are critics who contend that Reagan's eight-day, bicoastal journey to the next world never came close to the medieval pageantry practiced by our British brethren when they crown a King, for example.

For all their pomp, though, the Brits know it's pure "show biz." Simply Shakespearean theatre. Nobody's sacrificing their life for the new king, nor are they promoting a Crusade to smash the infidel. (Such assignments are reserved for George W's partner-in-crime, Tony Blair.)

The Reagan Event was more than a Hollywood epic: it was pure nationalism, elevating a B-grade movie actor into a mythological being, noble, kind, humorous, tough, principled and God-fearing, a giant worthy of supreme power. He could fight you "tooth and nail," but he was never mean-spirited.

He was—a god and everyman at the same time.

Hundreds of political hacks, all wearing $3,000 suits, trudged from one TV camera to another giving testament to the great man and telling their favorite "Dutch" anecdote.

I was getting groggy, but I think I heard the following. If so, it deserves the "Windbag Prize":

"Ron and myself were sitting alone talking about matters of state when Gorby entered the room and his fly was unzipped. We were on the brink of WWIII, but Ron said something so funny that Gorby nearly fell to the floor laughing, and the crisis passed."

The days droned on, and the incessant stream of testimonials never seemed to end. All the while, the main theme was jack-hammered home: Great men of power are ecumenical. They cut across party lines: Reagan. FDR. Lincoln.

Even die-hard California Democrats who still gag when they see Bonzo the chimp in late night movies, bought the package and now, like sleepwalkers, have come to terms with Reagan's surpassing greatness. Or at least they did for the eight days.

Things have quieted down. It's Sunday and the clean-up crews are sweeping up the confetti. My regular soap, pre-empted the entire week, returns on Monday. Thank the Lord.

It's as if we've been on holiday, and now we're back to life's banalities.

Back to those two bloody wars.

Back to watching Americans stumble through minefields, blindly following George W's leadership.

Back to politics as usual and the tedious presidential campaign.

Come to think of it, it wasn't really a holiday for the rest of us. This epic Reagan event was contrived to allow the state's present administration, its camp followers and the media (if there's a difference) to sort out the lies and deceit.

Ronald Reagan suffered two deaths, the first with the coming of his dementia. The second gave "Them" the opportunity to place him in the pantheon of state religion, and—

It provided the much-needed "breathing space" as indicated above.

But wait . . . while we were all teary-eyed and ecumenical, a seething power struggle was being fought out of camera range. The Reagan Loyalists, not satisfied with a federal airport carrying the great man's name, now required his imprint on the money.

The "Ronald Reagan Legacy Project" (there really is such a group) began its efforts years ago. In addition to a government Reagan memorial in every county in the United States, they favor a Reagan $10 bill, replacing Alexander Hamilton, who was not even a president, they argue.

Others, proud to compare Ronnie with FDR, feel he should supplant that great welfare-warfare president whose face has dominated the dime for almost six decades. Rumor has it that Nancy, outraged at the thought of "Ronnie's" likeness on small change, torpedoed the plan.

Mitch McConnell (R-KY), number two man in the federal senate, is pushing for the Reagan $10. Not to be outdone, "former libertarian," Dana Rohrabacher (R-CA) is doubling the ante by proposing a Reagan $20 bill.

Congressman Jeff Miller (R-FL) is the Reagan 50-cent piece "point man." He wants to eliminate JFK's countenance from the half dollar and substitute Reagan's image

(There are still customers at my coin company, who, when buying US silver half dollars, insist that 1964 Kennedy halves be EXCLUDED from their order.)

I suspect that the $10 Reagan may prevail, with one of those prettified (or is that deified) portraits that now adorn the fiat dollar in the various denominations.

All of this reminds me of my father Max's strong views about retaining the "dollar" as the name of our currency. He felt it was a mistake.

For those who have not suffered amnesia of the monetary past, the US dollar once had terrific buying power, thanks to gold and silver and carried a worldwide prestige unlike the current buck.

Retaining the name of something that no longer exists leads to confusion. Other countries think nothing of knocking off zeros and renaming their currency.

"Let's call it a 'Schmollar'," Max used to say.

Well, here's my plan: Let's eliminate the word, "dollar," no longer defined as a weight of precious metal and, in its place, substitute "Reagan." This will silence the combatants vying for their favorite place for Reagan's face.

Ronnie will be on every denomination of coin and currency.

It won't take us long to get accustomed to hearing the following while people exchange currency or make change:

"How many drachma to the Reagan?"

"Can you give me two Reagan tens for a twenty?"

"I need three 25-cent Reagans for the meter. Can you break a Reagan buck?"

"I'll bet you a 5 Reagan that George W wins the election."

Who knows, the "Reagan" might circulate for eternity.

Fortunately, to quote a former, prescient French finance minister, "eternity in monetary affairs is of short duration."

June 14, 2004

THE ONLY TIME THE US MINT GET'S IT RIGHT IS WHEN THEY DO IT WRONG

Speaking of stupidity, I've been there and the
US Congress wins awards for theirs.

I never thought I'd be drawing a line in the sand at Radio Shack.

"Why must I fill out anything? I'm buying the digital telephone with cash," I said through clenched teeth. "It shouldn't matter that I'm prepaying for phone time."

"I don't care how you pay. If you don't fill out the form I can't sell you the phone. It's a rule," Assitant Manager Ned responded, not realizing we were hurtling toward a Constitutional confrontation.

"OK, I'll give my name and address but I refuse to fill in 'Occupation' on Line 2."

"No 'Occupation,' no phone," said Ned.

Ned was one of these "virtual" young people I seem to encounter all over these days and I trust he will worry a bit when he reads how I answered, 'Occupation' on Line 2 : 'Luddite Assassin, Specializing in Low-end, High-techers'."

All of which started me thinking about "Occupations." I formerly held the belief that what one did for a living told everything about him like the old quiz show, "What's My Line?" Once the guest's occupation was finally revealed, there was little else we needed to know.

I'm not so sure about that now. After all, one's occupation is not ordained, but includes luck (good or bad), ambition (often misguided), compromise (selling-out?) and, most significantly, decisions made by others.

To demonstrate how unpredictable the career path can be, I submit this brief biographical note. In 1951, I was a twenty-two-year-old determined to avoid the draft and the certain death that followed in Korea. There was nothing ideological about it. It was fear and cowardice, pure and simple.

Draft day closed in and it was like awaiting the executioner's call. Finally, fate intervened. The Air Force, suffering a severe shortage of pilots, cut their enlistment term from four to two years to attract aspiring aviation cadets who were reluctant to enlist for four years, fearing they might wash out of flight training. The two year deal was terrific and I was first in line the next morning at the Air Force Recruiting Office.

I breezed through the rigid Flight Training medical exams (it was amazing how much my general state of health had improved since the Draft Board physical exam I took weeks earlier) and I began to think career.

Fantasizing:

The gorgeous blonde asks, "What business are you in?"

"I'm an Air Force jet pilot," I modestly admit.

Years later, now grey at the temples:

The gorgeous blond asks, "What business are you in?"

"I'm a commercial airline captain," I modestly admit.

Not bad as "occupations" go, especially to a twenty-two-year-old.

Unfortunately, the Air Force decided that my flight training would be as a navigator/bombardier. That didn't offer much promise for the future, as one could hardly go through life listing "bombardier" as an "occupation." Although Ned at Radio Shack might have been impressed.

Pay no attention to "occupations." If you want to know the "real person," check out what he or she does at leisure. A friend, Doc Arnold, makes his living as a gynecologist and his waiting room is always filled to capacity. A few years ago his wife, concerned that he was becoming too involved with his work, pressured him to take up some hobby. She had no idea what her advice would lead to.

It may be hard to believe, but friend Arnold actually reads insurance policies for recreation and exchanges Christmas cards with the US Bureau of Weights and Measures. It goes without saying that he is the dullest fellow in the county, unless you need help deciphering the clouded language of your Blue Cross Health Plan.

I must confess that I, too, have a hidden interest, which approaches addiction. And causes great concern to family members. They bring my meals on trays as I sit glued to the TV watching tapes of Congressional hearings on C-SPAN. Don't mock. Once you get to know the actors and capture the rhythm of the dialogue you realize you're witnessing high drama.

It hardly matters the topic: the pollution of streams in New Mexico, or the funding of the FBI, the panels are always the same; boring testimony, prepared by boring lawyers, read by boring people. Fortunately, most of the transcripts and prepared testimony never again see the light of day. Only Congressional staff members are forced to take the material seriously.

I'll admit that getting anything out of watching these bozos is like learning to enjoy caviar. It's sort of an acquired taste. But, should you ever forget how pompous, arrogant, and dangerous government could be, tune in to some Congressional hearings and "watch them make sausage."

Which brings us to that exciting time of the year when the "Making Sausage Congressional Awards" are about due. 2002 has produced some memorable events and here is a peek at some of the award highlights:

BEST VOTING RECORD FOR AN INDICTED CONGRESSMAN
—Rep. James Traficant, D-OH

WORST VOTING RECORD FOR A NON-INDICTED SENATOR—
Sen. Robert Torricelli, D-NJ

LIFETIME ACHIEVEMENT AWARD
—Sen. Strom Thurmond, R-SC

Sen. Thurman nicely symbolizes the disintegration of the Republic over the past four decades.

The Democrat and Republican Congressional Leadership announced the striking of a gold medal honoring Rep. Ron Paul, R-TX. The medallion is inscribed as follows:

"We Deeply Respect You, But Hope You Soon Return to the Practice of Medicine."

And, finally, the "Making Sausage Award For the Best Congressional Hearing of 2002."

This award goes to the Congressional proceeding which best portrays the waste, arrogance, and ineptitude of a government program.

The winner is—the US Senate Appropriation Committee's Treasury Subcommittee Hearing on the Sacagawea Dollar.

LRC and Mises.org readers know a great deal about the "disastrous Golden Dollar."

The Subcommittee hearing took place on Friday, May 17, 2002. The critical matter at hand was the Sacagawea Dollar. Why was it not circulating? What could be done to increase demand, and the BIG question: Should the program be continued with additional funding?

There was no debate, little disagreement, and few accusations with just a wee bit of blame placed on the Fed. The room reeked of bipartisan embarrassment.

Here are some highlights from the hearings:

Senator Byron Dorgan (D-ND), Chairman, very much in favor of the Sacagawea because the Shoshone Indian was from his home state, made some telling observations:

"I never received a Sacagawea coin in change."

"My contention is the program is a failure."

"We must determine what must be done to turn the situation around."

"The banks haven't seen much demand for them," one expert said. "Retailers and businesses say there hasn't been much demand for them."

Prime witness, Mint Director Henrietta Holsman Fore, is a charming lady, clearly someone the senators were not about to attack.

With pride she reminded the Senators that under a recent deal ten million Sacagaweas would be distributed at NASCAR racetracks this year. (At the end of fiscal 2001 over three-hundred-twenty million coins were in storage.) She implored these important men to support any program to get the federal government to use the coins more.

It's Fore's opinion that the Susan B. Anthony Dollar is part of the problem. On occasions when Sacagaweas are ordered from the Fed, they come mixed with the despised Susan B. Anthony. To solve this problem, Fore advised that the Mint is considering removing the Susan B. from circulation.

A highlight of the hearings was the appearance of Amy Mossett, wearing traditional Indian garb. She testified that on the cab trip to the hearing she tipped the driver a Sacagawea. Dismayed, she reported that he didn't know what it was.

There is a tag line to this Sacagawea story.

Earlier this month it was reported that two US Mint employees were charged with stealing and selling five $1 Sacagawea coins that eventually resold for $138,000. That's an average of about $28,000 each. What's that? A coin that they can't give away fetches five figures?

The five coins were mint errors. In this instance the Sacagawea planchet (coin blank) was struck by a faulty die. The front (obverse) of this die contained a Washington quarter. The underside (reverse) of the die held the Sacagawea. The result was a "mule," an error of such consequence that many coin dealers would sell their children into slavery just to obtain one.

There's an irony here. Since they ceased producing silver coinage the only way the US mint can make their products desirable is to screw them up.

July 8, 2002

THE WAR BETWEEN THE SEXES AND
EMULATING "MR. FIRST NIGHTER"

H.L. MENCKEN'S
IN DEFENSE OF WOMEN

G ive me a minute and I'll list the advantages that accrue with aging. Unhhh. Can I have another minute? If the years provide any accumulated wisdom, it is buried under layers of scar tissue. The other, overrated reward of surviving seven decades, "experience," was once defined as the residue of failure.

Strange, but it is in the war of ideas that senior citizen status brings some relief. Critics become less venomous when dealing with older folks. Which leads to Blumert's Fifth Law:

"The assault on career and reputation abates as defamers move on to younger, more vigorous targets." Or, put another way, why should the enemy expend energy and resources destroying the victim when the "grim reaper" will be doing it soon enough at lower cost?

"I've reached the age when nobody cares what I write about," I advised a friend.

"Nobody ever cares what you write about," he muttered.

"I'm free at last, and safe in my dotage. I can write on the most controversial subjects and nobody will care."

"You can write on any subject and nobody will care," the muttering continued.

293

294 — Bagels, Barry Bonds, and Rotten Politicians

"I'll blow the lid off the hottest subjects: The Differences Between the Races; Stalin, Hitler, Roosevelt, and Churchill: Who Were The Real Criminals? Homosexuality: Is It Genetics, the Environment, or Moral Decadence?"

To begin our search for truth at any cost, consider this question: "What is the single greatest threat to the economic well-being of the average man?" Illness? Corrupt government? Wrong. The correct answer is, Woman.

Our exposé: "How Women Have Manipulated Men Economically And Generally Hoodwinked Them From Time Immemorial."

There is little scholarship on the subject, no conferences, and the struggle between the sexes is so one-sided that the brainwashed victims are not even aware of their plight.

I have extensive files that conclusively reveal the insidious plot women have devised to dominate men. Unfortunately, my wife won't let me use them. She has also confiscated my autographed picture of Jessie Helms and my Wilt Chamberlain sports card.

She thinks she's in total control, but I smoke my cigars in the garage whenever I want to, whether she likes it or not.

But who needs my files? We have H.L. Mencken, America's greatest essayist and man of letters, and his brilliant two-hundred-dred-page book, *In Defense of Women* (New York: Alfred Knopf, 1918). The book continues to be controversial through its many printings. Mencken was perplexed that women viewed his classic as an attack. The point he was making was that it was the superiority of women that had led to their dominance over men in the important aspects of life.

Following, the great man makes his case and helps mine as well. All the quotes are from Mencken's *In Defense of Women.*

H.L.M. ON WOMEN AND THEIR UNDERSTANDING OF MEN

"A man's womenfolk, whatever their outward show of respect for his merit and authority, always regard him secretly as an ass, and with something akin to pity."

"She may envy her husband, true enough in certain details. She may envy him his masculine liberties, his invulnerable complacency, his talent for petty vices, his soothing romanticism. But she never envies him his puerile ego; she never envies him his shoddy and preposterous soul."

H.L.M. ON MARRIAGE

"The very fact that marriages occur at all is a proof, indeed, that they are more cool-headed and more adept in employing their intellectual resources, for it is plainly to a man's interest to avoid marriage as long as possible, and as plainly to a woman's interests to make a favorable marriage as soon as she can."

"He may want a cook and not a partner in his business, or a partner in his business and not a cook. But in order to get the precise thing or things that he wants, he has to take a lot of other things that he doesn't want."

"The truth is that, in a world almost divested of intelligible idealism, and hence dominated by a senseless worship of the practical, marriage offers the best career that the average woman can reasonably aspire to."

"But of all things that a woman gains by marriage the most valuable is economic security."

H.L.M. on "Good Looks" and How Much More Sensibly Women Deal with the Subject than Men

"A shop girl, perhaps, may plausibly fall in love with a moving-picture actor, and a half-idiotic old widow may succumb to a college boy with shoulders like the Parthenon. Women know how little such purely superficial values are worth."

"The weight of opinion among women is decidedly against the woman who falls in love with an Apollo. She is regarded, at best, as a flighty creature, and at worst, as one pushing bad taste to the verge of indecency."

H.L.M. on Sentimentality (Men Are and Women Aren't)

"One frequently hears of remarried widowers who continue to moon about their dead first wives, but for a remarried widow to show any such sentimentality would be a nine days wonder. Once replaced, a dead husband is expunged from the minutes. And so is a dead love."

"A man, speaking of his wife to other men, always praises her extravagantly. Boasting about her soothes his vanity—but when two women talk of their husbands it is mainly atrocities that they describe."

H.L.M. on Women in Present American Society (and How They Created It)

"If the average American husband wants a sound dinner he must go to a restaurant to get it, just as if he wants to refresh himself with the society of charming and well-behaved children, he has to go to an orphan asylum."

"The result is that they swarm in the women's clubs, and waste their time listening to bad poetry, worse music, and still worse lectures on Maeterlinck, Balkan politics and the subconscious."

"It is among such women that one observes the periodic rages for Bergsonism, paper-bag cookery, the Montessori method—and other such follies, so pathetically characteristic of our culture."

"She may neglect her home, gossip and lounge about all day, put impossible food upon his table, steal his small change, pry into his private papers—accuse him falsely of preposterous adulteries, affront his friends, and lie about him to the neighbors—and he can do nothing."

"Let him undertake the slightest rebellion, over and beyond mere rhetorical protest, and the whole force of the state comes down upon him."

"Today, by the laws of most American states-laws proposed, in most cases, by maudlin and often notoriously extravagant agitators, and passed by sentimental orgy—all of the old rights of the husband have been converted into obligations."

H.L.M. ON HOW THEY DID IT

"I am convinced that the average American woman, whatever her deficiencies, is greatly superior to the average American man."

"There was no weakness of man that she did not penetrate and take advantage of. There was no trick that she did not put to effective use. There was no device so bold and inordinate that it daunted her."

"Women, as a class, believe in none of the preposterous rights, duties and pious obligations that men are forever gabbling about. Their habitual attitude toward men is one of aloof disdain, and their habitual attitude toward what men believe in, and get into sweats about, and bellow for, is substantially the same. It takes twice as long to convert a body of women to some new fallacy as it takes to convert a body of men."

H.L.M. ON WOMEN AND THE LAW

"Women litigants almost always win their cases, not as is commonly assumed, because the jurymen fall in love with them but simply and solely because they are clear-headed, resourceful, implacable and without qualms."

"Any man who is so unfortunate as to have a serious controversy with a woman, say in the departments of finance, theology or amour, must inevitably carry away from it a sense of having passed through a dangerous and almost gruesome experience."

Today, *In Defense of Women* is sort of a reverse-cult classic. Women intuit that what Mencken disseminates is dangerous and sheds light on what their sorority would just as soon see remain dormant. The small group of men who discover *In Defense of Women*, usually too late to help themselves, pass tattered copies on to their sons.

If you buy one, conceal it as you used to your *Playboy* magazine.

If you get caught, blame me, as I'm over seventy and totally exempt from being indicted.

October 2, 2000

SHANGHEI AND MAO

MAO: THE UNKNOWN STORY
BURTON S. BLUMERT AND JUNE MORRALL
REVIEW THIS SHOCKING BOOK

L ike a bolt of lightening, Alexander Solzhenitsyn's master-piece *Gulag Archipelago*, published in 1974, destroyed in an instant over fifty years of lies and deceit about the Soviet Union and its leaders. Stalin would never again be seen as kindly Uncle Joe, but as a ruthless killer of millions.

Some scholars suggest that it was Solzhenitsyn's revelations that led to the collapse of the Soviet Union rather than Ronald Reagan's strategy of "spending the 'evil empire' into oblivion."

Like the "Gulag," we finally have this extraordinary work by Jung Chang and husband Jon Halliday that will forever end the web of lies that has insulated Chairman Mao from his true place in history as the worst murderer the world has known.

Mao: The Unknown Story (Jung Chang and Jon Halliday, New York: Knopf, 2005) is a step-by-step guide to how this evil man used terror as a tool to subjugate every Chinese citizen. Fear of a horrible, slow death, torture, and humiliation silenced every voice. Only what the Chairman said or thought mattered.

You must read this book.

It wasn't fashionable to criticize Mao in the West, particularly in the US. In San Francisco's Chinatown, only the local Kuomintang, Chiang Kai-shek's Nationalist Party, attacked Mao and they were marginalized as "reactionaries."

During the hippie era of the 1960s, in many households, Mao's *Little Red Book* was a popular Christmas stocking stuffer.

Mao was thought of as a modern Confucius, a gentle peasant who had freed China from its corrupt warlords.

Was it the media that promoted this false image about the worst tyrant who ever lived? It's time to know the real Mao.

You must read this book.

Clearly the authors despise Mao, so it was essential that they support their 650-page treatise with an additional 200 pages of meticulously researched notes. Not just scholarly citations, but countless interviews with people who worked for, or otherwise knew Mao personally, and survived the violence of his regime. The notes also include many official documents that have not been seen in the West before.

Mao wanted to impress Stalin and modeled his state after that killer-thug. He then proceeded to "one-up" his Soviet teacher. Stalin would wait for the right moment to use violence and treachery against his enemies. Mao was brazen and did not need a timetable. He used torture and murder on a daily basis to control fellow communists.

Chairman Mao made it known that his tactics were never on holiday. Often his punishment was meted out in front of huge crowds. This was certain to spread the news quickly. "Watch out! Everyone is a potential spy. And you could be next."

The masses were easy to control. He simply starved them to death.

In the end, Mao had either killed or imprisoned, or sent to work camps so many of his former officials that he had run out of credible bureaucrats to run the day-to-day business of government.

He had no choice but to "rehabilitate" some that he had purged earlier, like the "Capitalist Roader," Deng Xiao-ping. These men hated Mao, and the Chairman made a critical error in underestimating how they would undermine him as his health began to fail.

Most interesting was the revelation that the Nationalist leader Chiang Kai-shek (who later fled to Taiwan) was thwarted in his earlier negotiations with Mao because the Soviets were holding Chiang's son "hostage." By appeasing Stalin and Mao, Chiang hoped he would get his son back.

During his reign of terror, Mao forced the peasants to grow huge amounts of wheat and eggs and other foodstuffs to give to Stalin in return for technical information on how to build The Bomb. Mao starved his already poverty-stricken people and conducted public executions if quotas were not met. Business as usual for Chairman Mao.

Mao turned the country into one big concentration camp and he was the gatekeeper, allowing in selected outsiders, controlling what they saw so that when they returned home they would glorify what the Chairman had accomplished for his people.

Mao had little difficulty locating western media whores who would promote the lies about Mao and life in Red China and spread them like a deadly virus. There should be a special place in Hell for these people.

If there is a deficiency in this book, *Mao: The Unknown Story*, it is that after hundreds of pages outlining Mao's unspeakable cruelty, the reader becomes numb and desensitized. The fault is not the author's, but with the endless crush of evidence present.

As an antidote to becoming desensitized, keep in mind that this is not about a madman like Pol Pot. Mao may, in fact, match the crazed Cambodian in savagery. But, there's a major difference; Today, Pol Pot, often considered a protégé of Mao's, is a statistic in the World List of Lunatics, while Mao retains his place as a great figure in world history. This remains true twenty years after the Chairman's death. Well, until this Chang and Halliday masterpiece.

You must read this book.

Here are some tidbits from *Mao: The Unknown Story*:

- A conservative estimate is that 70 million perished—in peacetime—as a result of Mao's misrule.

- During the famous, "Long March," rather than trudging along with the troops, Mao reclined in an elaborate "litter" weighted down with his favorite books and other comforts, all carried by peasants forced to perform like pack animals.

- Mao spent about US$4.1 billion to create a Chinese atomic bomb. That money if spent on food would have saved the 38 million Chinese lives lost in the famine.

In a recent TV ad promoting the 2008 Summer Olympic Games to be held in Beijing, China, the camera focused on what appears to be Tiananmen Square. In the center of the screen, lo and behold, is a giant portrait of the despicable Chairman Mao.

Why do nations continue to show reverence for their tyrants?

Yes an economic miracle is taking place in today's China. The by-product of such an explosion is always freedom. China is a long way from being a totally free society, but, if this book, *Mao: The Unknown Story*, leads to the Mao portraits finally being torn down, that will be a giant symbolic stride toward individual freedom in China.

And maybe in other countries as well.

August 18, 2005

THE QUEEN

PORTRAYED BY THE MAGNIFICENT HELEN MIRREN

The commute over Devil's Slide was uneventful but I still sighed with relief as I pulled into the garage and shut down the engine. The fog was rolling in, Pumpkin days were behind us, and it was good to be home.

But, it was not to be.

"We can just make the 4:20 showing of *The Queen* in Palo Alto if we leave right now," my dear wife said breathlessly. There was no negotiating. She's all business when she dons those Grand Prix driving gloves.

"Look, isn't this the movie about Queen Elizabeth I, who reigned in the sixteenth century?" I whined. "Wasn't she beheaded, or locked up in the tower? In any case, do we really want to see a period piece movie, where they all talk funny?"

She rolled her eyes once or twice, and I noted that we were already on Highway 280 heading south.

The Queen, she sniffed, "is about Queen Elizabeth II, the present monarch, stars the great actor Helen Mirren, and is directed by Stephen Frears, whose 1985 film, *My Beautiful Launderette*, is a cult classic."

My spirits improved as we exited at Page Mill Road. I was now minutes away from a large-sized popcorn with the hope that they used real butter and, more importantly, I reflected that Helen Mirren is one of the finest actors of our time. She was dazzling as Jane Tennison in PBS's *Prime Suspect* series, and remarkable as the brilliant but difficult Russian émigré in *The*

Passion of Ayn Rand. Helen Mirren does not disappoint as The Queen. She is at the top of her game.

The story line of the film covers those shattering events in the UK during 1997. Tony Blair, amazingly portrayed by Michael Sheen, has become the first Labour Prime Minister in about twenty years. He is young—Blair was born in 1953, the year Elizabeth ascended the throne—and handsome. Although raised in privilege and properly educated, he is a socialist "new man."

His first official meeting with the Queen sets the tone for the entire film. Elizabeth, reserved, formal, but armed with a rapier wit, duels with Blair. She advises that he is her fourteenth Prime Minister. He is amused by the monarch, but remains respectful throughout.

Blair's wife, Cherie, does not share this respect. She is in sympathy with the 25 percent of the British population who believe the monarchy is an expensive anachronism and should be abolished.

To the tradition-bound Elizabeth, Blair might as well be a rock-star.

And then . . . the dark event that turns our story from a gentle tale of a collision of manners to a political crisis that could threaten the UK's constitutional monarchy:

Princess Diana is tragically killed in a motor accident in Paris.

To Elizabeth, this event is the final act of the dismal drama that Diana created for the Royal family. The movie, *The Queen*, does not dwell on the "sordid" events that led to Diana's divorce from Prince Charles. The audience is reminded, however, that Diana has been "excommunicated" from the royal family.

The only potential problem Elizabeth sees is the need to protect the young princes, Harry and William, from the evil media. In this she is supported by her consort Prince Philip— well portrayed by American actor James Cromwell. Her mother, "the Queen mum," is also quick to offer her full support.

The royal family never once considers that the young princes should be mourning the dead mother they dearly loved. Shut off the TV sets, hide the newspapers, this was the royal strategy. Prince Philip decides that fresh air is the best remedy and takes the boys hunting on the 40,000 acres that make up the Balmoral Castle grounds.

As the days pass the outpouring of grief for the dead princess rages like a forest fire. To the royal family this outpouring is incomprehensible.

The headlines begin to turn ugly; why is the flag at Buckingham not flying at half-mast? Why is Princess Diana not being afforded a royal funeral? When will Queen Elizabeth break her silence and acknowledge the tragedy of Diana's death?

From this point, *The Queen* becomes an elegant nail-biter. On the one hand, we have the intractable Elizabeth and her royal entourage clinging to traditions and views forged through 1,000 years.

On the other—average Brits who revere a different stripe of royalty: Elton John, Madonna, Elizabeth Taylor, the Spice Girls, and even the likes of Tony Blair.

To these subjects, Diana was the real princess.

The Queen relies heavily on archived tapes and films. It is a sticky matter to successfully weave old images into a screenplay. Director Frears does it artfully.

First, we see old BBC tapes of an ocean of flowers placed by grieving Brits around Buckingham and the other palaces. Then, seamlessly, Mirren's Elizabeth walking amidst the bouquets. She reads some of the attached messages and is stunned by the anger directed against the Royal family. She is in agony, yet, never buckles, never loses the royal demeanor that defined her life.

There is a sadness as Mirren's queen grudgingly accedes to the pressures put upon her. She is powerless, yet, never loses her grace.

Finally, Helen Mirren's Elizabeth realizes what we knew all along. We live in a "Pop Culture" and even tradition is fading fast.

This article first appeared on HalfMoonBayMemories.com.

October 31, 2006

BURT GOES TO THE MOVIES KICKING AND SCREAMING

When my dear wife begins to sound like her mother, I know there's no room for negotiations.

"We're going to see *Million Dollar Baby* on Tuesday and *The Aviator* on Thursday. I want to see these movies NOW, not on TV in 2008."

"And, there's no room for negotiations on this one, Blumert."

"But, we were at the movies just last month," I responded without much hope.

"Last month? It was the summer of 2003 and we saw *Seabiscuit*. How could you forget? Yours was the only review that panned that wonderful movie. The people at Bay Meadows Race Track, Seabiscuit's 'home,' were so offended that they actually considered barring you from their track."

"Just another example of the Power Elite suppressing dissenting views, but that's history, and my present concern is dealing with two movies in one week. I have an idea. Let's see them at the Drive-In. At least we can have a beer and a burger while watching, and if the movie drags a bit, I can take a nap. That Drive-In just south of Candlestick Park is my favorite."

"The last Drive-In anywhere near San Francisco was moth-balled by 1991. Get with it, Blumert. We're going to see *Million Dollar Baby* on Tuesday at the Cinema 12 Multiplex in the Mall and on Thursday, *The Aviator* is playing at the new Cinema 47 Megaplex, downtown San Francisco. We will be there."

"Look, it's not that I don't enjoy Clint Eastwood and DiCaprio, it's the multi- and mega-atrocities they call theatres that I despise. They remind me of bus stations, where finding your movie is like locating the platform your bus departs from."

In the old days, going to the movies was something special. It hardly mattered what film was showing. An evening at your neighborhood movie house was a social event. When I went I never failed to encounter neighbors and school chums. On special occasions, we went "downtown" to the "Roxy," or "Paramount." They were breathtaking examples of Hollywood's Golden Age; magnificent movie palaces of the sort found in almost every major urban center. (A few have been restored, like the Paramount in Oakland, California.)

At New York City's Paramount in the late 1930s and early '40s, the customer was treated to more than a First Run movie. You got an Organ Recital AND a star-studded variety show. This was my first taste of "live" entertainment. There they were, I could almost touch them: Louis Armstrong, Danny Kaye, and Sinatra creating memories that endured a lifetime.

Back to reality and Tuesday at the Cinema 12 Multiplex. As my wife had predicted, there we were, standing in the ticket line.

"Don't forget to tell them that we want to see *Million Dollar Baby* in Theatre #7 and that you get a senior's discount," my wife reminded. On a past occasion, I had forgotten which movie we came to see, panicked when asked, bought the wrong ticket and suffered through Disney's *101 Dalmatians*, engulfed by screaming, microbe-infested children.

Our fellow ticket buyers were grim-faced. If you didn't know otherwise, you'd think we were all waiting in line for a flu shot.

Built in the late 1960s, Cinema 12 was an early multiplex and like many similar across the nation, located near a Regional Shopping Center. I'm no construction maven, but I suspect that they were all slapped together cheaply and quickly.

The Men's Room was too small; the popcorn too expensive ($4 for a small bucket) and the butter-like substance squirted on the popcorn, close to rancid. The candy bars offered came in super jumbo size only, at super jumbo prices, and every soft drink dispensed was different than the one before or after.

"Small, medium or large," the youngster asked, pointing to varied red plastic cups.

"Can I get a bottle of Coke instead of that thing you're mixing back there?" I snickered.

Her answer exposed me as a pretentious horse's rear-end.

"Gee, sir, I don't know if we have those, but I'll ask my manager.

We finally located the small room they called "Theatre # 7," which was showing *Million Dollar Baby*. It was so dark that we nervously groped our way looking for empty seats. In the process I stepped on one fellow's foot and almost sat on his wife.

Fortunately, there was little danger of falling down as our shoes were glued to the floor by a sticky, sugary substance that is a nuisance to the moviegoer, but a deadly trap for small animals.

Local gossip has it that Cinema 12 is scheduled for demolition, and if true, it's not a moment too soon.

"Don't despair, Blumert. On Thursday, we see *The Aviator* at the brand new Megaplex in San Francisco. People are raving about the place."

They're "raving," huh? Well, nobody's asked, but here is my critique of that monstrosity; the most unusual aspect of watching a movie at the Megaplex is that you might be 800 feet above street level. As Tony Bennett might put it, you're "half way to the stars."

The facility is built vertically, with each of the 4 levels connected by hundreds of feet of escalator. As we ground our way up to level 4, I couldn't shake the mental image of being a patron at the Megaflex 47 during an 8.5 earthquake.

The tub of popcorn is $6; the candy bars the most expensive in town and the fancy European-style coffee house, a resounding dud. We had our coffee and biscuits across the street at Starbucks after the show.

"I hate to admit it, Blumert, but I totally agree with your opinions about these dismal modern movie factories and how much more we enjoyed our neighborhood theatres."

"Hold everything. I've got to get that on tape. Having you agree with me on anything qualifies for the archives."

From the 1920s through the '50s every small town in America had a movie theatre on Main Street. In the larger cities, each neighborhood had its own version.

They are all gone; disappeared from the face of the earth. Well, almost all gone. San Francisco had forty-five neighborhood movie houses through the early 1950s. Remarkably, twelve still exist. The unusual cultural make-up of San Francisco's neighborhoods may account for this anomaly, but that analysis is for another day.

Growing up in my neighborhood in New York City, the Waldorf Theatre was our entertainment Mecca. Any kid who could raise the 10 or 25-cent admission showed up for the Saturday matinee.

We got our money's worth: an Errol Flynn swashbuckler and a Jean Arthur comedy, a Hanna-Barbera cartoon, a Flash Gordon or Buck Rogers chapter episode with the superhero facing sure death every week only to survive at the beginning of next Saturday's Chapter, a black and white Newsreel, hosted by the avuncular Lowell Thomas that even entertained the kids— and "Coming Attractions" that gave moviegoers a peek into next week's thrills and spills.

You could sit through the Saturday matinee show three times if you managed to avoid the dreaded "Matron." She wore a white nurse's uniform and was armed with a large metal flashlight that she'd shine on a guilty kid's face with uncanny precision. She ferreted out those who had been there too long and swiftly rotated them through the exit door. They were not to be seen again until next Saturday.

At some point the more adventurous filmgoer started to cross neighborhood boundary lines and tasted the flavor of another neighborhood's movie house. In order to keep their old customers and attract new ones, every theater manager became intensely competitive.

The "free set of dishes" promotion caught on fast across the nation. You'd buy a ticket for a movie and get a free glass dish.

If you went to seventy-two movies you could build a complete set. If you missed a week, you might be short a butter dish. Acquiring one wasn't easy.

I don't recall many of the movies that I saw at the Waldorf, but I'll never forget *Camille* (1936) starring the mysterious Swedish beauty, Greta Garbo. It was a tragic love story and not the sort of movie suited for an eight-year-old. I don't know what I was doing there, but it was clear mother wanted me next to her.

Garbo's Camille lies near death from consumption. Her lover, played by Robert Taylor, handsome as a god, conceals his grief at her bedside. The men in the audience suppressed their tears but the women were openly sobbing. At that heart-wrenching moment, my mother's free soup dish slipped out of my hand and crashed to the floor. The sound of shattering glass resonated throughout the theater. I thought I would never breathe again.

Lew Rockwell tells me that today some of these cheap old dishes fetch big bucks on eBay.

As usual my wife summed up: "Well you've told us about grand movie palaces, neighborhood theaters, and your childhood—but you never said a word about *Million Dollar Baby* or *The Aviator*.

Ok, here's my review: *The Aviator* is a technically brilliant depiction of aviation history, and Howard Hughes's significant part in it. Beautifully acted, although a bit long, the film focused too much on some of the negative aspects of Howard Hughes's life.

As for *Million Dollar Baby*, Hilary Swank's work will be remembered as one of the finest performances EVER.

You'd better see them both.

February 5, 2005

THERE WAS LIFE BEFORE *GILLIGAN'S ISLAND*

Either Walter Cronkite, Ed Sullivan, *Gilligan's Island* and dancing "Old Gold" Cigarette packages were part of your childhood, or they weren't.

There aren't many of them left, but a still-breathing minority of this nation's population was born and toilet trained before there was such a thing as television. These folks are easy to recognize—they're old.

Okay, I'm one of the above. A TV set never served as my surrogate parent, and the only 12-inch screen we had at home was built into the front door of our washing machine.

The "electronically weaned" majority accepts their birthright and regards those of us born BTV (before television) as old and irrelevant. It's like being part of a victim group, and I don't like it.

At times, the pressure had become so intense that I began to deny my own heritage and tried "to pass" as one of THEM.

Faking not being "old" was easy. I maintained my youthful appearance through the discreet use of botox and bourbon. Friends tell me I easily passed for under seventy.

I also polished my persona, becoming "TV hip." My reaction to almost everybody and everything was a quiet snap of the fingers and a confident, "That's cool."

But I wasn't fooling anybody.

There I was, adrift, near despair, at a San Francisco Book Fair, standing in line for a copy of Hillary Clinton's book. I had hit bottom.

Then, a voice: It was "Captain Marvel" Marvin, one of California's leading dealers of Collector Comic Books, seated behind a display table covered with treasures from the 1940s and 50s.

Captain Marvel Marvin (*CMM*): "Shazam! Blumert, you look awful. There's botox on your shirt collar, you look well over seventy, and it's clear that you've hit bottom."

Blumert: "That's cool, and 'Shazam!' to you Captain. It's been a tough time pretending to be one of THEM."

CMM: Never mind those TV-weaned wimps. This is your heritage," he shouted, juggling musty comic book originals of "Superman," "Batman," and "Wonder Woman."

Blumert: "I hated comic books, With all respect, Captain, it was the dumb kids who liked them."

CMM: "Dumb kids, huh? And I suppose it was the REALLY dumb kids who didn't throw their comic books away and now have collections worth millions?"

Blumert: "I meant no offense, but I was raised during the Golden Age of Radio. 'Amos n' Andy,' 'Fibber McGee and Molly,' 'Jack Armstrong, The All American Boy.' And my favorites, 'The Shadow' and 'Captain Midnight'."

CMM: "Your luck is changing, Blumert. I have an original Captain Midnight Decoder Ring. For old times sake, I'll let you have it for only $2,800. It's a steal at that price."

I hammered the price on the ring down to $2,500, thanked Captain Marvel, and left the Book Fair a new man. I didn't buy Hillary's book, and proudly wore my decoder ring although it was designed to fit a nine-year-old's finger.

Oblivious to the hubbub at the Book Fair, I thought about those "Radio Days" and remembered Woody Allen's warm movie carrying that title. It was one of his few good films in recent years.

During those golden radio years—parents knew their kids were safe listening to the zany feud between radio legends Fred Allen and Jack Benny. They also knew that radio heroes like Captain Midnight and The Shadow always treated women with dignity and respect.

Pornography was in the closet and obscenity considered tasteless.

I never outgrew radio, but as we kids ranged further from home the movies became the dominant influence. I stumbled through adolescence with Mickey Rooney and the "Andy Hardy" series, aspired to be a great American like Jimmy Stewart and had a teenage crush on the elegant actress Ann Sheridan which has endured a lifetime.

That was Hollywood's Golden age.

Yeah, we had an occasional war or depression, but I think my generation had it better than the Gilligan Island TV Kids that followed us. This is a minority view, getting more minority everyday.

June 13, 2003

GERMS AND THE MOVIES

The anthrax scare has been very bad for Democrat politicians, the US Post Office and cocaine dealers.

Public health officials, on the other hand, seem to be doing just fine.

The official government line on anthrax is so bizarre it's like a bad script for a B movie. Every day we get a fresh version, things gets murkier and the questions pile up.

Are the spores coming from Islamabad or Hoboken?

Is it natural anthrax or militarized?

What if the bug-bomber's next virus of choice is smallpox? Do we have sufficient vaccine? Will the vaccine still work? Can the public be kept informed while at the same time unpanicked?

In search of answers I turn to that great font of truth, the American Movie. Hollywood's treatment of epidemics and bugs over the past seventy years can surely provide us with some blueprint for the future.

With credit to *Halliwell's Film Guide*, Google, and thousands of hours of movie-watching research during the mid-part of the last century, what follows is an evaluation of the quality and social impact of the selected films.

The bug movies fall into four categories.

1. THE GLORY DAYS OR, WESTERN CIVILIZATION 2: BUGS 0

In 1926, Paul De Kruif's book, *Microbe Hunters*—required reading in many pre-WWII high schools—glorified man's triumph over disease. In inspirational terms the powerful volume told how brave medical heroes often had to battle the existing order as well as the bugs.

The message was clear: science had no limits.

Hollywood picked up the celebratory theme of *Microbe Hunters* with the 1936 Paul Muni film, *The Story of Louis Pasteur*. This black and white drama portrays the great French biologist's struggle to vanquish the bugs, a tale every schoolboy was familiar with.

In the same spirit, Hollywood produced the 1940 movie, *Dr. Erhlich's Magic Bullet*. Erhlich, the German scientist, is portrayed by veteran actor Edward G. Robinson. The theme is a recurrent one—the brilliant bug-hunter encounters more diffi-culty with administrators than he does finding a cure for vene-real disease.

In the 1950 Elia Kazan film, *Panic in the Streets*, the pub-lic health official tracks down a carrier of bubonic plague in New Orlean's seamy waterfront district. Reflecting the times, this public health detective is a dedicated and respected pub-lic servant.

Note to the reader: Science's conquest of bugs reached its pinnacle in the 1970s.

As decades go, the 1970s was no bargain. The Vietnam War had sapped resources and morality, but at least the killing had stopped and the troops were home. The Civil Rights legislation of 1964 and the social upheaval of that decade had set in motion an attack on property and a political correctness that endure to this day. Watergate mucked up the political scene, but it was a scandal either enjoyed or suffered by beltway and media insiders only. To most everybody else, it was simply good theater.

Medical science had earned our undying faith. Tuberculosis and polio were something only our grandparents remembered. Smallpox was nearly eradicated and "wonder drugs" reinforced the growing faith that science was omnipotent. The wonder drugs also helped create a perverse sexual revolution that would burn out of control until the end of the decade and the arrival of AIDS.

2. MOVIES ABOUT AIDS. SCORE: EVERYBODY LOSES

Although dozens of films have been made about AIDS, only *The Band Played On* (1993), based on Randy Shilts's best seller, made a serious effort to discover the origins and spread of the killer virus.

All other movies like *Parting Glances* (1986) and *Philadelphia* (1994) were sentimental, politically-driven vehicles to raise consciousness and money for the virus's lobbyists.

3. SCIENCE FICTION MOVIES. SCORE: SCI FI: ONE, BUGS: ONE

Two major films best represent the genre. *The Andromeda Strain* (1971) is a well-crafted adaptation of Michael Crichton's best seller. The bug hunters are detectives seeking to find and stamp out a fictional killer. This deadly bug arrives in a spaceship and carelessness allows it to escape the decontamination process. Suspense builds, and the viewer is irresistibly drawn into the drama. (One wonders if Crichton had to import his killer bug from outer space because science had eliminated all the domestic varieties.)

In the 1953 film adaptation of socialist H.G. Wells's book, *War of the Worlds*, our bad bugs do good things. In this epic, the inhuman invaders from Mars are terrorizing, ruthless, unfeeling, indestructible—and just when the earthlings are ready to pack it in, the Martian war vessels start to crash to earth, their occupants all dead.

The Martians were immune to any weapons earthlings could muster, but they were unable to deal with the lowest of Earth's life forms, our bugs.

4. EBOLA. SCORE: EVERYONE LOSES

Ebola is the mother of all bugs. In the real world it's a quick killing African virus. We don't know the origins, we don't know the cure.

What Aids does to its host in ten years, Ebola accomplishes in ten days, author Richard Preston reminds us in his bestselling book, *The Hot Zone*.

Outbreak (1995), based on Preston's book, may be the only film dealing with Ebola. It's no surprise that the movie version scares the bejesus out of audiences.

In the film Dustin Hoffman heads up the team of germ sleuths tracking the fictionalized version of the Ebola virus.

Although *Outbreak* won critical acclaim, after forty minutes of watching Dustin Hoffman mumbling in a space-like suit, this viewer began to root for the virus.

The movie is flawed. It presumes to be based on a real event, but as horrible as the disease is, there has never been an instance when its spread would be considered epidemic. For this reason it fails as a medical hunt, and it self-disqualifies as science fiction.

A physician friend asked if there were any movies dealing with the 1918 Spanish influenza pandemic. There weren't any, I told him, and wondered why he had asked.

He stunned me with the following data about the Spanish flu:

There were 25 million dead worldwide between August 1918 and March 1919—more than died during the bubonic plague 1347 AD–1352.

500,000 Americans succumbed to the dreaded flu. Not many cities or hamlets were spared.

Like the common cold, people learn to live with the flu, the runny nose, congestion, fever and cough. The discomfort is usually short-lived, however, and the victim generally recovers. (20,000 die annually from influenza.) Not in 1918.

Once stricken the victims of Spanish influenza suffered severe congestion and their lungs blackened. Bloody sputum and sudden nose bleeds soiled the bed linen. Within days the patient turned a tint of blue and was almost certainly dying.

Health authorities had never encountered anything like it before. This flu spread more rapidly than any previous strain, and the recovery rate was dismally low.

Unlike the garden variety influenza that strikes the elderly and very young, the 1918 edition attacked healthy, young adults. It took a deadly toll on those American troops returning from Europe at the end of WWI. These troops were the primary carriers of the virus, something else we can thank the Apostle Woodrow for.

It's one thing to ponder fictitious diseases and unlikely epidemics. It's something else to reflect on a real worldwide disaster.

The vaccines they tried in 1918 proved useless. To prevent the spread of the disease gauze surgical masks were required in San Francisco, but they were an effort in futility.

The country was so devastated by the epidemic that the end of WWI was a secondary event and hardly celebrated.

Now you can understand why people are so quick to forget the Spanish flu pandemic of 1918. It's a case of plain old denial.

The nagging question is ever present: How would our society in the year 2001 handle a 1918 variety strain of influenza?

Not too well, I fear.

Yes, today's medical environment could not have been imagined 80 years ago. We have better understanding of cellular structure, and made impressive strides in developing vaccines. But the influenza virus changes so rapidly that all our advances might not make a bit of difference.

So you thought anthrax was scary.

November 29, 2001

WHEW, THAT WAS A CLOSE ENCOUNTER

San Francisco Set To Add Sex Change Benefits
City would be first to include option
—headline *San Francisco Chronicle*, 16 February 2001

*D*amien: "Thanks for calling the San Francisco Health Services System. This is Damien and our motto is: 'We can make a BIG change in you'."

Burt: "Hello, Damien. I'm Burt Blumert from LewRockwell.com. I'm considering doing a story about San Francisco's plan to provide sex change benefits, and the *Chronicle* advised that you were the fellow, excuse me, uh, the person to contact."

Damien: "The last caller said he was from the *New York Times* but he didn't fool me a bit and his sex change surgery is scheduled for next Thursday."

Burt: "There will be no surgery on this dude, buster. I'm simply reporting to our readers and frankly, Damien, you don't really want to know what they think of your San Francisco lifestyle, and this latest perversion."

Damien: "You can cut out the pretense. You're either a cross-dresser, a transvestite, or a transsexual, and it's your civil right to have the City pay for your sex change operation."

Burt: "This is ridiculous. I'm not calling to arrange for a sex change operation."

Damien: "Ah ha. I finally understand. It's not you. You're calling on behalf of your domestic partner."

Burt (indignant): "Please leave my wife out of this."

Damien (hissing): "Wife? Wife? This is San Francisco. What kind of a weirdo are you?"

Burt: "Weirdo? We are taxpayers, that's who we are. I don't want to finance changing Jack into Jill." (Blumert obviously pleased with his snappy retort.)

Damien: "Jack and Jill? What are you, from Utah? It would only cost $37,000 to turn Jack into Jill, and $77,000 to go the other way."

Burt (curious): "Why would it cost almost double from Jill to Jack than from Jack to Jill?" (delivered in a compelling rap beat).

Damien (exasperated)· "If not Utah, you must be from Idaho. Let me explain. In the first instance, the surgeon removes . . ."

Burt (turning a shade of green): "STOP. I withdraw the question."

Damien: "It sounds to me as though you may still be in the closet, and I can't give you any more time as there are needy people on 'hold.' By the way, where ARE you from?"

Burt: "Not from Utah or Idaho. I live right here in the San Francisco Bay Area. Can I ask one more question?"

Damien (suspiciously): "Yeah."

Burt: "My doctor advises me I may require gall bladder surgery. Do you suppose there's enough money left in the program to help me out?"

Damien: "Homophobe!" (hangs up).

February 20, 2000

REMINISCENCES OF
MURRAY ROTHBARD
AND OTIIER GREAT MEN

REMINISCENCES OF MURRAY

C ontrary to wide misconception, Murray Rothbard never hated trees or mountains—he simply believed in keeping such natural intrusions in their place.

They were okay as long as they didn't threaten his safety or comfort. I recall once, when a pal of ours was off climbing a mountain, Murray commented: "Sam could save time and energy by walking around it."

Animals, particularly people's pets, presented a bit more of a problem for Murray. As a guest in somebody's home, his good manners wouldn't allow any expression of displeasure even when the house mongrel thrust its snoot at Murray's crotch.

I think he disliked cats even more, but since so many of his acquaintances fed and housed these germ carriers, he may have mumbled a complaint, but, to my knowledge, Murray never recorded his displeasure on paper.

Which leads to Murray's views on children. Like many who are childless, he had little patience for unruly, noisy, smelly little savages that disrupted civilized adult activity. He was often puzzled that parents with obvious intelligence could allow the "little monsters" to run amuck.

Murray greatly admired how the English upper classes dealt with their children. (As recorded in novels and bad English movies, the nanny would bring them in at an appointed time to visit their father. They always addressing him as "Sir," and after reporting on their activities for the day, were summarily dismissed.)

I think about Murray all the time and my midnight excursions to the fresh LRC page remind me that Lew is Rothbardian #1.

Read something Murray wrote a decade ago. Shake your head in wonderment. Whatever the subject, Murray comes armed with a rapier, while the rest of us blunder along with butter knives.

Except in the realm of machines and technology. In that struggle the best Murray could achieve was stalemate.

I can just see him reacting to the BLOG. He would smile, totally oblivious to the technology and then proceed to crank up his sixty-year-old typewriter and, in a first draft, produce the most dazzling material imaginable.

June 5, 2003

ROBERT NOZICK, ROTHBARD, AND ME AT THE WORLD TRADE CENTER

I only met Robert Nozick on one occasion, and learning of his death today brought a kaleidoscope of images surrounding that encounter.

Here's how I remember it, but please don't jump all over me if some of the dates and details are skewed.

I think it was 1981: the Center for Libertarian Studies was going through a difficult time.

For the first five years of its existence, CLS received funds from a major conservative foundation, but an antiwar essay by Murray Rothbard bothered them, and they unceremoniously cut us off. (Rothbard, like Mises, was uncompromising, intractable, they fumed.)

The Center, free from their clutches, found itself poor, proud, and independent—a condition maintained through the years.

At about the same time, CLS was having bad luck with its Executive Directors. One was lost in a tragic suicide, and his successor—the CLS board would sadly learn—was a partially recovered member of Gambler's Anonymous.

Some months later, Richard—let's call him—disappeared, and two fellows with hand-painted ties, representing a garbage disposal company from New Jersey, came to CLS's offices looking for him. (Today, they could audition for "The Sopranos.")

In spite of the fancy address on Park Avenue South in Manhattan, the CLS offices were appropriately grungy. The two "collectors" were disappointed to see the impoverished setting. They realized they weren't collecting any unpaid gambling debts in this dump and after looking around a bit, they gave CLS a $5 contribution. (It's all true except the donation.)

Bear with me. I haven't forgotten Robert Nozick.

Old Racing Forms and torn up pari-mutuel tickets were not Mr. Gambler's Anonymous' only legacy. He had decided that the Center For Libertarian Studies would honor the 100th anniversary of the birth of Ludwig von Mises with a bash at the ritzy "Windows on the World" atop the World Trade Center. Yes, Richard's event would not soon be forgotten and could bankrupt CLS.

The CLS board was horrified. I was the brand new member of that august body, a lone businessman amongst a bevy of academics. Only friend Lew Rockwell, on the brink of launching the Mises Institute, was there to help derail Richard's grandiose plans.

I soon learned that the contracts with Windows on the World had already been signed. The Center was guaranteeing two-hundred-and-fifty guests and a sumptuous menu. When I noted that the baked Alaska dessert alone was priced at $12.50, I feared we were doomed.

But Richard's sin cut far deeper. It was quietly known in libertarian circles that Murray Rothbard had overcome a list of phobias. It took a great deal of effort, but poor Murray could now deal with airplanes, tunnels, and bridges, but, one fear remained—he was not about to enter an elevator in a skyscraper; a moving, sealed coffin that propelled a body over one hundred stories in a few seconds.

Given the recent horrid event on 9/11 at that very site, Murray's "phobia" now seems quite understandable.

How in heaven's name could the Center for Libertarian Studies schedule a celebration like the 100th anniversary of the birth of Ludwig von Mises knowing full well that Murray Rothbard would never show up?

I tried everything to break the contract with Windows on the World and cancel the event but it was too late. Richard had locked us in with substantial deposits we could not recover. CLS was committed to the dinner on the 108th floor, and Murray Rothbard wasn't going to be there.

And finally to Robert Nozick. Nozick was our first libertarian "pop-star." His award-winning book, *Anarchy, State and Utopia*, published in 1974, brought semi-radical libertarian concepts to the Establishment.

Many of us felt Nozick's book drew heavily upon Murray Rothbard's work without sufficient credit—indeed, that the whole work was intended as a limited-governnment response to Murray's anarcho-capitalism—though Nozick did grudgingly recognize Murray in the book's "Acknowledgements."

In balance, the success of the book was a breakthrough for the movement. Nozick was movie-star handsome and eloquent and—you guessed it—Mr. Gamblers Anonymous had contracted with Nozick to be the main speaker at the Mises dinner.

The elaborately engraved invitations went out and Nozick proved to be a powerful draw. The dinner was over-subscribed and although the mercy of time has obliterated the memory of Nozick's exact fee, there is no question that he helped fill the room

As the night of the dinner drew closer we became more worried about Murray. We begged, we implored, we threatened. We even considered taking the entire day to walk him up the 100-plus floors.

Not a chance. He wasn't getting near those elevators.

Dear Joey Rothbard, Murray's lifelong companion, finally asked that we stop badgering him and that we leave the matter in her hands.

At the elegant reception prior to the banquet tuxedoed waiters splashed French champagne into everybody's glass. Any wasted drops that might have spilled to the carpet set off the cash register in my head.

The guests milled about on the 108th floor in the clouds looking down on New York's old skyscrapers, the Empire State and the Chrysler Building.

But our joy was tempered. There was no Murray.

Suddenly all eyes turned to the giant elevator doors as they rolled open. There was JoAnn Rothbard with her trophy, poor Murray. He was ghastly white. The applause started slowly and mounted to cheers as most in the room realized what Murray had overcome to make that ascent.

JoAnn led him to the lectern and the room grew silent. Murray leaned over, grasped the microphone, and said: "I bring you greetings from Planet Earth."

Robert Nozick's entrance was almost as dramatic. Not copying Murray's rumpled appearance, Nozick wore a fashionable turtleneck under his jacket. His hair was perfectly coiffed and a fashion critic might report that he was exquisitely casual. Only a Harvard philosopher could bring it off.

Not only was he thin and tall and god-like, he was articulate and born to dazzle women. It was as if they were melting at his feet. Women were lining up to present him with their hotel room keys.

But most of the men in the room would have most likely murdered him.

The rest of the evening remains blurry. The program was well received, and as the blood began to course again through Rothbard's veins, his speech turned out to be the hit of the evening.

Nozick did not disappoint, but there was a surprise yet to come.

The near-bankrupt CLS had provided a limo for super-star Nozick, and pre-paid his hotel accommodations for one night. But he never used our reservation, and I was to learn why.

Weeks later I received a bill in the mail. It was for an expensive suite for an entire weekend at the fanciest East Side hotel.

Murray once said he never met a billionaire he liked. I never met a Harvard philosopher super-star that I understood. N.B.: We devoted much of the first issue of the *Journal of Libertarian Studies* to his book.

January 26, 2002

REST IN PEACE, REV. "RUSH"

I have no claim to scholarship. I was never his disciple, nor could I afford being a patron. For heaven's sake, I was not even a Christian. Yet, I was proud to share forty years of friendship with the great Christian scholar and charismatic spiritual leader, Rousas J. Rushdoony.

In 1973, Rushdoony's monumental tome, *The Institutes of Biblical Law*, was published and immediately recognized as an extraordinary contribution to Christian thought. As the years passed, the Institutes became the foundational influence for the Christian Reconstruction Movement.

In the preface to this historic work, "Rush" wrote: "Many of the ideas developed in this study were discussed at times with Burton S. Blumert, who in more ways than one has been a source of encouragement."

Although the reference was hardly deserved, it meant more to me than a Nobel Prize for Coin Dealing. What had prompted this giant of a man to be so generous? The answer is clear: I was a friend.

But spiritual leaders, you might say, don't have friends. It's unlikely that the Archbishop of Canterbury has any pals, but Rush and his wife, dear Dorothy, were my true, enduring friends.

I was introduced to the great man in 1962 by financial newsletter writer H.D. Bryan. As is often the case when searching for beginnings, specifics are difficult to recall, but before long Rush and I were on the phone at least once a week. Our chats covered every subject ranging from medieval history (of which I knew nothing), the evils of the modern church (of which I knew little) to plain old gossip about folks in the freedom movement (of which I was a minor authority).

As the seasons passed, we drifted a bit. Rush was traveling all the time, testifying before varied official bodies on behalf of homeschooling. I would see him but a few times a year, and his demeanor changed from that of the vibrant Christian scholar to that of an Old Testament patriarch. There were occasions when I expected to see small lightning bolts around his head and magnificent gray beard.

Others have covered the life, career, and enormous impact R.J. Rushdoony has had on Christianity, conservatism, and individual liberty.

I can only share with you some personal reflections of small moments during our decades-long friendship.

THE GOLD COINS THAT DIDN'T EXIST

The memories are jumbled but it was probably during the late 1960s that I had consigned an array of world gold coins to a weekend charity church bazaar Rush had organized. He phoned on Monday morning to report that the event was a smashing success, and the gold coins sold like "hotcakes."

The next day's mail included payment and a group of returned coins. Surprised, I'd thought every item was sold. I examined the rejects, and red-faced, realized they were all Turkish. (Rushdoony's Armenian heritage could never forget the holocaust the Turks perpetrated upon his people). We never exchanged a word about it, but it was as though I had never sent the satanic coins and he had never returned them.

THE CARTON OF PAPER MONEY

August 16, 1968, was the final day US $1, $5, and $10 silver certificate notes were to be redeemed by the US Treasury Department for actual silver. As the day approached, activity in the coin and precious metal industry turned frantic. Rush was visiting my office in San Mateo, and I jokingly handed him a carton containing ten thousand silver certificates that we were shipping for redemption.

I proceeded to say something as unbelievably stupid as, "What do you think of this as a Christmas gift?"

"Rush" accepted the "gift" with a graciousness that comes only to men of the cloth, long accustomed to the charity that sustains their flock. It took several agonizing moments to recover the valuable package. Years later I realized that, as the saying goes, he was "putting me on" all along.

THE LAST CONFERENCE

Although it was heart wrenching to see him so frail, his 80th birthday celebration was a grand event in San Jose, California.

Rush's face brightened when I told him of a forthcoming conference *The Rothbard-Rockwell Report* was sponsoring. Wouldn't it be terrific if he could attend?

Andrew Sandlin and the other folks at Chalcedon, Rush's foundation, made all the arrangements and Rush was comfortable during the seven hour round-trip between his home in Vallecito and the Villa Hotel in San Mateo

It was a magical moment for the two-hundred conference attendees when Rush entered the banquet room.

"Burt, ask Rush if he would like to address the group," Lew Rockwell said.

"But, Lew, he may not be up to it."

"I think you should ask him," Lew persisted.

The next fifteen minutes were amazing. I was so apprehensive that I can't even recall his subject but his presentation was impeccable. Not a mumbled word, not a hesitation, not a break in the flow. It was pure Rushdoony.

I needn't have worried. The crowd was enthralled.

POWER OF CONCENTRATION

Rush and Dorothy had come to my office, and we were to have dinner in San Francisco with Christian school educator Reverend Bob Thoburn who was visiting from Virginia. I advised Rush and Dorothy I needed fifteen minutes to prepare for departure. He smiled, removed a small volume from his leather briefcase, and started to read.

I don't recall the nature of the calamity. It might have been a fire, a flood, or an armed robbery, but my office was in total chaos that afternoon. I do know that Rushdoony's eyes never left the page of the book. From someone whose attention span is about thirty-five seconds, I marveled at his power of concentration.

No surprise he could read a book a day.

The Christian Reconstructionists have lost their inspirational leader. The homeschooling movement mourns the passing of the great man who provided its life's blood. His students and parishioners will never replace this magnificent educator.

And I will miss my good pal, Rush.

February 14, 2000

LEW ROCKWELL'S DOER'S PROFILE

Llewellyn H. Rockwell, Jr.
International Playboy and Bon Vivant

- Favorite food: Any endangered species

- Favorite sport: Four-dimensional chess

- Favorite US president: William Henry Harrison (served as president for only few hours)

- Favorite century: Eighteenth

- Favorite flower: Pillsbury

- Favorite pastime: Studying Bolivian maritime law

- Hobby: Collecting political buttons of winners he's supported (so far he has one)

- Next project: Founding the "Committee To Relocate the Nation's Capital to Butte, Montana

- And what does Lew Rockwell drink? Liquid Mylanta (12 years old)

March 19, 2001

INDEX